ELIZABETH & PHILIP

Also by Tessa Dunlop

History

Army Girls: The Secrets and Stories of Military Service from the Final Few Women Who Fought in World War II

The Century Girls: The Final Word from the Women Who've Lived the Past Hundred Years of British History

The Bletchley Girls: War, Secrecy, Love and Loss: The Women of Bletchley Park Tell Their Story

Memoir

To Romania with Love

ELIZABETH & PHILIP

A STORY OF YOUNG LOVE, MARRIAGE, AND MONARCHY

TESSA DUNLOP

PEGASUS BOOKS
NEW YORK LONDON

ELIZABETH & PHILIP

Pegasus Books, Ltd.
148 West 37th Street, 13th Floor
New York, NY 10018

First Pegasus Books cloth edition April 2023

ISBN: 978-1-63936-398-8

10 9 8 7 6 5 4 3 2 1

Printed in the United States of America
Distributed by Simon & Schuster
www.pegasusbooks.com

CONTENTS

INTRODUCTION

◆◇◆

The late Queen was very old, exceptionally so, and yet I did not expect to be starting this book with such a definitive ending. Omnipresent until her departure, working from her Scottish home just two days before death, aged ninety-six, Elizabeth II managed to surprise us with her exit from the stage of life. The Queen was mortal after all. Of course she was; it is the institution of monarchy that endures, in part thanks to Her Majesty's extraordinary century of service. I write these words in the immediate aftermath of her death – ceremony unfolding up and down the country, newscasters intoning in black, obituary films extolling Elizabeth's many understated virtues – and I am struck by the timing.

In the last year of her life, the Queen joshed with Paddington Bear in a CGI film, waved off her Platinum Jubilee in eye-catching green from the Buckingham Palace balcony and welcomed in her umpteenth prime minister. The loose ends of the Elizabethan age dispatched with, she went to meet her maker, leaving us to pause for thought. How had Elizabeth pulled off the contradiction of ancient monarchy in the modern era? The possible answers are legion, but amid all the commemoration and reminiscing, one aspect of the Queen's life towers above all else: her enduring union with Prince Philip, the late Duke of Edinburgh. Only in the last eighteen months of her reign did Elizabeth walk alone, the stick perhaps a metaphor for the sovereign's missing husband.

Introduction

The Queen and the Duke of Edinburgh's marriage helped define the post-war world, and later they would become Britain's golden couple, with Philip's characteristic bluntness and humour neatly offsetting his wife's propriety and restraint. When the Duke died it was hard to imagine the Queen without him. Elizabeth sat in St George's Chapel – masked, dignified and regal – and said goodbye to her husband of seventy-three years, and whole world was struck by that solitary image. Our sovereign had lost her 'strength and stay'; it wouldn't be long before Elizabeth also bid us her farewell.

Famously, their relationship was based on mutual respect, deep love and a resolute belief in monarchy, but despite its essential nature, the marriage was never straightforward, nor balanced. In death, even the couple's respective funerals served as a reminder of the disparities within their union. Unlike the Queen's almighty and solemn state funeral, choreographed with the full heft of governmental support and infrastructure, Philip's was a private, streamlined ceremony inside the grounds of Windsor Castle, pared down to conform with both Covid-19 restrictions and his modest expectations and lesser rank.

Likewise the media coverage in the wake of the Duke's death, although comprehensive and respectful, was nowhere near the scale of the late Queen's wall-to-wall global commemorations extended across a two-week period of mourning. In death as in life, Philip assumed his place behind the Queen. And yet, in Britain, a vocal minority still took umbrage when television and radio stations abandoned their schedules and dedicated output to honour the deceased Prince in April 2021. The BBC felt compelled to put a complaints form on its website. Well-known public historians even got involved in the debate; one, irked after yet another broadcast outlet contacted her for comment on Philip's life, tweeted: 'I am not, and never will be, a royal historian. History is of the many not the few'.[1]

It was that backlash, partially driven by social media, which inspired this book. Here, I should declare my hand. While I have a doctorate in History, including the role of royalty in national imaging, I also spend a lot of time with society's outliers – the extremely elderly. I write about their lives in oral history books and count some of them among my best friends. They are part of an exceptional generation; aged ninety-five and over, most don't have access to the internet: they rely on television for companionship and news, and are direct contemporaries of the late Queen and the Duke of Edinburgh. Together they fought in the same war and enjoyed similar wartime romances. The Queen was not their fantasy grandmother; she was their peer. For them remembering Philip's and now Elizabeth's life is a poignant and important trip down memory lane to a time when monarchy was truly magical and marriage between a prince and a princess the imagined gateway to a long and happy life. Back then, Elizabeth and Philip stood for the many, not the few.

I wanted to explore those ideas in this book and take a final opportunity to examine not just what we know (or think we know) about Elizabeth's early relationship with Philip, but how their royal love story was portrayed and received by their own generation. In recent years, Her Majesty became the world's most famous nonagenarian; it is easy to forget that, once upon a time, Elizabeth was a young girl, living an extraordinarily confined life in the grounds of Windsor Castle during World War II. Service in uniform and access to men of her own age came late for the heir to the British throne.

This story starts in that war, which is where I uncovered the future Queen in an archival search for my last book, *Army Girls*. Uniform is an incredible leveller, and HRH Princess

Elizabeth looked like all the other Auxiliary Territorial Service (ATS) recruits, with waved hair, a smooth make-up free face and compulsory cap, but, of course, she was nothing like them. The future Queen was already adept at making the extraordinary look ordinary. Subsequently, I returned to that same archive to make an obituary programme about Her Majesty's wartime service[2] – I pulled open a long flat drawer and, there, beneath a sheath of cellophane, lay a poster-sized image of a young Prince Philip in all his naval regalia. I was staggered by his unapologetic good looks. He was, to use an old-fashioned phrase, quite simply a 'knockout'.

'Oh, yes,' agrees Daphne, who was two years his junior and also served in the ATS. 'Prince Philip was ridiculously handsome. But I often thought people were very unfair about him.' Her comment, a throwaway line from a woman who is now ninety-nine, piqued my interest. In the wake of the 1936 abdication, and up against the constraints of war and her unique position, Elizabeth had managed to marry the man she wanted. Even more impressive was their union's enduring success. In many respects the Queen's marriage to Philip was her greatest coup.

However, in the 1990s, when the Windsor children's broken marriages were headline news, commentators often suggested that Elizabeth and Philip's own relationship had not been subjected to equivalent press intrusion. It is true: 24/7 media coverage didn't exist back then, but newspaper archives confirm it was never easy. Interest in Elizabeth's love life, tied as it was to an institution of state, proved relentless and, for Philip, sometimes unforgiving. Why did this young man irk courtiers and newspaper editors alike? Was it his outsider status? His flirtatious blond aesthetic? Or simply his gumption? Would any suitor intending to marry the nation's most eligible girl have been given a similar reception?

Introduction

This book tries to answer those questions, but it is also a love story and the tale of a marriage born in a tense post-war world. As a fellow veteran married for an equally long time explains, 'we felt lucky to have survived the war and we were keen to try our luck in marriage as well'.[3] But Philip and Elizabeth were no ordinary couple. The growing celebrity of royalty ensured they had to negotiate their own relationship (not always easy) at the same time as they fulfilled society's expectations of love, family and, from 1952, monarchy. The margin for error was small and doubts about Philip persisted.

There was little ambiguity in late 1940s' Britain. Young girls were expected to get on and marry, and the vast majority did. In 1947, Elizabeth and Philip led a generation down the aisle that broke records. Never before had so many couples got married so young. Occasionally in this book I touch base with my nonagenarian (and centenarian) friends. They remind me that the mid-twentieth century was an era when the sanctity of marriage really meant something and, out in front, leading the way, for better or for worse, was the heir to the British throne and her foreign prince. We know how the story ends, in a remarkable seventy-three-year marriage. This is how it began. I hope you enjoy getting to know young Elizabeth and Philip as much as I did.

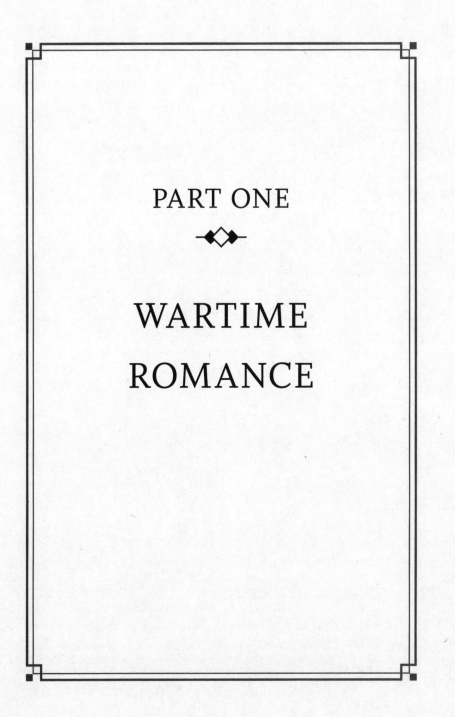

PART ONE

WARTIME
ROMANCE

ONE

◆

A Windsor Lockdown

Ronald was a fine stripling of a lad; over six foot tall and not yet sixteen, he'd left school a year earlier and daily travelled into the city, where he shovelled rubble, pushed a barrow and heaved bricks. Outdoors, whistling as he worked, his life with London's bomb clearance division was infinitely preferable to the classroom or the office. And there was an end in sight. From mid-1944, with the Allies in France, thoughts had started to turn to the peace; by March 1945, the very last V-1 rocket hit the capital and Britain held its breath: finally the sirens were silenced. Surely, sometime soon the Germans would surrender?

At the beginning of May, newspapers reported that Hitler was dead, the *Daily Mail* concluding 'the probability is that he was mad', and Berlin finally fell to the Russians.[1] Back in London, rumours of when Victory in Europe Day would be declared reached a frenzied pitch. The week-long speculation gave Ronald long enough to plan. He was living with his Aunt Lizzie in Harrow; he couldn't complain – she'd given him a roof over his head and food on the table throughout the war. His mum was back in the Rhonda Valley, ill in hospital with consumption, and his dad had long since disappeared (an attractive midwife, by all accounts). He'd brought himself up,

9

got a job and enjoyed his freedom. Spring was here, the sap was rising and, at fifteen, he fully intended to enjoy VE Day.

Dawn broke on 8 May warm and clear and Ronald set off, with a friend, from Harrow to the West End. Apparently that's where it was all happening, with Buckingham Palace the focal point. 'We want the King!' roared the crowd. It was on days like these that monarchy came into its own. Bonfires had been burning overnight, pretty young girls in bobby socks sported red, white and blue ribbons in their hair and carts carrying fruit and refreshments were draped in Union Jacks. The streets were mobbed, and the nearer to the Mall Ronald got, the closer the atmosphere became – beer, endorphins and the delicious human scent of unadulterated delight.

Recollections from that exceptional day are plentiful. Memory is selective but few forget one of the happiest moments of their lives. Girls and boys danced the Hokey Cokey and scrambled up lampposts, men gave them a heave-ho and a cheer, and, once again, those small specks in the distance, the Royal Family, trooped out on to the balcony, waving at the heaving mass of humanity below. Box Brownie cameras caught the moment, ticker tape fell from the sky as if by magic, and Winston Churchill famously joined his new chum, King George VI. Young Ronald was somewhere in the crowd dancing a jig and, over there, beyond the iron railing, flanking the Prime Minister on the Buckingham Palace balcony, was Princess Elizabeth.

How times had changed in five years. Despite her father's predictable protestations that military uniform was not appropriate for a girl, eighteen-year-old Elizabeth had eventually got her way. Sometimes mistaken for shy (she was around her peers), the Princess possessed a quiet certainty and steely determination. That evening she remained in her ATS uniform: a symbol for women's unprecedented service during a long war in resolute and not particularly flattering khaki. Her mother, Queen Elizabeth, wore folds of turquoise (and later reappeared dressed in white, with a sparkly tiara) and little sister Margaret Rose posed in baby blue, but not Elizabeth. Hers was no honorary uniform: the young subaltern had served in the People's War and, now, she too wanted to be part of the celebrations.

Decades later, as Queen, she recalled: 'I think we went on the balcony every hour, six times, and then, when the excitement of the floodlights being switched on got through to us, my sister and I realised we couldn't see what the crowds were enjoying.'[2] Unlike Ronald, Elizabeth was not free to roam at leisure. Led by her precocious sister, the pair had to ask parental permission to leave their gilded cage and, on this occasion, the King relented. Peace in Europe was not an everyday occurrence and so a group of sixteen appropriate minders and friends were duly assembled. Having endured a childhood scorched by unending curious onlookers, with innocent expeditions frequently upturned when her identity was exposed, Elizabeth was determined not to be recognised. She pulled her cap down over her forehead, dark hair neatly rolled above a regulation collar. The Grenadier officer in charge reprimanded this sloppy attempt at disguise: 'he refused to be seen in the company of another officer improperly dressed'. The Princess (temporarily) complied and so out they stepped into the evening throng.[3]

After enjoying the novelty of cheering her own parents from the ground, the group slipped discreetly across to Parliament Square and then onwards to Piccadilly, St James's Street, Berkeley Square and down Park Lane, briefly pushing through the revolving doors of two grand London hotels – the Dorchester and the Ritz. The crowds and distance covered suggests the Princesses were out amid the crush for several hours, with Green Park the final thoroughfare back to the Palace.[4] Was it there, somewhere near the Mall, that Ronald established eye contact with what looked like a familiar face? She saw him and he very definitely saw her. Briefly the pair came together, close enough to talk.

'I know you!' insisted the young Welshman.

'No, you don't,' replied the girl. Was her cap pulled down once more? Ronald remembers she wore it lower than was standard practice.

'Yes! You're Princess Elizabeth, aren't you?'

'No, I'm not.'

'You are! I'd recognise your face anywhere!'

'Ok, I am, but you mustn't tell anyone. It's a secret. Ok?'

Ronald nodded his head and solemnly promised. And then, bonded in secrecy, they danced together in the close night air. Elizabeth never breathed a word. The King's private secretary, Sir Alan Lascelles, later noted, with smug satisfaction, 'the Princesses, under escort, went out and, unrecognised, walked about'.[5]

'Apparently it was one of the chaperones that moved her on,' Jo Kavakeb sighs.

We never believed him, you see. Our stepdad dancing with the Queen! We just laughed and he didn't mention it again. It became part of family folklore. And then, in 2015, the film *A Royal Night Out* was released and the penny dropped. My son said, 'Granddad, when was it that you danced with the Queen?' Turns out it was VE Day and suddenly his story made sense.

Ronald is dead now – he slipped away mid-pandemic, aged ninety – but his stepdaughter, Jo, has laid photographs of him out on the table. Staring back from the sepia pictures is a tall, confident young man; he has a long, handsome face and neatly parted fair hair. The likeness is unmistakable: Ronald was the spitting image of Prince Philip, a naval first lieutenant still serving in the Far East in May 1945. Jo laughs. 'I think Elizabeth definitely saw something in my stepdad, don't you?'

The future Queen later described that evening as 'one of the most memorable nights of my life'. Meanwhile, Ronald would never hear a word said against Her Majesty and he always stood for the national anthem. Jo pauses before answering a final question. 'Prince Philip? No, funnily enough my stepdad wasn't quite so keen on him!'[6]

◆

Briefly, on 8 May 1945, Elizabeth was drawn towards Ronald – two comrades freed from the grind of war on their very own big night out. When they danced between pools of electric light, perhaps Elizabeth saw a fleeting physical resemblance to the man she'd held a torch for since 1939. And, yes, even at thirteen, the age when the Princess first meaningfully met Philip, it is certainly possible to have a full-on crush. Ask any girl, no matter if she is flanked by her parents and dressed to match her little sister in buckled shoes, a sun bonnet and buttoned coat on a mild summer's day. Visiting Dartmouth Naval College two months before the outbreak of war, Elizabeth had been introduced to a stunning older boy and she couldn't take her eyes off him. Five years her senior, he had a direct gaze, bags of confidence and a royal title – cue Philip, Prince of Greece and Denmark, and a top notch naval cadet to boot.

The story of 'Their Majesties at the Royal Naval College' was featured on page sixteen of *The Times*. The paper might have made more of the visit if only they had guessed its long-term implications. But how could they? Elizabeth was so very young and war was on its way, hence the royal inspection. There was a march past for the King and Queen and lunch on the *Victoria and Albert*.[7] Philip, briefly charged with chaperoning the two Princesses, played with toy trains, leapt over a tennis net and famously took on the Royal Yacht in his row boat. According to Elizabeth's governess, Marion Crawford (aka Crawfie), all the cadets turned back at the insistence of the King once they were out in the Channel,

> except this one solitary figure whom we saw rowing away as hard as he could, who was, of course Philip. Lilibet* took the glasses and had a long look at him. In the end the King said, 'The young fool. He must go back otherwise we will have to send him back.' . . . we gazed at him until he became just a very small speck in the distance.[8]

Eighteen-year-old Philip was fighting fit, eager to impress and longing to earn his British stripes at sea. A cousin aptly remembered him as a 'huge hungry dog; perhaps a collie who had never had a basket of his own and responded to every overture with eager tail-wagging'.[9] The 'pink-faced' girl from the Palace had just been confronted with a fairytale prince in playful packaging.[10] But the game that loomed on the horizon was not child's play. To survive the dark years of war, Philip, the 'Viking'-style naval trainee, would need courage and luck, in spades.[11] Ditto Elizabeth, now the unexpected teenage heir to the British throne. The task that lay ahead of the Princess was onerous and her exposure to life limited, a situation improved neither by the arrival of war nor by her overprotective father.

It is well known that George VI, Elizabeth's papa, was a reluctant monarch. Born the second son of a second son, he had inherited the throne in December 1936 courtesy of a hapless hedonistic brother who'd reneged on his royal duties in

---

*   Princess Elizabeth's pet name among friends and family.

favour of wedded bliss to an American divorcée. The impact of Edward VIII's abdication had ramifications that are still felt today, and will be dealt with in due course. But while there has been much hand wringing and sympathy for dear shy Bertie's kingly plight (apparently his reaction at the prospect of inheriting the throne was 'one of horror and despair', a disposition milked by his comely little wife, Elizabeth),[12] much less attention has been paid to the undoubted perks of arriving on the adult scene as the King's second son.

Unlike his older brother, David (as Edward was known), whose marriage was always destined to be a matter of state, as long as Bertie's bride was sufficiently aristocratic and virginal, he was the author of his own domestic destiny and permitted to marry his first choice: a self-possessed and charismatic wife who suited his personal needs, plucked from the craggy bosom of Scotland's aristocracy. To call Elizabeth Bowes-Lyon a commoner is somewhat stretching the truth. In fact, this ninth child of the 14th and 1st Earl of Strathmore and Kinghorne could trace her lineage back to Robert the Bruce, arguably a purer line than the House of Windsor, and certainly less Germanic. But more important, from Bertie's point of view, was her impact on his timorous, insubstantial personality. He chose well. As the ubiquitous royal observer Henry 'Chips' Channon noted of Bertie's bride shortly after their wedding in 1923: 'everyone agrees that she has improved Prince Bertie enormously. He is better-mannered, better-tempered and certainly better looking since he married.'[13]

With a happy marriage under his belt long before he became King, George VI presumably wanted the same for his beloved Lilibet, who would never enjoy the relative anonymity or freedom available to her parents in their early years. But, despite his best intentions, the nervous King proceeded to ruthlessly restrict his eldest daughter's access to young people her own age. Here, a degree of sympathy is required; royals have long been inherently distrustful of outsiders, often with good reason. Prime Minister James Callaghan's observation that 'what senior royalty offer you is friendliness not friendship' is backed up by Queen Victoria's earlier cautioning: 'Never make friendships . . . friendships and intimacies are very bad & often lead to great mischief.'[14] Messaging that appears to have stuck. George VI had very few close friends and derived most his pleasure from 'us four', a cosy domestic quartet consisting of the King, the Queen and the two Princesses. There was mutual respect and love in abundance, but Elizabeth and Margaret, who unlike their predecessors lacked a 'royal mob' of siblings, lost out socially.

Lady Martha Bruce, still alive and aged one hundred at the time of writing, is the daughter of the 10th Earl of Elgin. Another Scottish aristocrat of impressive lineage, Martha, along with her siblings, had been the recipient of Crawfie's schooling before the governess was headhunted by the neighbouring Bowes-Lyons at Glamis Castle and sent south to educate Elizabeth and Margaret.[15] This aristocratic poach appears to have had little impact on Martha. Like so many girls from society's 'top drawer', before the war she had been sent to one of a burgeoning number of single-sex boarding schools in the south of England. Apparently the education was patchy, but at least she rubbed shoulders with female peers away from the strictures of home. Not so Princess Elizabeth. Growing up, she spent an inordinate amount of time with a sister four years her junior, a clutch of royal staff, and Crawfie, by all accounts good fun but a governess nonetheless.

If, before September 1939, the Princesses enjoyed occasional excursions, swimming and dancing lessons – and, in Elizabeth's case, scheduled trips to Eton College for lectures in constitutional history – after the outbreak of war the noose tightened. An initial five-month stint in Birkhall on Balmoral estate taxed even Crawfie's capacity for solitary teaching, a situation exacerbated by the absence of the girls' most regular companions, the King and Queen.* The Princesses' isolated world had been reinforced. Meanwhile, beyond the perimeter of their Highland retreat, war was never far away. As with so many girls at the end of 1939, Princess Elizabeth was about to discover what it felt like to be trapped in a private setting without recourse to action.

◆

It was the dead of night on 14 October 1939 when Günther Prien made an early name for himself as one of Germany's most notorious U-boat aces, slipping into Orkney's Scapa Flow, the naval base for Britain's Home Fleet, and firing three torpedoes with deadly effect at HMS *Royal Oak*. The anchored battleship was a sitting duck. Eight-hundred and thirty-three seamen drowned, most mere lads, some not yet eighteen. The news could not be covered up; back in Westminster, Parliament demanded answers from the First Lord of the Admiralty, Winston Churchill, who was devastated by the attack. 'Poor fellows, poor fellows, trapped in those black depths.'[16]

Further north, the grim news penetrated the confines of Balmoral estate – the Princesses were avid listeners to the wireless. (What else was there?) Thirteen-year-old Elizabeth was profoundly affected. 'Crawfie, it can't be! All those nice sailors.' Her little voice piqued with deep sadness and the injustice of it all. The loss contrasted cruelly with the gleaming naval cadets' full-bodied vim during the Princesses' final pre-war outing to Dartmouth just months earlier. The tragedy

---

* To ease the pressure on their governess at Balmoral, a Mrs Montaudon-Smith was employed to teach the girls French and singing.

repeated on her; that Christmas, Elizabeth's thoughts kept returning to the dead sailors and their families.[17] And almost certainly to Philip, Prince of Greece, that 'strange creature out of another world' who could so easily have been numbered among the dead.[18]

In fact, Philip was just fine. It was small, and easily missed, but beyond all the military news, troop inspections and weather warnings, the blond naval cadet, who had made such an impression on young Elizabeth before the war, briefly popped up in the British press on 30 January 1940. With his glamorous cousin, Marina, Duchess of Kent, and Elizabeth's parents, the King and Queen, Prince Philip attended London's West End; the play was *Funny Side Up* (the Royal Family loved musical theatre and comedies).[19]

The outing came at a watershed moment. Philip had finally been granted permission to serve in the Royal Navy, albeit with limitations. An accomplished cadet who had trumped his fellow trainees at Dartmouth, winning the King's Dirk for best all-rounder (to the chagrin of a few), the sweet scent of success had been mired by uncertainty over his status. Although proud of his royal title (he always signed himself 'Philip, Prince of Greece'), his native country's neutrality initially complicated the boy's wish to serve in the Royal Navy.

It was Philip's well-connected, violently ambitious uncle, Lord Louis Mountbatten (a second cousin of George VI), who took matters in hand and, by the end of January, the situation had been temporarily resolved. The young Prince was assigned a British ship, though admittedly one on the outskirts of war, accompanying Australian and New Zealand vessels. The theatre trip was a final night out in London before his posting to the other side of the world. Elizabeth didn't attend, but at least, by then, she had been moved to the more proximate Windsor Castle, a royal seat blessed with built-in defences. Did she see

Philip that January? Quite possibly, he was family in the loosest sense of the word (Queen Victoria's prolific progeny made sure of that). Certainly Elizabeth's ardour had not dimmed. Two months later, amid much giggling and in the company of a governess and her little sister, she confided to a friend that Philip 'was her "boy"'. She reinforced meagre memories by 'cutting his photos out of a paper'.[20]

In the early years of World War II, centuries-old traditional military thinking framed men as heroes compelled to serve in a dangerous conflict for their womenfolk and children – the peaceful, fecund ideal back at home. The Princess, with her scrapbook on Philip's war, was the archetypal young and vulnerable female. Enjoying hazy dreams of a prince at sea, in theory she had the space and time to grow up and ideally meet other people. After all, as her father would later admit, a first crush is rarely more than a beginner's step in matters of the heart. But there was a war on. Like most men, rather than deal with the thorny issue of his daughter's adolescence, the King preferred the option of safety first: the Princesses rarely left the heavily fortified grounds of Windsor Castle.

At one level, the precautions were very sensible. Although fifteen miles outside of London, Windsor was vulnerable during the Blitz, and a German target more than once. Numerous Grenadier Guards flanked the castle, a ring of anti-aircraft guns encircled its impressive walls, sirens frequently wailed and a dungeon-cum-air raid shelter (where Elizabeth bagged the top bunk) became part of daily life. At the beginning of October 1940, bombs even fell on Windsor's Long Walk and Bishops Gate, and a Messerschmitt was downed in the vicinity. Great craters pock-marked the Royal Park, reinforcements shook, trees fell and, less than two weeks later, the Princess made her first radio address with (what became) hallmark equanimity.[21]

We know, every one of us, that in the end all will be well; for God will care for us and give us victory and peace. And when peace comes, remember it will be for us, the children of today, to make the world of tomorrow a better and happier place.[22]

A carefully curated adolescent existence appears to have reinforced imperturbability in the Princess. The chapel in which she was christened at Buckingham Palace was destroyed, likewise the family's pre-abdication town house, which contained her happiest childhood memories – 145 Piccadilly. The war blazed around her. Meanwhile, Elizabeth ploughed on with a restricted routine inside a small Windsor social circle, the limitations of which are laid bare in *The Windsor Diaries*.

The publication of Alathea Fitzalan Howard's daily journals while Her Majesty was still alive surely justifies Queen Victoria's concern that friends can 'lead to great mischief'. Here was a rare childhood acquaintance of Elizabeth's who slipped through the net. From a dysfunctional aristocratic family that missed out on a ducal inheritance because Alathea was a girl, she made up for this loss of status by ingratiating herself with the Princesses during the war. Washed up on the other side of Windsor Park, fey, lonely and prone to self harm, Alathea meticulously charted the daily ups and downs of a peculiar and privileged wartime lockdown, where her best friends were two years and six years her junior: Elizabeth and Margaret, respectively.

Teenage Elizabeth was emotionally young for her age. Held back by the constant presence of little sister Margaret, the picture painted is of an unworldly princess, even undeveloped. Her pursuits were simple – bike rides, art, girl guiding, dance classes and parlour games; her tastes unsophisticated – Aertex shirts, slapstick comedies, pantomimes, horses and dogs; and her temperament ill suited to large groups and gadding about. While Alathea was distracted by school, then VAD nursing, Elizabeth remained 'high and dry' in her ivory tower.[23]

On the surface, their existence was serviceable if somewhat 'bleak'. Despite protestations of restraint in public and Queen Mary's claim that wartime Windsor, shrouded in blackout curtains, without its chandeliers and crown jewels, was 'no fun', the girls ate well, wore pretty silk dresses aplenty and had a constant entourage of adult assistance. But, as Alathea marvelled, it was impossible to speak to the Princess frankly – one-to-one, as girls do – because she was almost never alone.[24] There were nannies, governesses, vicars, detectives, and upper bracket Grenadier Guards, who came and went and were occasionally killed in battle (they might have doubled as suitors but the setting was hardly conducive to flirtation) – and, of course, the Royal Family. Which begs the question, how does one develop without personal space?

Differently, is the answer. The Princess was an exception and she knew it; implacably, calmly, she got on with growing up in the shadow of the King and her destiny. During her gauche teenage years, she uncomplainingly pushed through the standard 'rather fat', 'puffy', and 'stolid' stages. In an era that judged women on their looks (Alathea's diary is testimony to that), Elizabeth was fairly plain and remarkably free of vanity. She wore 'terrible' shoes, 'ugly'-shaped dresses and, according to Crawfie, lacked taste. But the Princess could also be 'pretty, animated' and enigmatic; yet, no matter how hard Alathea tried, she rarely penetrated Elizabeth's unyielding exterior: Lilibet was 'v matter of fact and uncurious and above all untemperamental'.[25]

The impression is of a 'dispassionate' princess, entirely different from her affectionate, challenging younger sister. This was an heir to the throne who kept her distance in these peculiar wartime circumstances, which *The Times* tersely referred to as 'cramping'.[26] According to Alathea, Elizabeth's temperament was 'quite unsuited to forming strong or violent attachments', unless, of course, that individual was a sailor-prince far away at sea.[27]

The Princess's world was drawn in simple unquestioning lines: Hitler was 'horrid', Britain would win the war, and her unspoken destiny was to be Queen.[28] Equally consistent (and interesting, given observers found Elizabeth young for her age) was the commitment to her abiding wartime crush. Philip pops up throughout Alathea's diary, ditto in Crawfie's memoir, *The Little Princesses*, as almost the only man Elizabeth expressed an interest in. In December 1941, the usually 'placid and unemotional' fifteen-year-old became 'very excited' about the prospect of a Christmas visit from the Prince, and, sure enough, 'her Philip came'.[29] He was not Alathea's type. Jealousy perhaps? Unlike Alathea, Philip had penetrated the inner sanctuary of the Royal Family. No wonder Elizabeth felt at home around him: he was like one of her own in a household that had recently hosted Philip's cousin, George II of Greece, and King Peter of Yugoslavia (married to another cousin of his). What more could she possibly want from a pin-up? Here was a handsome prince, a distant relative and a man in uniform serving in her father's navy.[30] Needless to say, not everyone was quite so enamoured.

TWO

◆◇◆

The Aphrodisiac of War

'I can tell you, she was a very pretty girl. Stunning. And, yes, she dated Prince Philip for a while, it was fairly common knowledge.' Pamela pauses to take in the picture. Osla Benning stares out of a pre-war photograph. Flanked by a friend, she's leaning on the roof of a car at the Whaddon point-to-point the year she came out as a debutante: 1939. Her gamine features are framed with a stylish fur hood and her gloved hand holds a race card. Osla's aristocratic allure still stands the test of time, and her wartime story has filmic qualities – she worked at the now famous Bletchley Park.[1] And if anyone knew about this girl's routines at Britain's top-secret code-breaking centre, it was Pamela Rose, who, six years Osla's senior and her immediate boss, was tasked with organising the rotas for the girls working in the Park's Naval Hut 4.

'Well, I suppose she was quite "debby". A lot of us were.' Pamela, a reluctant debutante herself and an actress, was an intimidating prospect. In charge of a gaggle of entitled girls who'd grown up with no real expectation of working, she had to be.

It wasn't easy. They all wanted leave at the same time to attend dances in London. Yes, Osla was very much among them. She spoke German and had money and confidence. She was tremendous fun. They'd catch the milk float from London to Bletchley at the crack of dawn and do their shift in party dresses.

Osla is preserved for posterity in Bletchley Park folklore. She was one of three debs who careened down the corridor of Hut 4 in a laundry basket with Jean Campbell-Harris (later better known as Baroness Trumpington). The girls were duly punished for their high jinks and didn't work together for the next three weeks.[2]

Pamela shrugs, she is very old (one-hundred-and-three), and we have been through her Bletchley story before. 'They needed linguists at the Park to help the code breakers and a lot of the girls who spoke German were rather grand. In the mid-1930s it was still fashionable to be "finished off" in Germany. I was in Munich in 1936.' Pamela knows why I have returned to the subject of Bletchley Park. It is 2021, Prince Philip has just died and I want to find out more about his wartime girlfriend, Osla Benning.

> What more can I tell you? She was fabulous looking. They were dating when I was at the Park, so sometime around 1941–42, and we all knew he was a Greek Prince. I remember meeting him years later when he was the Duke of Edinburgh and being struck by just how traditional and English he seemed![3]

Recently, with ramped-up interest in the late Duke, Osla has acquired near legendary status. Biographers refer to her as 'larky', with a love for practical jokes, and they gently skirt around the issue of her relationship with Philip.[4] A subject the late Duke was always quick to contain. Yes, she was 'fun', yes, he was the godfather to her first-born son, named Philip, and, no, he would not answer any more gossip-related questions.[5] Osla was best friends and wartime colleagues with fellow debutante and grandee Sarah Norton.* But the unspoken rules around discretion that royals and their circle hold dear ensure the latter's published memoir steers clear of Osla's royal boyfriend.[6] It is Pamela, a friend, a bohemian and contrarian, who confirms that Osla and Philip were very definitely an item.

Of course they were. Who could resist Osla Benning? Not many, according to Sarah, who remembers her 'innumerable' male admirers.[7] This was a girl who lived life on the edge. Canadian born, by 1939 her parents were divorced, her father was dead, her mother had remarried and, living back in England, was determined to launch her daughter into society. Osla more than looked the part in a gown of blue silk net, embroidered with iridescent paillettes, and a train to match.[8] *Tatler* had a field day featuring this 'attractive' girl whose final polish had been applied in Vienna and Paris. The head shot is sultry if a little stern, the complexion flawless, and, notably, the caption insists Osla was being presented not by her divorced mother but rather by a certain Lady Beatty.[9] Foreign-born, presumably the ambition was to find Osla a suitable British man on the circuit. Although minus the pedigree of landed aristocracy, she was still a stunning girl in a milieu that valued highly the aesthetic qualities of someone predestined to be a future society wife (indicative of the time, her stepfather found fault with her 'quite thick legs', which were duly bound to slim them down[10]). Hopes ran high for Canadian Osla; that is, until war broke out and muddied the rules of the upper-class dating game.

Osla was immediately bundled off to distant cousins in Canada, where she soon revolted and got herself back to

---

* In 1945 Sarah married William, Viscount Astor, and later Lieutenant-Colonel Thomas Baring. She divorced both.

war-torn Europe, extorting a ticket through flirtation and arriving in Portugal in an aeroplane (very daring back then). To hell with sitting on the sidelines, this was a girl who liked to be at the centre of things. A cargo ship to Liverpool returned Osla to England, where there was a stint of menial work in Slough, drilling sheets of metal for aeroplane parts at a Hawker Siddeley factory with her friend Sarah, before they and their German language skills were headhunted by top-secret Bletchley Park.

It wasn't all bad, far from it. Slough was a stone's throw from Windsor, where the girls found plenty of Life Guards and military men at Victoria Barracks for entertainment purposes[11] (there is no mention of the locked-down Princesses, several years the women's junior). Sarah's father, the filmmaker Richard Norton,* brought a cottage (aptly named Penny Royal) in the vicinity and proceeded to cook porridge and cater for the girls, while back in London they shared a mutual godfather – none other than Lord Louis Mountbatten (the ruling class was a relatively small clique who relied on their connections with each other). Mountbatten and his beautiful heiress wife, Edwina, had a penchant for politicking and networking at their London penthouse in Park Lane (replete with private express elevator and cinema) and were on the lookout for pretty girls to entertain their nephew, Prince Philip of Greece. The son of Mountbatten's sister, Princess Alice, he was the family's intermittent house guest and lacked a stable British base. Like Osla, he too was foreign, beautiful and homeless. Both came from splintered, international families, both relied on their wits and looks to get by and, keen for adventure and structure, both were longing to get involved in the war.

---

*   Later the 6th Baron Grantley.

Pamela pauses: 'It was quite an obvious match, when you think about it. Back then we very much lived in the moment.'

◆

Britain's aristocratic hierarchy, in which the Royal Family sits at the apex, has a history of guarding its internal strata with coded language, behaviour and status. Sweeping up into the golden branches of privilege was not something that could be done overnight; access to a higher class required much more than money, it required breeding. And when it came to breeding, few could compete with Prince Philip of Greece and Denmark. European kings and queens littered both sides of his family – his maternal grandmother, Victoria, Dowager Marchioness of Milford Haven (Queen Victoria's granddaughter), was born in Windsor Castle; his paternal grandfather, King George I, had sat on the Greek throne for fifty years; his cousin, George II, still occupied it. The family's blood line was predominantly German not Hellenic, and it was through George I that they laid claim to both Greek and Danish titles; George I's father had been heir to the Danish throne. In other words, Philip was a young man from ancient stock and he wore his royal badge with pride; throughout World War II, he was a Prince of Greece who exuded a 'special' status.'[12]

In the game of class, social confidence was crucial, and Philip had it in spades, but the reality of this young man's existence in 1939 was far more precarious than his titles or manner let on. Based in Britain, he was occasionally included in royal excursions courtesy of his Greek cousin, Marina, Duchess of Kent (married to the George VI's brother), and his uncle Louis Mountbatten, but in the latter's Park Lane apartment the young Prince was often relegated to a camp bed. Philip didn't have a consistent home and his broad assortment of glamorous relations were scattered across Europe, pitched on different sides of an ugly war. Queen Victoria had been a strong advocate of cosmopolitanism in monarchy; in her opinion, Dutch William III and her own German Prince Consort were Britain's greatest royal leaders,[13] but the rule book had been brutally torn up in World War I. In 1917, George V declared his children no longer had to marry (foreign) royals but could marry English men and women. The decision was an obvious one when Europe's mightiest dynasties found themselves forced to choose sides, and first cousins fought first cousins in a conflict that saw the demise of numerous royal houses. The Greek monarch Constantine I (Philip's uncle) was exiled in 1917, only to return to Greece three years later, where a maelstrom that ended in another abdication had a direct impact on baby Prince Philip, born in Corfu's Mon Repos in 1921.

The boy's birth had been met with much euphoria; here at last was a longed-for son after four daughters for Prince Andreas,* brother of the Greek King, and his wife, Princess Alice of Greece. But what came next was ugly by anybody's standards. Greece's British-backed war against Turkey had overstretched itself and the reinstated royal family provided the desperate country with a convenient whipping boy. Another coup d'état followed. Philip's father, Prince Andreas, a major-general in the army, escaped execution but was stripped of his titles, nationality and dignity. Andreas lived out the rest of his life in France, more specifically the Riviera – a sybarite who loathed exile and lacked money – and never really recovered his identity. His wife, Princess Alice, was also badly affected. The couple's marriage, which began as one of

---

* Andrew, the British version of Andreas, was also sometimes used in reference to Philip's father.

the last hurrahs of royalty in fin-de-siècle Europe, fizzled out. The Princess had a breakdown and was sent to a sanatorium in Switzerland. By the time she reappeared on the scene in the late 1930s, her daughter, Cécile, had been killed in a plane crash and soon both Europe and her international family would be irrevocably cleaved into warring factions.

For Philip, what began as childhood exile with his family in a salubrious Parisian suburb, Saint-Cloud, by 1939 had become a solitary, dislocated existence. His financially and mentally depleted father and mother lived in France and Greece respectively and their remaining three daughters were all married to Germans actively engaged in the Nazi regime's war against Britain. In contrast, Philip's secondary education in an experimental Scottish boarding school, Gordonstoun, and his close affiliation with Victoria, his English-based maternal grandmother, and her sons (George, 2nd Marquess of Milford Haven, and his younger brother, Louis Mountbatten) saw him keen to assert his Britishness – as yet emotional rather than official. The war was the perfect opportunity to do just that and Mountbatten (known to Philip as Uncle Dickie) the ideal sponsor.

Mountbatten's own father, Prince Louis Alexander of Battenburg and for a time Britain's first sea lord, had been hounded out of office at the beginning of World War I for his German heritage. Dickie, in the absence of any sons of his own, had no intention of allowing a similar fate to befall his nephew, Philip. The path had been smoothed early on with the rebranding of the Battenburgs who had emerged from the wreckage of World War I with the new English title of Marquess of Milford Haven and the name Mountbatten. That Philip was not a Mountbatten, but instead, through his exiled father, a snappy Germanic Schleswig-Holstein-Sonderberg-Glücksburg, did not put Mountbatten off. Quite the reverse. Although Uncle Dickie failed to clinch British naturalisation for Philip before the out-break of war, he successfully steered him into the Royal Navy, where he oversaw his progress.*

Biographers are prone to pick at Philip's past and surmise that his renowned offhand manner was the product of a nomadic, insecure childhood, during which he was subjected to an assortment of schools and relations in several European countries.[14] Perhaps. But certainly it was that same childhood that equipped him well for war. Here was a boy who knew how to stand on his own two feet, an individual more than ready for his first military challenge.

It was the Italian dictator Benito Mussolini, desperately playing catch up with Nazi Germany, his ally and military superior, who gifted Philip an early break at sea. Italy's ill-advised invasion of Greece through Albania in October 1940 quickly unravelled, but the attack was sufficient to end Greek neutrality and Philip's sidelined war. The Prince's subsequent posting as midshipman on the HMS *Valiant* placed him in the eye of the storm; he was part of a British fleet convoying troops into Greece ahead of Germany's arrival to reinforce the com-promised Italians.

By March 1941 anticipation leaps from the page in Philip's diary. All shore leave had been cancelled; Italian cruisers were reportedly planning an attack, their location was identified off Cape Matapan in the Peloponnese. The intelligence came from Bletchley Park and Britain's subsequent manoeuvring was complex – the enemy could not know their encrypted commu-nications had been compromised. Code breaking wasn't

---

* Although his lifelong passion was flying and early on he harboured ambitions to join the RAF, it is significant that Philip allowed himself to be steered into the Royal Navy, a more conventional option that followed the Mountbatten family tradition. It was also the service George VI had belonged to as a young man.

Britain's only advantage, however; the Italian fleet was significantly weaker, with only one battleship, no radar and no aircraft carrier. After a successful initial attack, Britain's Commander-in-Chief of the Mediterranean, Alan Cunningham, launched a second in the middle of the night from close range at the hobbled, unsuspecting Italians. *Valiant* and a second battleship, *Barham*, opened fire – midshipman Philip was tasked with operating the searchlights, picking out the enemy across the inky black.

'As if it were broad daylight', a first cruiser was exposed and annihilated. Next the Prince trained his light left, identifying another 'enemy so close the light did not illuminate the whole ship'. Salvo after salvo smashed at point-blank range into the cruiser 'stern to stern'. The vessel 'completely vanished in clouds of smoke'.[15] The Battle of Cape Matapan cost Italy five vessels and their dead numbered over two thousand. Britain lost three airmen. Later Philip would shrug and say 'it was as near murder as anything could be in war. The cruisers just burst into tremendous sheets of flame.'[16]

That night the Prince had been party to a rare British victory before a much bigger defeat in Greece, which saw the Greek monarch evacuated to Crete in April 1941. By May the German counterattack had begun and HMS *Valiant* was strafed from the air and hit twice on the quarterdeck. But war is about winning, and from now on Philip could claim his own small part in that much longer process. On the night of 29 March, his opportunistic technical support saw him named in dispatches for his 'alertness and appreciation of the situation'.[17] This was not leadership, and the midshipman was not in contention for a medal, but he'd held his nerve and fought for two countries. The Prince of Greece had more than earned his leave.

◄◇►

'I suppose I was unusual. Avant garde? You could say that. My parents were frightfully preoccupied with singing and left me to my own devices.' Pamela was an actress who had forgone her first role on the West End stage for work at Bletchley Park, where she met her future husband. 'Yes, Jim and I were lovers. I'd had a few boyfriends and I knew he was the one.' Pamela is matter-of-fact. In 1930s' theatreland, sex outside marriage wasn't uncommon, but it was accompanied with risk. 'The men provided a sheath. And there was Dutch cap. Well, yes, some did slip up, none of the bits and pieces were terribly reliable.' She pauses. 'Bletchley Park was more mixed, there were plenty doing much worse than me – partner swapping and all sorts – but a lot of the girls were very young and naive.'

Indicative of that naivety was Pamela's friend, Rozanne Colchester, also at the Park, and so struck by the former's confession of intercourse that she later noted in her memoir: 'Pam and Jim were lovers.' Rozanne, a mere nineteen, was far too terrified to have sex.

> I promised my parents I wouldn't go to bed with anybody until I was going to marry them, because Father said darkly 'if you have a baby you will jolly well look after it yourself. We are not going to pay for it!' It was good to be tough because it was a stigma, no man would marry shop-soiled goods.

Mistakes were costly and, even at Bletchley Park, impossible to keep secret. According to one testimony, a 'sad girl had a baby and hid it in a drawer, dead of course'.[18] During the war Britain's sexual contract was only partially revised; it was older women between the ages of thirty and forty-five who had double the number of illegitimate births, not those just out of

school. Along with her friend, Sarah, nineteen-year-old Osla
Benning fell into the 'young and naive' category of Bletchley
recruit, and, in the context of the time, Sarah's protestations
of their innocence ring true.

> On the subject of boyfriends, I suppose I should mention
> sex, or the lack of it . . . during permissible social activi-
> ties it was considered all right to hold hands, accept a
> chaste kiss and a dance cheek to cheek, but the possibil-
> ity of going any further was condemned because it was
> certain to lead to pregnancy and result in ostracism.[19]

She would later confide: 'Certainly, I and all my close friends
would have considered ourselves defiled if we hadn't come to
marriage as virgins'. As for Osla, she didn't even know what an
erection was and believed a male suitor when he explained
he'd misplaced a torch in his front pocket.[20] This was a generation of women who had grown up in the dark about their own
biology. Ignorance collided with fear and, irrespective of
desire, many girls were simply too afraid to take a risk. On the
whole men, aware of the stakes, did not pressure them unduly
to do so. Sarah recalled that their 'boyfriends were decent
enough not to take advantage'.[21]

When it came to his relationship with Osla, its likely Prince
Philip was one such man. Returning from sea, with a promotion under his belt and a lieutenant's training course on the
horizon, the couple continued to see each other. By all accounts
Osla was one of the first people he telephoned when on leave.
They enjoyed rendezvous in Leicester Square's 400 Club and at
Sarah's cottage in Windsor, where her father, Richard Norton,
recalled a youthful prince with a 'forceful intellect'.[22] But sex
with this freshly pressed, one-to-watch debutante was out of
the question. Neither Philip nor Osla had their own home

(hence the cottage), and neither could afford to slip up. Their social standing and reputation were paramount in an uncertain world and, for Philip, abstention wasn't out of character. The etiquette demanded in royal households, the rigours and responsibilities as head boy at Gordonstoun, and life in the navy – they all demanded considerable discipline from an otherwise wilful young man.

But nor was blanket abstention compulsory. Sarah noted in her memoir how it was presumed that the excited young men they prohibited from having sex found gratification elsewhere. 'We imagined they would ease their frustrations by taking themselves off to a high-class brothel.'[23] Certainly this course of action, or similar, had long provided relief for royalty. George VI's father, George V, indulged in this rite of passage while in the navy, with a girl at Southsea, and he shared another with his brother. The notation in his diary – 'she is a ripper' – suggests the Prince enjoyed himself.[24] His notorious eldest son, later Edward VIII, the abdicated King, acquired an early taste for women among World War I prostitutes in France, and although his brother, later George VI, was an altogether more gauche prospect, there were regular visits to an actress, Phyllis Monkman, in London's theatreland. When she finally died in 1976, among her effects, carefully contained in a scuffed leather wallet, was a portrait of the Prince in a naval uniform and cap.[25]

At sea, miles from home, travelling from port to port, handsome lads like Philip could behave as they saw fit. Discretion was the key. For many young men, the war brokered new opportunities and encounters, sexually transmitted disease rates soared, and fallen women were the scapegoats. Philip travelled extensively, including stints of leave in Port Said, Cape Town and Sydney, where even girls from the smart set conceded that sometimes in war: 'what would seem like shocking promiscuity in peacetime, was felt as a beneficence of the heart.'[26] But back among pristine debutantes from within the bosom of upper-class British society, the Prince could not afford to put a foot wrong.

Playful was as good as it got – and according to his cousin Alexandra, it was an art form Philip knew well. When visiting his aunt, Princess Aspasia of Greece and Denmark, Alexandra described one of Philip's pre-war liaisons in a Venetian speed-boat. The phut-phut-phut of his motor suddenly cut out; the Prince was dabbling with his latest passion – Miss Cobina Wright, the sumptuous daughter of a New York socialite. Within earshot of impressionable young Alexandra and his aunt, it is hard to believe seventeen-year-old Philip did more than whet his appetite. The next morning he sheepishly blamed faulty spark plugs.[27] Early on the Prince learned when and where to walk the line between decency and indulgence. He would keep seeing Cobina for several weeks, and they even had a dalliance in London, but, by 1941, she was an established movie star and Philip was at sea. Six years later and a married woman, her showy wedding gift* to Britain's most famous bridegroom suggests neither party had anything to hide.[28] But, if nothing else, Cobina, like Osla, proves that Philip had a weakness for very beautiful, glamorous women.

His relationship with Osla also gradually petered out, despite Pamela's astute observation that theirs was 'an obvious match'. Certainly much united the pair: beyond bundles of charisma, good looks and social verve, 'neither of them, even by the standards of their time, had experienced much emotional warmth or security as children'.[29] They could take solace in each other; Philip wrote letters, Osla wore a jewelled naval cipher as a brooch and confessed she loved a naval officer, but

---

* See page 108.

there was no prospect of a future. Philip was a prince without money, a home or realm, and Osla, with a dead father and a thrice-married mother, likewise lacked a home and country to call her own. They could not give each other what they most wanted. By 1944 the fun was over and Osla was engaged to someone else; it was time to move on.* Philip had probably always intended to.

---

* Her first engagement in 1944 to diplomat Guy E. Millard (later Sir Guy) didn't last. Osla eventually married British civil servant and diplomat John Henniker-Major, 8th Baron Henniker, in 1946.

THREE

◆◇◆

'Destined for Princess Elizabeth'

It was the mid-1930s, and that bright young thing from the previous decade, dear Uncle David, otherwise known as the Prince of Wales, still enjoyed filmstar glamour and an eye for the zeitgeist. Fair-haired and debonair, this first-born son of George V managed to do what no Hanoverian or Windsor had ever done: he brought the dazzling allure of celebrity to the ancient British monarchy. The Dominions and America were enchanted by the Prince of Wales. He chewed gum, loved jazz music, dancing and diving, hung out with his own American-style brat-pack, and had a well-known weakness for Stateside divorcées. Pennsylvanian Mrs Wallis Simpson was yet more proof that David did things differently.[1] But if the Prince had spent twenty years getting away with it, kingship proved a very different game.

His modish arrival at Daddy's funeral in January 1936, 'hat-less from the air', as John Betjeman put it, was a harbinger of things to come.[2] Before the storm broke, Stanley Baldwin, Britain's avuncular Prime Minister, who stood for warm beer, village cricket and family solidarity, conceded of the forty-one-year-old new King, 'it is a tragedy he is not married'.[3] In terms of notoriety, Edward VIII's insistence over his intended bride would soon trump his bachelor reputation.

'She was a dreadful woman. An American, she wanted to be the Queen of England!' Edna Cripps, born in 1915, was the oldest person I've met with a clear recollection of the abdication.* A servant girl from Lincolnshire in the 1930s, she'd fully bought into the idea of the Royal Family as pillars of rectitude and decency. Their presence gave majesty and order to the deferential world in which Edna operated. She eagerly read royalty titbits in the local papers; her favourite was the Duchess of Kent: 'Ooh, yes, I knew all about Princess Marina's wedding. She always tended to wear blue – she was definitely the prettiest royal.' The prospect of modish Edward with his American floozy butting into this decorous scene and discrediting the throne with their 'revolting' behaviour was a step too far for Edna, and much of provincial Britain. They 'were both a bloody nuisance. He was devil of a ladies' man . . . We didn't want this American woman, who had been married twice, but she, the horrible so-and-so, was determined she was going to be Queen.'[4]

Britain's press finally confirmed what the public already knew: Edward VIII was having an affair with a twice-married American woman, and now he wanted to marry her. A few cosmopolitan youths marched in favour of the King outside Buckingham Palace, and Winston Churchill volubly declared the monarch should marry whom he liked, but conservative Britain thought otherwise. Public life and divorce did not mix. Nor Anglicanism and divorce; after all, the King was supreme governor of the Church of England. The matrimonial union of Edward and Wallis threatened the very facade of moral, upright Britain. The King had to accept the advice of his ministers – for once dear David did not get his own way. Edward VIII was duly sacrificed on the altar of monarchy.

---

* Edna Cripps, 1915–2019.

You must believe me when I tell you that I found it impossible to carry the heavy burden of responsibility and to discharge my duties as King as I would wish to do without the help and support of the woman I love.[5]

By December 1936, the newly styled Duke of Windsor was gone, and he never really returned. When it comes to monarchy, second chances are thin on the ground. The press didn't completely lose their fascination with the ex-King – Americans were particularly enamoured – but, from now on, the Duke was a sideshow, a man cut adrift for 'the woman he loved', destined to spend the rest of his life perfecting the 'art of doing nothing' with his Duchess, Wallis Simpson. (Edna nods. Quite right too.) The message going forward was uncompromising. When it came to the next British heir to the throne, winning the war would not be enough. A secure monarchy needed a state-approved secure marriage. Nothing could be left to chance. Cavalier David had left the House of Windsor dangling by a thread; it must never happen again.

The abdication, marked in her childhood diary, placed immense pressure on one small girl, HRH Princess Elizabeth. Until 1936, her family had enjoyed the trappings of monarchy without its more onerous implications – that changed overnight. From Elizabeth's point of view, initial adjustments were mainly practical: she had to learn to curtsey to her father (a privilege previously reserved for her late grandfather), and there was the move to Buckingham Palace – apparently like camping in a museum – not to mention the hoo-ha surrounding the coronation.[6] The Princesses wore coronets and bare legs beneath long skirts and Elizabeth thought the prayers went on too long. As did the photographs: her mother, Britain's new Queen Consort, sighed, 'we aren't supposed to be human'.[7] The Duchess of York had not married her Bertie to become Queen – she never forgave 'that woman', Wallis Simpson, and refused to disguise her dismay at the 'intolerable honour' of becoming Queen.[8] Not so her eldest daughter; like many girls of her generation, Elizabeth was biddable and obedient. Britain, in the 1930s, operated under a strict hierarchical order, and if her place in that order had just irrevocably shifted, so be it.

Incrementally the Princess's life changed but little was openly discussed. The subject of 'handsome golden-headed' Uncle David who had loved a 'romp' with his nieces[9] (and bore more than a passing resemblance to a certain Philip of Greece) was never mentioned. It would be nearly twenty years before Elizabeth saw him again. For the time being the Princess was heir presumptive, not heir apparent, but any slither of hope that the thirty-six-year-old Queen might push out a son was soon extinguished. If everything went according to plan, Elizabeth would become Queen. Cordoned off behind palace doors, the Princess dutifully assumed the mantle of her destiny; she imbibed constitutional titbits, stayed abreast of politics and public affairs, posed for photographs, pronounced on the wireless and assumed an honorary role as Colonel of the Grenadier Guards. But Edward VIII's fate had taught Elizabeth that the one aspect of royal life that threatened the throne more than any other wasn't fully in her control. And that was wedlock.

Most girls in wartime Britain valued a good solid marriage above all else: it was the bedrock of mid-twentieth century society. Many worried about finding the right man or, indeed, finding any man during the war. But, for Elizabeth, the stakes were dauntingly high and help explain the future monarch's early, tenacious crush on Prince Philip. A couple of other teenage encounters are indicative of the pressure she was under. They included a 1943 family get-together

with Andrew Elphinstone, about whom the Princess mourn-
fully wrote: 'I wish he wasn't my first cousin, as he's just the
sort of husband any girl would love to have',[10] and an evening
with a chinless Grenadier Guard who hurt Elizabeth's feelings when he didn't offer her more than the first dance.[11] 'War
has a little narrowed her social contacts' was how *The Times*
lightly described Elizabeth's predicament.[12] Stuck in Windsor, the subject of marriage preyed on the mind of the future
Queen. In June 1942, the sixteen-year-old briefly and unchar-
acteristically let down her royal guard and confided in her
friend Alathea, who, ears pricked and heart pounding, jotted
down the Princess's confidences.

> She said she wondered if she'd ever marry, and I assured
> her she would, and she said if she really wanted to marry
> someone she'd run way, but I know she wouldn't really –
> her sense of duty's too strong.[13]

Constricted and compromised, Uncle David's shadow was
never far away. Philip, her poster-boy prince, who was at last
enjoying his 'hot war', needed to live up to expectations.

-◇-

Edward's affair with Wallis Simpson and his subsequent abdication had enveloped the Royal Family's majesty with a
soap-opera sheen. While the British press had pandered to the
Establishment and restricted much of the pre-abdication
coverage, international papers operated under no such restraint. Nor did the removal of the disgraced King in December
1936 see interest immediately abate. Matters of the heart so
illogically, fatally entwined with the head of state proved irre-
sistible stuff. Edward had exposed the flaw at the heart of
modern monarchy and readers were eager to consume the next
instalment. The fallen King had only just arrived in Austria

(had Wallis received a ring yet, the papers mused)[14] when the American press leap-frogged over Britain's new monarch, George VI, and started speculating about the next generation, sniffing out a replacement royal celebrity. Little Elizabeth, just ten years old, was considered fair game in the January 1937 edition of *Literary Review*. The American publication had no qualms about segueing between the Princess at play, with touch tag, green hoops and toy horses, and a list of future prospective husbands for the prepubescent child. Names included a swathe of minor European royals, several of whom the pending war in Europe would exclude. As the *Review* aptly noted, royalty was an endangered species. Lucky, then, that one of her named potential suitors – 'Prince Philippe of Greece, [aged] fifteen' – landed on the right side of the conflict.[15]

Speculative press reports are important context for what's invariably seen as a one-sided game, in which Philip's Greek family is identified as scheming with English-based relatives (read Mountbatten) to manoeuvre their itinerant prince into prime position for the biggest royal prize in existence. It is true enquiries were made on Philip's behalf and vigorously pursued by Mountbatten early in the war. Visiting Greece in 1941, Henry 'Chips' Channon was full of it. Apparently Philip 'was extraordinarily handsome', and Channon gleaned from the Greek royals that he was 'to be the Prince Consort and it is for that he is serving in our Navy!!?'[16]* But this early gambit is unsurprising when the subject of Elizabeth's betrothal was being openly discussed in the press before the family had even moved into Buckingham Palace. The sharks were circling from

---

* In January 1941, Henry 'Chips' Channon was sceptical about the match, but within a year he'd come around to the idea. In January 1942, he pronounced Philip an 'absolute "charmer" aged only 20' and 'about the best-looking boy I have ever seen', and again repeated he had 'been selected as the Prince Consort of the future!' (Citation in Henry 'Chips' Channon, *The Diaries*, vol. 2, p. 702).

the very beginning. Some compassion is needed here, not just for Elizabeth but also her doting parents. Given the public interest, on one level war and their daughter's lockdown in Windsor must have been a welcome reprieve for the anxious King and Queen.

Philip, meanwhile, grappled with a very different set of problems; he was a prince whose reduced circumstances had always been horribly out of kilter with his royal pedigree. Since 1922, just a year after his birth in Corfu, the pattern was clear: instability, ignominy and insanity were the hallmarks of exile. Things had settled down a bit for his mother and father by the late 1930s, but they were still living in different countries and neither regularly saw their son. As a young boy, Prince Philip would 'take a stick and trace on the path the plans of the home he meant to build one day'.[17] Oh, for the privilege of abdicating a throne in the playboy style of Romania's King Carol or Britain's King Edward. Instead Philip grew up the recipient of holidays and humiliating hand-outs from various rich relatives; money which paid for an American school in France, a prep school in England and boarding schools in Germany and Scotland. Nothing could be taken for granted. As a naturally competitive boy, self betterment was the only option and a solid royal marriage the only means of procuring a realm.

During the war, June Hutchinson, daughter of the Countess of Westmoreland and a contemporary of Philip's, had a friend with a deep and abiding crush on the Prince. The anecdote that stems from this young woman's obsession is often cited: she and Philip lay side by side in bed and talked for hours with a bolster strategically placed between them. In all that time and despite being 'very much in love with him', the girl wasn't even the recipient of a kiss. Philip 'would not transgress the bolster'. Given what was at stake, this behaviour is

unsurprising. As discussed, sexual restraint was the only reliable form of contraception. However, the reasoning behind
Philip's piety is striking. 'He was,' he told his admirer, 'destined
for Princess Elizabeth.'[18]

This recollection came from a diary extract written decades after the event; it is not possible to pin an exact date on
the above incident, but it does suggest that those Windsor
festivities when the Prince was an occasional guest at the
beginning of the war laid firm foundations. Elizabeth, with
her pink cheeks and scrapbook, was not the only one who harboured feelings, or at least ambitions, for the future. In later
life, whenever Philip was asked about his time spent with the
Royal Family, he was disdainful. 'I suppose if I'd just been a
casual acquaintance it would all have been frightfully significant. But if you're related . . . it isn't so extraordinary to be on
kind of family relationship terms. You don't necessarily have
to think about marriage.'[19] Perhaps not, but nor is it hugely
common to write to a third cousin you hardly know.

It turns out Osla wasn't the only recipient of Philip's wartime missives. In South Africa, shortly after the Battle of Cape
Mataplan in 1941, he admitted to his cousin Alexandra he was
writing to 'Princess Elizabeth, in England'. 'But she's only a
baby', challenged Alexandra, and presumed he was wangling a
Christmas invitation. Later she retrospectively reviewed her
judgement and wondered 'had they already begun then, the
gentle assurances and recognition of the heart?'[20] In her own
sweet way, we know that Elizabeth had, and like Alexandra, I
believe Philip was also invested in the idea. It is possible to see
in an adolescent the imprint of the future adult.

Perhaps here it is helpful to draw on my own experience as
a testimony for early attachments and how they can develop
into deep relationships. I met my husband (a Romanian peas-
ant, not a Greek prince) when he was twelve and I nineteen.

We maintained intermittent contact across a continent and fell in love when he was seventeen. Our wedding came six years later.[21] Sending those letters back to England, to Osla and to Elizabeth, Philip was hedging his bets and investing in the future. Can you blame him? Britain's future prince consort was displaying canny foresight under the guise of 'family'.

-◇-

In December 1943, Philip was on leave in England and sitting in the front row of an *Aladdin* seasonal special, feasting his eyes on a dewy seventeen-year-old princess tap dancing in utility shorts and tights.[22] Shimmering inside a sequined jacket, Elizabeth was playing the male lead – of course she was. The teenager shone in what had become the Windsors' local Christmas extravaganza. With so little to go on throughout the war, the press honed in on this annual performance to affirm the future monarch's musical and theatrical accomplishments. No matter that Margaret was infinitely more talented, Elizabeth had a 'true ear and a melodious soprano voice', she was an 'excellent pianist' and 'has learnt to rub shoulders easily with her contemporaries'. In fact, Elizabeth did more than that: she patted the cast of village children and evacuees on the back, linked arms and danced with them, and indulged in several slap-stick pranks, including popping out of a laundry basket dressed as a charwoman. The King and Queen howled with delight.[23]

Amid festive ideas of Merrie England, this was the stuff of dreams. And it didn't escape the press's notice that lapping it up next to his freshly widowed cousin, Marina, Duchess of Kent,* was 'a very fair, older looking' Prince Philip.[24] People

---

* The Duke of Kent (the King's younger brother) was killed in a plane crash in Caithness, Scotland, on 25 August 1942. In an RAF Short Sunderland Flying boat heading for Iceland, it was the first time a Royal Family member had been killed on active service for over 450 years.

outside the family were starting to join the dots, and those with a ringside seat began to realise that love might be in the air, or at least in the offing. Even jealous Alathea noted in her diary that a wedding would be a 'most desirable event', while cautioning Philip 'could not be in love' with an Elizabeth who persisted in childish pantomime antics.[25] Rigid aristocratic Alathea couldn't comprehend the appeal of Elizabeth's naive charm. Blanching at a future sovereign backslapping commoners and cross dressing, so too did she miss the point of modern monarchy. The special bond between the royals and their people that the newspapers picked up on was in fact the Windsor family's secret weapon. The Queen had shown an appreciation of its importance when she'd refused to abandon a bombed Buckingham Palace, insisting she could finally look the East End in the eye. The Royal Family's success depended on their popularity with the masses; it was a formula that Philip, a prince without a people, instinctively understood.

'Weather-beaten and strained', a 'grave charming young man' recently back from assisting in the Allied landings on Sicily, the Prince had been through the mill in the Mediterranean and acquitted himself well. Appointed First Lieutenant and second-in-command of a destroyer, at twenty-one he became the youngest officer to hold such a post, and physically the stress of war and his part in it had taken its toll (as did a bout of pre-Christmas flu). Crawfie found Philip 'greatly changed', presumably so did the Princess, but in a good way, for she had 'a sparkle about her none of us had seen before'.[26] Equally changed, almost buxom, the Princess and her affirming performance tickled the Prince. Despite her shy exterior, here was proof that she didn't take herself too seriously. The pantomime was the very essence of light relief and afterwards came a weekend of capering, when Philip and his cousin,

David, the 3rd Marquess of Milford Haven, 'went mad' and 'danced and dance and danced' with the two Princesses.[27] Philip and Elizabeth remained in contact for the rest of the war.

In fact they did more than that. They swapped photographs, and the delight Philip's picture gave Elizabeth saw her dance around the room.[28] Crawfie cautioned against the Princess putting the photograph on her mantelpiece: as future Queen, people came and went in her newly appointed, chintzy pink apartment: word would get out. Elizabeth rebelled with a replacement photo – Philip not quite incognito under a bushy beard.[29] Amid these sweetheart anecdotes is a sense that Elizabeth wanted to show off her brave sailor, and certainly Crawfie suspected as much. But what girl didn't want to show off her beau in 1940s wartime Britain?

This was a conflict where women remained strictly non-combatants; despite unprecedented female conscription and military uniforms, the hero narrative was almost exclusively reserved for men, and traditional gendered spheres changed surprisingly little. In a world where young boys were risking their lives and dying, the soldier's masculine appeal increased exponentially. Almost every girl in Britain dreamt of a hero's return when peace came. Elizabeth might have been a princess but she was also an impressionable young teenager; 'Viking' Philip ticked all the right boxes.

Certainly the Prince had a rough charm rarely seen within the confines of Windsor. He arrived at the castle with his cousins, genetic proof of his royal stamp, but from an early age his life had been informed by male-dominated institutions and communal living, sharp-edged discipline and rowdy humour. Even among his peers, Philip could occasionally appear abrasive. His final school report noted that his impressive 'leadership qualities' were 'marred at times by impatience and intolerance'.[30] Likewise in the navy, his competitiveness and brusque exterior occasionally put noses out of joint. As a guest in Windsor Castle, he laughed 'v. loudly' at films in front of the Royal Family, and his manners 'left nothing to be desired'.[31] This alpha male approach evidently worked for the smitten Princess – he was a breath of fresh air blowing through the stuffy castle – but her elders were less than impressed. Crawfie found him rude, so too other members of the royal household.[32]

Philip's capacity to rub people up the wrong way proved a lifelong Achilles heel, one of which he was acutely aware. What he could get away with at sea under the guise of leadership and princely presumption was less easy to disguise among middle-aged monarchs. The Queen received a cagey thank-you note after Philip's winter visit in 1943, when he hoped his behaviour 'did not get out of hand'. The Prince had fired off notes like this before, writing to a bereaved family friend in January 1943:

> Dear Zia, I know you will never think very much of me. I am rude and unmannerly and I say many things out of turn which I realise afterwards may have hurt someone. Then I am filled with remorse and I try to get matters right . . .[33]

Private Secretary Alan Lascelles's tight-lipped observation 'I prefer the latter' in reference to Philip's cousin, David Milford Haven, said it all. The Prince's entitled bumptiousness ruffled feathers. As one courtier observed: 'the family were at first horrified when they saw that Prince Philip was making up to Princess Elizabeth. They felt he was rough, ill mannered, uneducated and would probably not be faithful.'[34]

In the context of family, the King and Queen had given a scion of a disreputable royal house access to their inner most sanctuary. In breezed Prince Philip, the very embodiment of jocular, challenging service life, a world they had gone out of their way to shield the young Princess from.

FOUR

◆◇◆

Demob Happy

'I signed up when I was seventeen-and-a-half. That was the youngest age you could join the military services.' Barbara Weatherill is ninety-seven years old and until very recently her life shadowed the Queen's. 'I am definitely a royalist. Oh, yes. I had a lovely sepia picture book on the Princess when I was a little girl with pictures and so forth.' Tucked away in the Yorkshire Dales, the only child of a policeman from the West Riding Constabulary, Barbara grew up knowing that the future monarch loved the colour yellow, belonged to the Girl Guides and preferred ponies to bicycles.

She sighs. 'Everybody compares me to the Queen these days because there aren't many of us left and I was in same the military service as her – the ATS.' The Auxiliary Territorial Service was established in 1938 as a catch-all to solve the army's 'manpower' problems in World War II. Although denigrated as attracting the 'wrong sort of girls', nick-named the Auxiliary Tarts Service and renowned for its unattractive khaki uniform, the ATS quickly became the largest of the three women's services; it was responsible for recruiting girls to operate the technology on Britain's gun-sites and later drafting them overseas in support of the Allied army on the Continent.[1]

Of all the ATS trades available to women, driving was seen

as the most glamorous. Barbara is adamant. 'I always knew I wanted to drive. When I grew up it was only upper-bracket girls who had access to a car. So I made it very clear that only driving would do.' Champing at the bit to get away from the confines of domestic life in Yorkshire and a dull telephonist job, Barbara challenged her parents' reticence and signed up as soon as she could, stoutly insisting, 'I served from 1943, that was two years earlier than Her Royal Highness. Bless her.'[2]

Down south, trapped in Windsor, Princess Elizabeth also wanted a slice of the action and waged her own war of attrition against a reluctant father, who, like so many men of his generation, did not approve of women in uniform. There had been considerable national anxiety at the prospect of 'the wives and mothers of the future' being exposed to the 'wholesale hardening process' that came with military service and Elizabeth was more than just a future wife and mother.[3] But as the parent of the future Queen, the King had to bear in mind the changing optics of the day. From December 1941, women between twenty and thirty years old were obliged to join the war effort, with the conscription age soon dropping to nineteen. Like so many girls, Barbara got in early, but Elizabeth, who'd set her heart on the Wrens (Women's Royal Naval Service), had less luck. Convincing the ancient machinery of crown and state was a laborious process; despite numerous honorary roles, no female member of the Royal Family had ever served in the military fulltime.

For Elizabeth's eighteenth birthday in April 1944, *The Times* pitched the future monarch to a war-weary nation. The Princess had accomplishments, a love of the outdoors, musical abilities and a firm grasp of history, but beyond the platitudes there was something missing.[4] A war story. No, Britain wasn't ready for female soldiers, but it had performed an almighty U-turn on female service, and if the monarchy was going to reflect the people, then the Princess was right: she needed to serve.

What came next happened slowly. The paper trail between the ATS and Buckingham Palace was extensive, and the minute attention to detail indicative of a life that was controlled by the institution to which it belonged.[5] Elizabeth would join up but not with the classier Wrens, rather the much bigger ATS, where the Princess's stodgy Aunt Mary (the Princess Royal) was already Controller Commandant. The ATS needed the publicity and the numbers, the Wrens did not. Alathea, who had opted for nursing in the VAD, was horrified by Elizabeth in her 'ATS battle dress, which consists of trousers' and thought she 'looked awful'. The Princess went to 'Camberley for a course every day for three weeks and after that she ceases it – thank Heaven!'[6]* Elizabeth was now officially part of the People's War, but the Royal Household had done everything in its powers to limit the experience.

Barbara, who also trained in Camberley, looks at Elizabeth's ATS training schedule and tuts. We have been through this before. 'You see, her course was very pared down. There was no physical training, no gas drill, no fatigues. Well, yes, I suppose she did serve, but she didn't even sleep in the barracks.' Rather than feeling resentful, Barbara is sorry that Elizabeth missed out. Every morning and evening, bottle-green royal transport swept up to take the future Queen back to her castle. Recruits who trained alongside Elizabeth remember a 'quiet girl'. Someone who 'didn't put herself forward.'[7] And no wonder. She was in the war – the press regaled the public with stories of a princess proficient behind the wheel of a Bedford truck – but she wasn't one of them, not really.

---

* In fact, Elizabeth's training spanned almost two months between March and April 1945.

53

Barbara recalls: 'in Camberley we stayed in huts in the grounds, at least twelve of us in each, and we'd chat away in the evenings'. The experience was an eye opener for a seventeen-year-old from the Yorkshire Dales. A favourite story is the Glaswegian woman three beds down. At forty-four years old, from the Gorbals, Marianne MacDonald had 'an accent you could cut with a knife – as rough as they come', and was 'quite open about being a prostitute. In fact, I think she still was. She was a blousy sort, not the escort type.' Barbara was terrified but soon discovered that Marianne had 'a heart of gold'.

> She came in one evening and said 'can I have a word, young'un!' Well, she started asking me all these questions about the woman in the bed next door to me. Had she made any approaches? And then she stopped and said 'you haven't a clue what I am talking about have you?'

Rumours were rife that the girl in bed number two was a 'lesbian' and Marianne was determined to 'protect' innocent Barbara. 'I hadn't a clue about such things in those days. I could have got mixed up in a world I didn't understand!' Barbara chuckles and concludes that it was 'inevitable' the Princess didn't sleep in barracks. 'It's a pity, really, but that is just how it was.'

The story is of its time: hundreds of thousands of girls all over Britain burst out of the confines of their small parent-governed routines and were exposed to the habits, behaviours and desires of recruits from very different walks of life. After an initial training course, there were evenings socialising with different regiments, girls met boys on their own terms, they shared a smoke and a drink in the NAAFI* and, if there was no corporal in the vicinity, enjoyed a quick pet behind the barracks. That was service life in the 1940s Britain. But it was not the life of a future Queen, the Royal Family made sure of that. A safe fifteen miles away from Camberley, Elizabeth went to bed every night in Windsor Castle.

Given the Princess's heavily curated wartime existence and his part in its restrictive nature, it's not surprising that, on VE Day night, the King closed his diary with a rueful comment about his daughters: 'Poor Darlings, they have never had any fun yet.'[8] Flushed and fresh from 'walking miles' and dancing with an attractive 'Philip look-alike', Elizabeth gleefully noted in her diary: 'ate, partied, bed 3am!' The Princess had bided her time, served in a limited capacity, and done what she was told, but now she was nineteen and had clear ideas about what she wanted for the future.

Three months later, on VJ Day, 15 August 1945, Elizabeth was out again. This time she 'congered into house† . . . sang till 2am. Bed at 3am.'[9] And the Princess had plenty to sing about – the end of the Pacific War signalled the end of Philip's war. Soon her prince would be coming back to Britain.

◆

In the wake of Prince Philip's death in 2021, considerable attention was given to his wartime service – here was a naval hero with a track record of derring-do, a man whose lifetime of Great British public service began in the war, first as a midshipman in the Mediterranean Fleet and then a lieutenant in the British Pacific Fleet. Hailed as one of the Great Generation, his death

---

* The Navy, Army and Air Force Institutes were run by the British Armed Forces for recreational purposes and sold sundries and refreshments to servicemen and women.

† Buckingham Palace.

coincided with the high noon of World War II nostalgia, as Britain in the grip of a pandemic reflected on the service of a prince with 'Hans Anderson fairytale good looks' who had defied the odds at sea.[10]

Cast through the prism of time, Philip's story does have a fairytale quality to it, but, as is so often the case, the reality was more complex. It's true that his 'great war' did not stop with a dispatches mention in 1941. Prior to Philip's appearance at the Princesses' *Aladdin* spectacle in December 1943, he had played his own dazzling part in the Sicily landings, with feats recorded in hagiographical detail by the ship's yeoman. 'The stars were bright and sea was black', and the vision for enemy bombers dangerously clear. Here was a brave prince and 'a brilliant plan that was destined to save our lives.'[11] With *Boys Own* verve, under Philip's supervision the crew 'lashed together large planks of wood', which were duly set alight, providing 'billowing clouds of smoke' and the pretence of a vessel burning at sea.[12] A perfect cover that allowed Philip and his good ship *Wallace* to escape to (relative) safety.

Subsequently posted to the Pacific as the First Lieutenant of HMS *Whelp*, there are more stories of bravery: pulling survivors from an Allied bomber out of the sea and retrieving a drowning pilot in *Whelp*'s whaler. These heroics are matched with high days and holidays onshore in India and Australia. When he wasn't serving, Philip was apparently either surrounded by 'armfuls' of girls with his main mucker, the Australian First Lieutenant Mike Parker, or being entertained by his stunningly successful Uncle Dickie in Egypt and India respectively.[13]

On the surface it was a blessed life, and, for sure, every man standing in 1945 had to contend with the issue of survivor's guilt. How the hell had they made it through? But beyond his impressive wartime narrative with its trajectory of action and promotions, an insecure thread persists in Philip's story. What started as an unstable childhood ('everybody has a family to go back to and I don't', his end-of-term refrain)[14] developed into a series of family tragedies compounded by the complexity of war.

Mike Parker's oft quoted line 'we were both orphans' (neither were) carried some truth in relation to Philip. A lot of attention has been paid to the key role Louis Mountbatten played in the Prince's formative years. But it was Louis's older brother, Uncle Georgie, the 2nd Marquess of Milford Haven, and a British naval commander, who provided Philip with his first surrogate father-figure, guiding him into prep school and offering succour and shelter in the holidays. Then, suddenly and prematurely, Uncle Georgie died in 1938. The death shook schoolboy Philip, who was already coping with another tragedy.

The preceding year his favourite sister, Cécile, her husband, the Hereditary Grand Duke of Hesse, and two of their children were wiped out in an aeroplane crash. The loss was grave – Philip became very quiet upon receipt of the news – and the backdrop tense; fraught geopolitics overshadowed the pitiful family situation. At the funeral, amid all the British-based Mountbatten relatives and Philip's own father and mother, was Hermann Wilhelm Göring, founder of the Gestapo and head of the Luftwaffe. The presence of this high-ranking Nazi symbolised a deepening political divide that would further fracture Philip's already disparate family.[15] Like Cécile, his three remaining sisters were married to Germans who fought for their Fatherland in World War II. (Prince Christoph of Hesse, Sophie's husband, was an early member of the SS – Hilter's elite bodyguard.) Meanwhile, Philip's mother, Alice, returned to her beloved Greece in 1939 and refused to leave when the Germans came. She wrote to Philip of her two-bedroom flat, wondered why he was fighting in the British fleet not the Greek Navy, and took refuge in her Orthodox faith and various missions to save orphans and Jews.[16]

But it was the premature death of his father in 1944 that underscored a loss dating all the way back to Philip's childhood. Although Prince Andreas had kept an eye on his son's school reports (as his only boy, the reputation of the family was at stake), contact was intermittent at best.[17] This did not dim Philip's devotion to his father, quite the opposite, but something had been missing and now it was gone. Receiving news of Andreas's death when aboard HMS *Whelp*, Philip was unable to attend the funeral, just as he had been unable to visit his father in Vichy France earlier in the war. It wasn't until 1946 that he visited Monte Carlo and picked up Prince Andreas's meagre effects from his girlfriend, the Comtesse de La Bigne. Philip appreciated her eccentric glamour, and perhaps, also, the care she had shown his father.

As per his past, the Prince's future was unsettled, a worrying prospect for a man who liked to be in control. The end of the war signalled the end of Philip's structured existence as part of a naval fleet. In 1946, the itinerant Prince of Greece and Denmark came back to Britain, where he still had no home.* And no immediate family. In this context, it is easy to understand the appeal of constant, sensible, no-frills Elizabeth; his affection for her had been common knowledge among his crew. Philip carried the Princess's picture in a brown leather frame: broad face, curled hair, reassuring kind eyes.[18] Elizabeth, with her devoted parents, steadfast manner and vast guaranteed inheritance, represented everything that eluded him. She was a million miles away from the beautiful society girls whom Philip 'squired' and flirted with en route to

---

* 'Of no fixed abode' was his strapline in visitor books.

marriage. The Princess promised a world both entirely different from his own and enticingly familiar. In July 1943 he wrote to her mother, the Queen, acknowledging 'the simple enjoyment of family pleasures and amusements and the feeling that I am welcome to share them'.[19] And he probably meant it.

Philip wanted Elizabeth and, a desire kindled early, it grew. He had mooted the possibility of their marriage to the exiled Greek King, shortly after his Christmas visit to Windsor in 1943. George II informed George VI, who pressed pause. It was too soon. Is any father ready to relinquish their daughter into the arms of another man? The King certainly wasn't and he didn't believe Elizabeth was ready either. George VI was mindful that his own (highly successful) marriage had been to a woman aged twenty-three, while the Princess was still just a teenager. Elizabeth is 'too young for that now' and had not yet met 'any young men her own age', he explained to his mother.[20]

Stalling was easy during the war – Philip was on the other side of the world. But after his 1946 return to England, the Prince, desk-bound with a dull naval job in Corsham, Wiltshire, was harder to keep at bay. Roaring up to Buckingham Palace in a MG sports car (by all accounts his only material asset), he was a man on a mission and refused to apologise for it, explaining to the Queen: 'there is always a small voice that keeps saying "nothing ventured, nothing gained" – well, I did venture and I gained a wonderful time.'[21] Renowned for her appeasing demeanour, the Queen let it pass. She said nothing. How could she do otherwise when her daughter was shiny eyed? 'Someone is coming tonight!'[22]

Elizabeth now had her own suite and household at Buckingham Palace, but invariably the couple dined together in the old nursery – Philip in his shirt sleeves and Margaret in tow. Fish, pudding and orange juice, and a game of catch in the hall. Hidden as much as possible from public sight, the couple were clearly in love, but love is not enough when you are destined for the British throne. Crawfie, one of the many curtain twitchers in the Palace, surmised it was Philip's lack of 'home or a kingdom' that was the problem. He had the inescapable whiff of a fortune hunter about him, but it was more than that. Perspicacious Margaret got to the nub of the matter when she asked: 'He's not English. Would it make a difference?'[23]

◆◇◆

The vista is a roaring waterfall, candescent spray, deep black pooling burns, heathered hills. The Princess was staying at Balmoral and the footage was filmed by the family.[24] The impression given is liberating and uncluttered; there's a *Swallows and Amazons*' quality to these images – this is downtime, outside, in the open air and away from Joe-public. It was August 1946 and Elizabeth had at last escaped London, her post-war home, where the Princess's every outing had been tracked, her sartorial choices examined, the company she kept recorded, the music she danced to critiqued. Drab, down-at-heel Britain was hungry for a gilt-edged young love story and the tabloids didn't disappoint.

> *Daily Mail*, 27 March 1946: 'Lord St. Just, 24-year-old lieutenant of the King's Royal Rifle Corps' hosted a party and 'the Princess danced with him for 25 minutes on the crowded floor. They did a fast rumba, followed by a bahia, a samba and a slow bolero.' The partying continued after midnight.

> *Daily Mail*, 29 May 1946: 'Princess Elizabeth dances with Captain Humphreys, a Guards officer in her party at the Navy League dinner-ball at the Dorchester last night. The King . . . looked in at the ballroom for a few minutes – but there was no one dancing. He was too early.'

Daily Mail, 1 June 1946: At Windsor Hotel in 'a pink dress and white fur coat' dancing to Paul Jones 'the Princess started with a Grenadier Guards Officer, but quickly lost him, and then had a succession of partners.'[25]

In the summer of 1946, coverage of the heir to the throne's love preferences provided the heartbeat of high society's social scene. Philip and Elizabeth were occasionally at the same event but rarely danced together – that would've given the game away. Better surely to have newspapers peppered with the names of hopeful British gentlemen? Scrutiny was restrained by today's standards but intrusive nonetheless. Decades later Elizabeth reminisced: 'Balmoral is a place one looks forward to very much, it has an atmosphere of its own.'[26] And no wonder; amid Scotland's 'flood and mountain', the family were guaranteed some privacy. It was here that Prince Philip was invited in August 1946, at the height of speculation over Elizabeth's intentions.

In the home-shot footage, the fresh-faced Prince looks almost shy: his head is cocked, his glances cautious. In one frame he is paring a vegetable, in another rowing the Princess across a loch. He wears cotton slacks, she a crushed-raspberry-coloured blouse. It is impossible not to be moved: they are clearly in love. But despite the absence of the press, they were not alone – far from it.[27]

I grew up in feudal Highland Scotland in the 1970s and 80s. There the calendar revolved around the shooting season, in an existence where big houses, estate game keepers and terrifying highland women loomed large. Even then, posh Scotland had its own clannish exclusivity. It was a world the Princess had grown up in: her great great grandmother, Queen Victoria, sealed the affection between the royals and Highland life and her mother was from one of Scotland's grandest families – the Strathmores. So, yes, Elizabeth wore Balmoral tartan like a second skin; she wriggled on her tummy, handled a shot gun and could fell a stag. She belonged. Philip did not. He arrived without a pair of plus fours, was a 'rather erratic' shot (and stuck on the outside of the line as far away as possible from the King) and, in this pronounced feudal hierarchy, his manner, in the words of one gamekeeper, appeared 'rather unpolished.'[28] Foreign even? Yes, Philip had been to a Scottish school, but elite Scots were not educated at new-age experimental Gordonstoun, they went south to Eton College, where future courtiers and aristocrats had their edges rubbed off.

Britain's Scottish Queen had been a stalwart during World War II. She stuck out her chin, held on to her handbag* and picked her way through bombed London. Her royal stock rose, but the impact of the conflict was lasting. She did not like Germans. There is an irony to this antipathy, given the heritage of the family she'd married into. But the Windsors had worked so successfully at their everyman cosy English image that one almost forgot they were Hanoverian by descent. Not so Philip. He looked German, with a manner that certainly wasn't British, and in his family tree there were Teutons everywhere.

A good solid British aristocrat would have served the Princess's purposes much better, at least so thought the Queen. On her alleged list was one 'Johnnie' Spencer, Viscount Althorp,† but young Elizabeth was far too self possessed to fall for a dimmer member of the landed gentry.[29] Meanwhile, much of the court agreed with the Queen about Philip – according to Private Secretary Sir Edward Ford, their doubts had 'a great deal to do with the fact that he had

---

* But if you are in royal circles, it is bag never handbag.
† Later 8th Earl Spencer, Johnnie married (and divorced) Frances Fermoy. Their third child was Lady Diana Spencer.

so much German blood'. That sentiment also infested political circles. 'Anthony Eden, Harold Macmillan and others – it was extraordinary how anti-German they all were.'[30] In Scotland, the problem was compounded by the Queen's unpleasant younger brother, David Bowes-Lyon, another member of the cliquey Balmoral house party that summer, who 'had it in for Philip right from the start'.[31] This hostile backdrop contextualises a letter Philip sent to the Queen in late 1946, apologising for a 'rather heated discussion' he'd started at dinner and hoping that she didn't consider him too 'violently argumentative and an exponent of socialism'.[32] Among the Bowes-Lyons, a little of Philip went a very long way.

Perhaps, then, it was fortuitous that the Queen was incapacitated during the family's Scottish sojourn: the *Daily Express* reliably informed its readers Her Majesty 'slipped, fell and hurt her left leg while crossing the brook in lonely Glen Gairn'. She missed church, and presumably missed more than that. Without 'Mummy' breathing down her neck, the Princess had a freer rein.[33] Surely the King could not fail to notice how well the young couple got on? Philip shared the family's pratfall sense of humour and talked to Elizabeth as an equal – what other man could do that? Certainly, on a personal level, the two men had much in common. Retrospectively and reluctantly, Philip admitted it was here at Balmoral in 1946 that: 'one thing led to another. It was sort of fixed up.'[34] By all accounts, during the August visit the King acquiesced in principle to the couple's engagement, but there was to be no public announcement. While the sovereign's reluctant blessing was an important start,* it was just the beginning of a very convoluted process.

---

* The 1772 Royal Marriages Act stipulated that, under the age of twenty-five, the heir to the throne required permission from the monarch to marry.

George VI was the not the only family member intricately involved in the relationship between Elizabeth and Philip. His cousin, Louis Mountbatten, pursued the match from the outset with the unconcealed zeal of a fanatic – he had been the patron of Elizabeth and Philip's first proper meeting in Dartmouth 1939. Uncle Dickie was devoted to his young 'killingly funny' nephew – just talking about him made his 'sleepy strange eyes light up with an affectionate, almost paternal light'.[35] This affection fuelled Mountbatten's ambitious streak – he always went the extra mile for himself and his family.

Philip was fond of his uncle but took his scheming with a pinch of salt, wryly referring to himself as Dickie's 'Pygmalion' and cautioning against Mountbatten's more overt politicking: 'I beg of you, not too much advice in affairs of the heart or I shall be forced to do the wooing by proxy.' That Philip understood the pitfalls of Mountbatten as a backer is reflected in the note he wrote when Dickie was promoted, mid-war, to Supreme Allied Commander for South East Asia. 'As a string puller, of course, you have practically lost all value, you're so big now that it might smell of nepotism.'[36] Pushy and prone to name dropping, Uncle Dickie and his wife, Edwina, were regarded as too self serving and politically radical (and sexually louche) for many within court circles to countenance. The last thing they wanted was a placement prince in Buckingham Palace, with Mountbatten his puppeteer.

George VI knew exactly what his forceful cousin and entourage of Greek–German relations were up to and he did not approve, issuing a warning shot across Mountbatten's bows in 1944: 'I have come to the conclusion we are going too fast.'[37] Uncle Dickie continued to preoccupy himself with the outstanding issue of Philip's British naturalisation, but pretended it had nothing to do with a possible marriage. Few were fooled and Mountbatten had to watch his step on two fronts. If this thinly disguised Battenburg was prone to getting backs up in court, Fleet Street's henchmen were equally suspicious, and it was in the popular press that 'alien' Prince Philip also had to win hearts and minds. Post-war, the mood of the country had changed. In Prime Minister Clement Attlee's People's Britain, more than ever the future monarch and her marriage needed a public seal of approval.

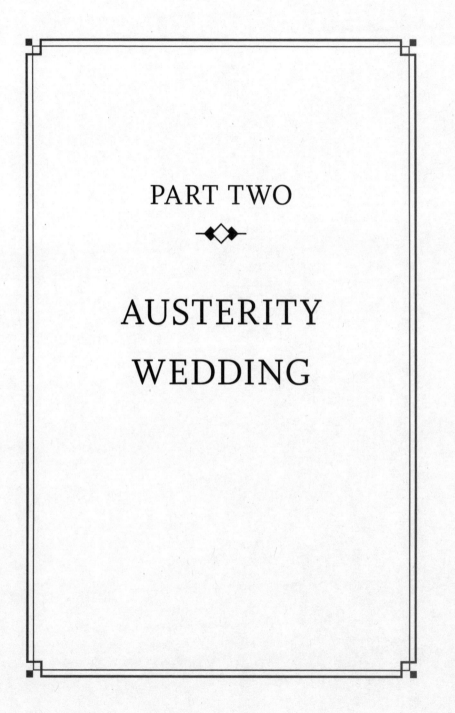

PART TWO

AUSTERITY
WEDDING

FIVE

◆◇◆

'Should Our Future Queen Wed Philip?'

Daphne Attridge is an ardent royalist. She always has been.

> I grew up thirty miles from Sandringham, in Feltwell,
> Norfolk. There was no bus service from the village
> back then but I knew all about the family and I always
> did like Philip. We share a birthday. I'm going to be
> ninety-nine tomorrow and he would've been one-
> hundred-and-one.

She pats her chestnut-coloured hair and examines the photograph I've taken on my mobile. 'Yes, I suppose you can post that one.' Appearance is very important to Daphne; she has exacting standards, both for herself and her royals.

> I suppose you could say he was *absolutely* handsome.
> Elizabeth did look lovely sometimes, but Philip was just
> so handsome. Certainly she wasn't as good looking as
> him or Margaret, but I think he saw the potential. He
> was drifting around in no man's land; he'd had a diffi-
> cult childhood so it made sense to marry Elizabeth.
> Well, yes, quite a lot of things were said about him at
> the time.

Daphne sighs. She remembers a 'debonair' prince, someone who 'had probably sowed his wild oats and the King wasn't happy about this. And of course he was foreign. So the Princess was sent on a cruise to forget about him. At least I think that's what happened.' She smiles; Philip and Elizabeth were part of her generation, talking about them anchors her back to a past when she was a pretty young thing in a post-war world where 'marriage was very very upfront'. Daphne was engaged at seventeen and a half (and six months later promptly unengaged).

> But the point is marriage was a big part of life. It was our focus. So, yes, there was a lot of talk about the Princess and Philip. I liked him myself. He spoke his mind and was always getting into trouble, a bit like I do.[1]

Daphne is proud of her exceptional memory and much of her testimony stands up to examination. While the Prince had been secluded from the press during his 1946 Balmoral sojourn, his appearance in Scotland had not gone unnoticed: 'Philip, who is 23, is at present at Balmoral Castle on one of his visits to the Royal Family.'[2] His inclusion at the Windsor's most intimate holiday home ramped up speculation that had already been in circulation for over a year. With a new challenging tone, *The Star* had led the fray in September 1945, writing: 'Rumour is again finding a husband for the most eligible bride in the world – nineteen-year-old Princess Elizabeth', before insisting that, 'Nobody, nowadays, would welcome a marriage to some young princeling just for the sake of finding a Royal bridegroom to be the eventual Prince Consort.' Philip, the 'Greek Prince', was named in the next paragraph. Even for the less than perceptive reader, the subtext was clear: the paper did not like the idea of a Johnny foreigner marrying their princess.* It had been a 'pleasure . . . when the present King, as Duke of York, chose a British girl for his bride and married Lady Elizabeth Bowes-Lyon in 1923.'[3]

The forthright nature of the article disturbed the Palace, which promptly issued the first of several denials regarding Elizabeth and Philip. A year later, in September 1946, the Palace was still denying the existence of a possible engagement. The court's unprecedented concern over tittle-tattle pointed towards a new relationship between royalty and a less deferential press. So much for The Star's disingenuous hope that 'the Princess will marry for love, as her parents did.'[4] Here was a girl not only beholden to the King, his courtiers and his ministers, but likewise to Britain's fourth estate. In this democratic new era, newspapers expected to have a voice in royal affairs like never before.

If The Star had the capacity to rattle the royal cage, there were other far bigger players that had to be held at bay. William Maxwell Aitken, 1st Baron Beaverbrook, was a pugnacious force in British public life; a Canadian self-made millionaire, Lord Beaverbrook had been building his media empire and arm-bending at the highest levels in British political life since before World War I. By the 1940s, his Express newspapers enjoyed the world's largest circulation: 2.25 million daily sales, for campaigning publications that were uncompromisingly patriotic. These conservative newspapers were the lifeblood that helped sustain the magic between the monarchy and its people, and in a country still nursing open wounds from fighting a world war, that monarchy had to be unstintingly British. This posed a problem for Philip once he had been spotted at

---

* In a further slight against the Prince, the article inferred that he was Elizabeth's second cousin. i.e. a little too close for comfort. He wasn't – he was her third cousin.

Balmoral, which was compounded by Beaverbrooke's well known disdain for his uncle, meddlesome Mountbatten. The Prince was tainted by association. Uncle Dickie understood the stakes were high: 'foreign Philip' needed an immediate facelift.

> [Any]thing you can do to get your . . . friends to realise that [Philip] has absolutely nothing whatever to do with the political set-up in Greece . . . will be to the good.

Tom Driberg, openly gay and an unlikely combination of gossip columnist and Labour MP, received a missive from his friend, Mountbatten. So too did a series of newspaper editors, with special attention paid to those at the *Express*.[5] Philip was being rebranded by his uncle and nothing was going to be left to chance. Newspaper reports that wrote anything along the lines of 'King George, while having the highest regard for Prince Philip, fears there might be political repercussions in Britain if the Princess marries a foreigner' had to stop.[6]

Long gone were the days when Greece was associated with a pantheon of greats – lofty Homeric ideals, ancient Athenian notions of freedom, Periclean levels of oration – even Lord Byron's romantic version of a thrusting new nineteenth-century nation-state was consigned to the past. In 1946, modern Greece had little to recommend it to a British public that lumped the country in with disparaging ideas about the perfidious Balkans. Coups, military weakness, communists and corrupt kings defined a people who, by 1946, had descended into a messy civil war. Philip was George II's nephew; worse still, he was sixth in line to a throne with unpleasant pre-war fascist associations, fighting the very communists who had pushed back against the Nazis. Mountbatten needed to keep his campaign simple.

Philip was not Greek (racially this much was true – the Greek royal family had not one drop of Hellenic blood). Driberg obliged, explaining to his readers that Prince Philip was 'an intelligent, broad-minded, fair, good-looking young man . . . he could not even speak Greek, having left Greece as an infant'.[7]

As for the Prince's naturalisation application, according to Mountbatten that was only unresolved because of the war; to all intents and purposes, the Prince was British. Uncle Dickie did not go in for subtleties. *The Times* got the message and helped spell it out: Philip was 'the grandson of one very distinguished British admiral and the nephew of another'. He 'joined the Royal Navy by open competition in the ordinary course and . . . but for the abnormal conditions arising from a state of war, he would ordinarily have become a British subject . . . in 1939'.[8] Mountbatten, 'ruthless in his approach to the royals', greased the wheels, or in the words of an astonished *Express* editor, pushed an extraordinary 'campaign of nobbling'.[9] The results were effective: the conservative press towed the line, and after audiences with both the Home Secretary and the Prime Minister, Mountbatten clinched an agreement for Philip's naturalisation. So far so good, but it was hardly romantic.[10]

Daphne shakes her head.

Poor Philip. He never sounded Greek to me. I spoke to him once about fifteen years ago in Ipswich. It was a royal visit and the Queen turned down the row with cadets. I knew she would: she likes men in uniform. And the Prince came over to us women. He joked about me living in the million-pound apartments on the dock. 'No, I don't!' I said, and he took hold of my gold sovereign necklace and said, 'Well, it looks like you could afford it!

73

Old Philip flirting with old Daphne.

> Funny to think he was the same man from all those years
> ago. He'd aged a fair bit. Back then what we really wanted
> to know was whether they were in love. That was impor-
> tant. We wanted to know they were happy.

◆

To Rachmaninoff's Piano Concerto No. 2, Laura impermissi-
bly and passionately fell in love. The year is 1945 and the
location somewhere in middle England. Dr Alec is (moder-
ately) handsome, dapper even, and he promises something yet
more profound than a pleasing aesthetic. This man is sensi-
tive, thoughtful, he understands Laura's needs, and when they
kiss, it is deep and tender. The tension is stretched taut across
the screen. But of course it could never happen. They were
married, each to someone else. In the end they chose to stay
apart, the relationship was never consummated but the longing almost consumed them. Laura returned home to Fred, her
dull husband, and Alec took a doctoring job far away in the
Empire, and so the credits rolled at the end of *Brief Encounter*.

The audience could breathe again, loosen their collars and
wonder what if? What if sexual desire had been allowed to
trump duty and marriage in 1940s Britain? Nöel Coward's art-
ful script, acted out exquisitely by Celia Johnson, manipulated
a predominantly female audience long accustomed to a world
of physical frustrations, pedestrian marriage and wifely com-
mitments. Whatever illicit blips there may have been during
the war were over. In late 1945, it was all about returning to a
steady domestic footing, a point which the morality tale sewn
into *Brief Encounter* neatly reinforced. The next few years
would prove a boom time for marriage, but many young ex-
service women who had enjoyed a degree of independence
harboured higher expectations of what that marriage might

mean. Looking down the lens of the late 1940s, they did not anticipate making a choice between duty and love (between Fred and Alec). They expected their twin needs to be fulfilled by one man, their husband, an ideal that has subsequently been termed a 'companionate' marriage.

If they couldn't immediately attain this goal in their own personal lives, girls like Daphne (who didn't get engaged again until 1953) at least wanted to believe true love and companionship existed between Elizabeth and her rumoured Prince Charming. For many young women, the kind of man Philip was and his romantic intentions towards the Princess were very important. Elizabeth's future betrothal and wedding, like no other national event, would reframe two sacred institutions at the heart of British identity – marriage and monarchy.

So the Princess's next steps were a big deal and, in new democratic Britain, fuelled by the burgeoning press, large parts of the population not only wanted to believe in her marriage, they also expected some degree of agency over it. After all, had not the monarchy caused unjustifiable upheaval and national disgrace with its martial shenanigans in 1936? The *Manchester Guardian* was unequivocal, quoting then Prime Minister Stanley Baldwin: 'I pointed out to him [Edward VIII] that the position of the King's wife was different from the position of the wife of any other citizen. It was part of the price which the King has to pay.' The paper concluded it was 'essentially a matter . . . in which the voice of the people must be heard'.[11] That final principle had belatedly been applied in 1936 and, by 1947, the press was determined to do things differently.

In the run up to the abdication, the obsequious British media had allowed itself to be muzzled, with foreign publications breaking the story (complete with pictures of Edward and Wallis in bathing outfits) that led to the departure of an Imperial British king. In 1946, international papers were still taking the lead. *France Soir* proved eerily accurate when it wrote: 'Philip of Greece will become a naturalised British subject within six months and, six months afterwards, his engagement to Princess Elizabeth will be officially announced.'[12] But this time Fleet Street was determined to stake its own claim over the narrative, with the initiative coming from more sceptical left-wing publications. Emboldened by the *Guardian*, early in January 1947 the *Sunday Pictorial* stunned the nation with an audacious headline: 'SHOULD OUR FUTURE QUEEN WED PHILIP?' The paper demanded that 'above all the loyal people over whom the young Princess will one day rule as Queen' needed the chance to express their views: 'NOT AFTER THE EVENT, AS WAS THE CASE WITH ANOTHER ROYAL CRISIS IN 1936, BUT BEFORE IT.'

Tapping into the will of the people was a new-fangled idea, with the polling of public opinion first introduced in 1938. The paper proclaimed there was no better, more 'democratic' way of testing the national temperature on 'foreign Philip' and his intentions with Britain's most precious asset: Elizabeth. Readers were invited to write in with their opinions – thousands did so – and the results were published over the subsequent two weeks. '55% IN FAVOUR OF THE MARRIAGE . . . 40% AGAINST A MARRIAGE WITH PRINCE PHILIP OF GREECE.'[13]

The poll lit a touch paper. Not everyone approved. Ironically, given their reputation today, in 1947 it was the conservative press, including the royalist *Daily Mail*, that cried humbug and bad form. How dare the *Sunday Pictorial* encourage readers to cast judgement on their social superiors? How could the Royal Family preserve their mystique when assailed in such 'gross bad taste'?[14] It was the Left that led the Right into a more challenging, certainly a more invasive, relationship with their monarchy. When Andrew Marr, in his *Diamond Queen* biography, writes that in the immediate post-war period only the 'most anodyne of references to royalty appeared' in the press, it isn't true.[15] Moreover, the polls conducted were worrying inconclusive. The results were not a unanimous victory for Philip. Far from it.

Across the country, Britain's feted war heroes – its male soldiers who had served overseas and come home to austerity and disappointment – sat in clubs and barracks and stewed over the idea of a Greek consort. The very thought stuck in their craw. 'Let's have no more foreigners in England' their fall-back position. 'Let us not link ourselves with Greece or any other royal household.' Lest there was any doubt: 'we would like the Princess to follow in the footsteps of her father and marry a commoner. That worked well.' The Russell Family, in Euston Road, London, spelled it out: 'a father and two sons who have served in both wars' say "Definitely no!" to a marriage with a foreign prince'.[16] Little Britain's military men wanted to pull up the draw bridge.

It was girls like Daphne who kept the romantic dream alive. 'I wanted to know if they were in love,' she repeats, before adding: 'I think Elizabeth was very in love with him.' As the *Sunday Pictorial* discovered: 'women form the overwhelming majority of those who favour a marriage' (and here was the deal breaker) 'provided the two young people are in love'.

Without a hint of irony, the phrases: 'The right to live their own lives', 'a purely private matter' and 'no interference in the dictates of Princess Elizabeth's heart' recurred in letter after letter.[17] Elizabeth was allowed a fairytale romance (if that is really what it was), and it should be a private matter, and yet girls wanted to share in it with her. Women were less inclined

to project ideas of realpolitik on to the Royal Family, preferring to indulge in their own romantic fantasies, with the
Princess at the pinnacle of a domestic paradise. As the English
writer Virginia Woolf astutely observed before the war, Britain
had an 'insatiable need to see' royalty because 'if they live then
we live in them too'.[18] The Princess's imagined love life was a
vindication for the post-war woman and her right to choose, if
not in the workplace, then at least behind closed doors.

As for hard evidence of this true love, the public hadn't
been given much to go on. Just one convincing celluloid frame
existed of the pair together. Philip, an usher at his first cousin
Patricia Mountbatten's large society wedding in October 1946,
was caught smiling gently at a coy Elizabeth in fur coat and
floral coronet. The effect was electric. The photograph is still
rerun in documentaries today. The *Sunday Pictorial* had
tapped in to the national mood with their ground-breaking
poll (including pictures of a beaming prince and updated over
several weeks with more encouraging results). The news
reverberated around the world. 'THE PRINCESS AND THE
PEOPLE – 64% OF PEOPLE NOW SAY YES.'[19] Who was
backing Elizabeth? After all 'a happy queen is always a good
queen'.[20] Could anyone resist this universal love story? Certainly not America, where radio networks blared out the latest
polling and papers pronounced: 'All the world still loves a lover
and the romance of Princess Elizabeth and Prince Philip is the
rightful common property of mankind.' The poll was also
'closely followed by the Greek people', who had just held a ref-
erendum on their own monarchy. Surely this union would
have the 'happiest effect on Anglo-Greek relations'?[21] (Unlikely
when the fact Philip hardly spoke Greek was framed as a virtue in nearly all the British papers.)

Meanwhile, inside her palace, Elizabeth had to adjust to a
new level of public intrusion at a time when her marriage was

not yet certain. Rival publication the *Picture Post* lamented that the polling would 'infinitely' wound 'the feeling of all those concerned'.[22] Perhaps. Certainly we know from Craw-fie's insights that Elizabeth hated the press speculation: 'It was horrible . . . they shouted at me "where's Philip?"' The attention compounded her insecurity at time when a silent royal fog was yet to lift over the question of her engagement. The Palace's denial of any pending nuptials in September 1946 had been accompanied by the announcement that the family, without Philip, would got on a four-month tour of Africa. The timing felt unnecessarily cruel.[23]

Daphne remembers the pending royal trip as a 'cruise to make Elizabeth forget about Philip'. Certainly it suited the King that the Princess would be out of Philip's way until after her twenty-first birthday. But, organised the year before to bolster South African leader Field Marshall Jan Christian Smuts' political fortunes internally and Britain's imperial prestige externally, the Royal Tour on an old battle cruiser, HMS *Vanguard*, was also about fulfilling the King's needs as a father and family man. George wasn't quite ready to let his daughter go.

◆

Edward VIII's abdication speech in December 1936, coming just a decade after the global embrace of the wireless (the term 'radio' was considered an unacceptable Americanism) is best remembered for that line about being unable to 'discharge my duties as King . . . without the help and support of the woman I love'. This focus on his dilemma between love and duty has obscured what he said next. Not only did the deposed King (somewhat disingenuously) recommend his brother as a man with a 'long training in the public affairs of this country' and 'fine qualities', Edward went beyond these platitudes and cited the crucial difference between him and the otherwise poorly equipped, gauche Bertie – he had 'one matchless blessing, enjoyed by so many of you and not bestowed on me – a happy home with his wife and children'.[24]

It has been lucidly argued by historian Rosalind Brunt that this domestic virtue – a happy home and hearth – which the Duke and Duchess of York had so carefully cultivated, was initially overlooked when George VI became King in December 1936. Pathé newsreel of his accession focused exclusively on the monarch's divine majesty, proclaiming 'High and Mighty Albert to the Imperial Crown' and filming him in formal ceremonial grab.[25] The results were clunky and underlined the new king's lack of suitability. Unlike Edward (with his uncanny knack of reading the moment), the press had not yet identified George VI's main selling point – here was the twentieth-century's archetypal family man. Loyal, devoted and doing his best with an appropriately unsexy wife in Elizabeth ('just above the average country house type')[26] and two dear, identically dressed, unsophisticated daughters.*

It was this familial idea that had been relentlessly pumped during World War II. 'Us four', or 'The Firm',† stayed put in Britain and did their bit; they were photographed visiting bomb sites, surveying march pasts and waving from their balcony. The shocking death of the Duke of Kent in a plane crash underscored the 'one of us' mentality. Even royalty understood

---

* In 1937, Surveyor of the King's Pictures Kenneth Clark was 'shocked' at how little the King and Queen actually did. 'She gets up at 11. Hardly anyone at Windsor and just as dreary in the evenings as under [George V and Mary].' The couple's primary pleasure came from being with their children; it took them a while to adjust to their new responsibilities as monarchs. Meanwhile, the picture Crawfie paints of the Duke and Duchess of York prior to becoming monarchs is of a couple whose life primarily revolved around their daughters at 145 Piccadilly.

† George VI first referred to the House of Windsor as 'The Firm' during his reign and the term stuck.

what grief meant. This new opiate for the masses – a pin-up nuclear family – helped whitewash memories of the abdication and reasserted the Windsors' popularity in the post-war era. A. J. Cummings, an astute political commentator, was quick to point out in early 1947, when the speculation over Philip reached frenzied levels, that: 'the British throne has never been held in such good esteem as it is today. It is of the utmost importance that the strong links of mutual confidence should be preserved.'[27]

It was against this picture-perfect familial backdrop that the Windsors' Royal Tour to Southern Africa in 1947 was framed. Once more the King neatly side stepped (or at least postponed) the Philip question. He knew that the Royal Family's departure from Portsmouth Harbour in the middle of a truly gruesome winter on 1 February 1947 wasn't just a reaffirmation of imperial Britain but also the final hurrah for his little unit. And the press promoted it as such. America's *Time* magazine couldn't get enough of Team Windsor. An anecdote from Rhodesia (now Zimbabwe) affectionately underlined the family's keen ability to look out for each other. The Queen struggled up 'the slope of the great granite dome of Malindidzimu'. Apparently it was her 'smooth-soled shoes' that held the middle-aged consort back. Thankfully, Elizabeth took a hit for her mother, sacrificing her own sensible 'low-heeled footwear' and reaching the summit in stocking feet (nylons, size 9 ½).

Onwards to South Africa (the apogee of the tour) and another cosy little story. Once more the Queen proved ill-clad for the conditions; a breeze on Table Mountain took off with her hat. No matter, their sturdy leader, seventy-seven-year-old Smuts, ran in pursuit of the missing item: 'He returned with the hat in one hand, a graceful blue feather in the other.' Cue the article's pièce de resistance:

The King, whose powers of observation are apparently not much better than the average husband's, wanted to know where Smuts had found such a lovely feather. 'It's from my hat' said the Queen sweetly.[28]

No matter that he was thousands of miles away from battered Britain (storms both economic and natural), basking in African sunshine, the King was first and foremost like every other husband. Here was the Empire's everyman with the perfect support act, his family, filmed waving and smiling on a loop. This was ideal gloss for a royal tour with dark undercurrents – it was the first time a reigning monarch had set foot in the thirty-seven-year-old Union of South Africa and Princess Elizabeth was not the only one disturbed by the ugly rhetoric of the nationalists. (The following year the National Party won the election, when a policy of extensive racial segregation was introduced.) Nor could intimate observers fail to notice how exhausted and irritable the King was – a trigger for Equerry Captain Peter Townsend's uncharacteristic outburst: 'For heaven's sake shut up, or there is going to be an accident.'[29]

Irrespective of granular detail, the trip was a great success for the Windsor brand – together they were greater than the sum of their parts, with a particular reverence reserved for Princess Elizabeth. She even managed to impress recalcitrant Private Secretary Alan Lascelles. He reported back to his wife: 'From the inside, the most satisfactory feature of the whole business is the remarkable development of P'cess E.' She was girl with 'a perfectly natural power of enjoying herself' and 'a healthy sense of fun' who,

can take on the old bores with much of her mother's skill and never spares herself in that exhausting part of royal duty. For a child of her years, she has got an astonishing solicitude for other people's comfort; such unselfishness is not a normal characteristic of that family.[30]

This was an extraordinary tribute given Elizabeth's inner turmoil during the four-month royal tour. HMS *Vanguard's* departure in the bleak midwinter marked the beginning of her first trip abroad (the war had a lot to answer for), and BBC newsreel reminded viewers that, for the Princesses, what came next 'was a great adventure'.[31] At least it should have been. But appearances can be deceptive. Crawfie recalls that Elizabeth cut a despondent figure in the weeks before she left. Outside the Palace, press speculation had reached new hurtful heights, while inside the Princess dutifully tried on frocks for a warmer climate, awaited Philip's evening telephone calls and methodically read up on distant lands marked out on an African map. Before they set sail there was a quiet dinner at Chester Street, Mountbatten's smaller post-war London home. In the intimate green dining room, the royal party sat on Chinese-lacquer chairs, enjoyed stuffed pheasants and Champagne from priceless silver and glass and chatted beneath soft lighting and a solitary Frans Hals painting. With Philip present, the atmosphere was heavy with anticipation but nothing was said. Elizabeth longed for certainty and an official announcement.[32] Instead what came next was another Palace denial.*

An intelligent girl, standing at *Vanguard's* rail 'looking back sadly towards England', Elizabeth knew she was at a crossroads.[33] The Princess left British shores as part of the world's most famous family. To succeed as the future Queen, she and Philip would

---

* According to the *Sunday Pictorial*, a fifth and final denial was issued 'from the Royal Train in South Africa, when reports said that the engagement would be announced in Cape Town on the Princess's twenty-first birthday'.

have to match the dizzy domestic heights established by her parents, and for that to happen she needed all the help she could get. Incrementally, behind the scenes, things were moving in the right direction. The King had already overcome any personal misgiving about the man Elizabeth was in love with, writing to his mother, Queen Mary, 'I like Philip. He is intelligent, has a good sense of humour and thinks about things in the right way.' And with the Princess's twenty-first birthday looming before the end of their South African Tour, he could no longer use her age as an excuse. Even Lascelles eventually warmed to 'the nice young man'.[34] Meanwhile, back at home, the press geared up for a big announcement – Philip's British naturalisation.

On ice initially over fears of jeopardising the outcome of the Greek Plebiscite which restored their monarchy, then worries about Philip's association with an unsavoury dynasty, finally the excuses ran out:

> Daily Mail, 19 March 1947: Prince Philip of Greece has become a British citizen . . . he has relinquished his title and has become a commoner . . . His name is now Lieutenant Philip Mountbatten, R.N.*

As if by magic, Philip's elongated Germanic tag, Schleswig-Holstein-Sonderburg-Glücksburg had vanished, replaced by the already anglicised name of his maternal uncle: Mountbatten. Yah boo sucks to all those thin-lipped Brits who worried about his heritage, now Philip was officially one of them. To squash any suggestion of favouritism, the newspaper pointed

---

* It has subsequently been proved that, courtesy of the 1705 Act of Naturalization, as a descendent of Sophia, Electress of Hanover, Philip was already a British subject. A rare oversight, it appears that in this case Mountbatten had not done his genealogical homework.

out his 'name was on a list of 817'. So, too, had the former Prince made a sacrifice – 'he has renounced his right of succession to the Greek throne, to which he was sixth in line'. But lest there was any confusion, 'it has been denied that the change of nationality has any connection with the persistent rumours of his forthcoming engagement to Princess Elizabeth'.[35]

There was still no announcement. But Elizabeth, who was writing constantly to Philip as she criss-crossed a different continent in a white train one-third of a mile long, had not changed her mind. During the war, royal riding master Horace Smith observed of the Princess that, once she committed herself to a subject, her interest did not 'wane with the passing of time'.[36] And nor had it with Philip, a man for whom the political obstacles were almost surmounted. Now a commoner, he'd laid himself bare for Elizabeth. To hell with what the stuffy courtiers thought – this lieutenant was a serviceman and a British one at that. However, before she returned home to face her romantic destiny, there was one more challenge to overcome. Elizabeth needed to win the hearts and minds of her future subjects. If the people understood the Princess, surely they would also understand Elizabeth needed Philip by her side?

SIX

◆

'People Will Say We're in Love!'

'I don't think it necessarily was their favourite song, but it was played on the radio a lot.' Barbara pauses. 1947 was a long time ago, but the tune stuck because it resonated for her too. What was it called? 'Yes, that's right – "People Will Say We're in Love!" And I was! There were a lot of us in love at that time.' A song from the musical *Oklahoma* has been for ever pinned to Elizabeth and Philip's romance, courtesy of their appearance together when the show came to the West End in the spring of '47.[1] But the association between the tune and the couple has since been pooh-poohed by the Prince. It wasn't *their* song. Absolute 'sentimental codswallop!'[2] Possibly not, but, as discussed, nor was the couple's romance entirely their own, and the show tune that Barbara aptly recalls neatly summed up their predicament.

> *Don't throw bouquets at me*
> *Don't please my folks too much*
> *Don't laugh at my jokes too much*
> *People will say we're in love.*

Quite so. Obvious vulgar displays of affection would never do. Even when Establishment circles had privately decided that the engagement could go ahead, a subtle approach was required to convince the nation that what Elizabeth and Philip shared was indeed a genuine affection for each other, not some gimmicky flight of fancy or dynastic arrangement. According to historian Edward Owens, this thinking was likely informed by that poll in the *Sunday Pictorial*. Ruby from County Durham summed it up best when she wrote in to the paper with: 'if these two young people are really in love, let them be united by all means and the best of luck to them both.'[3] Owens believes that 'the royal household . . . built on the positive reactions to the rumoured engagement', and it is in this light we should interpret what came next.[4]

Recorded in Cape Town to mark her twenty-first birthday, the Princess's landmark address to the Commonwealth and Empire on 21 April 1947 made history. Elizabeth will always be remembered for pledging to devote herself entirely to the service of others. In a simple virgin-white wrap dress, nipped at the waist and off set with white peep-toe shoes and a double string of pearls, the Princess delivered the oration of her lifetime. Neatly tucked in front of a BBC microphone placed on a small circular table, dark red lipstick and shoulder pads were the only aesthetic concessions to the Princess's increased maturity. This was not a speech that focused on Her Royal Highness's ability and majesty. It was a proclamation of her youthful commitment to serve; one which capitalised on Elizabeth's all-round 'wholesomeness'.[5] The Princess's fresh clipped voice had an inbuilt vulnerability, but it was the words she used that guaranteed the speech enjoyed an extraordinary, lasting impact.

As with everything royal, this was not a spontaneous address but rather a finely tuned work of art that had been checked and double checked. Its author was *The Times* journalist Dermot Morrah. On tour with the newspaper in South Africa, here was a man who had cut his teeth at the *Daily*

Mail and regularly combined lively text with a high moral tone and firm belief in monarchy.[6] The Princess's evocation was masterful:

> I declare before you all that my whole life, whether it be long or short, shall be devoted to your service and the service of our Great Imperial Family to which we all belong.

The text has subsequently been held up by royal biographer Ben Pimlott as a fine example of Princess Elizabeth, with a 'nun-like promise', offering her listeners 'the bromide of Commonwealth and imperial ideals'. As a royal speech, 'it reaffirmed the British Monarchy as the one reliable link in an association of nations and territories whose ties had become tenuous.'[7] But it did so much more than that. Crucially, the speech established Elizabeth's vulnerability. In a world where gender mattered, this was a girl deliberately capitalising on her femininity when she told the young people of the empire that she would 'not have the strength to carry out this resolution alone unless you join in it with me, as I now invite you to do.'

It was a speech so powerful that, at first reading, the words reduced the Princess to tears. Private Secretary Alan Lascelles's retort to this emotional confession is worth noting: 'Good, said I, for if it makes you cry now, it will make 200 million other people cry when they hear you deliver it, and that is what we want.'[8] His wish came true: the speech, transmitted in both cinemas and on the BBC's Home and Empire Service, brought 'a lump into millions of throats.'[9] Here was a dutiful young princess being frank about needing support just months before the announcement of her engagement to Philip, the man destined to become her 'strength and stay'. It is the connection between these two events that Edward Owens urges us to see. Elizabeth needed Philip and his support to do her job well.[10] Delivered in birdlike staccato sentences, the subliminal message was both intoxicating and emotional, and the timing critical. In three days HMS *Vanguard* would finally set sail for England.

In April 2021, *Vogue* magazine collated '31 Iconic Photographs of Queen Elizabeth', which travel right up to Her Majesty's solitary, masked appearance at the Duke's funeral in 2021. One stands out from all the others. This particular photograph was snapped on the deck of HMS *Vanguard* in early 1947; Elizabeth is tilted backwards, arms outstretched, writhing with unguarded joy in a bold floral dress. She is playing tag amid white-socked midshipmen and her delight is discernible.[11] Were they en route home? The impression is of a girl unburdened, with something (or someone?) to look forward to.

But away from the ocean's sunlit horizons, back in England, life had an apocalyptic quality. According to America's *Time* magazine, 'Like Job the British people had been "made to possess many months of misery" . . . Gales boiled over . . . fallen trees blocked many main roads . . . bomb ruins crashed into bomb-weakened houses.'[12] Peacetime Britain was a mess.

Barbara sighs. 'Yes, I was a taxi driver in Rotherham after the war and we couldn't get out because of the storms. We had to have something to look forward to. Perhaps that's why so many of us got engaged.' Barbara's boyfriend, airman Stan, had finally been demobbed. He came home from Gibraltar and sought her father's permission for his daughter's hand in marriage. 'Our dads knew each other. They were policemen on adjoining beats in different parts of the West Riding Constabulary.' In 1947, Barbara and thousands like her would tie the knot in greater numbers than peacetime Britain had ever seen before. 'Well, yes,

I suppose it is something else that links me to the Queen. Their families knew each other too. It was often the case in those days.'

That year records were broken, with a staggering 401,210 couples heading down the aisle,[13] and like Barbara and Stan, Elizabeth and Philip were among them, but first things had to be made official. The signs looked good. In May, the Princess 'danced a little gig of delight to be home again' and the Queen wrote 'very secretly' (underlined twice) to her sister, May Elphinstone, explaining that Elizabeth had 'made up her mind to get engaged to Philip Mountbatten. I think that she is *really* fond of him'.[14] As for Philip, it had been a long inauspicious winter training naval cadets wrapped in a greatcoat. The Princess's return heralded the late arrival of his spring. He wasn't there on the quayside to welcome the Royal Family back – far too obvious – but soon resumed visiting the Palace in that natty little MG sports car (black with green upholstery).[15] Lieutenant Mountbatten liked things to look good; he had a keen eye, enjoyed design and was well aware that, before any announcement could be made, he had to procure a ring for one of the richest girls in the world.

❖

Over the years Philip would acquire a reputation as an impressive amateur jewellery designer, a man capable of expressing commitment to his wife in touching combinations of precious stones and metals. After their marriage, one of the Prince's first gifts to Elizabeth was a diamond brooch in the shape of his naval badge. It was made by Garrard and Co., an exclusive London company, and given to the Princess shortly after the birth of baby Charles.[16] But, in 1947, prior to their official engagement, Philip lacked a crucial ingredient: money. To solve the conundrum of Elizabeth's engagement ring, he had to rely on his own (royal) family.

There are touching anecdotes about the great care the Prince took with his late father's modest effects. Upon receipt of Prince Andreas's signet ring, he immediately slipped it on to his own finger and never took it off, his father's shabby clothes he had refitted to wear himself, ditto his ivory-handled shaving brush.[17] Just as Philip told friends that marrying Elizabeth 'was his destiny', so too did he place great stock in his own family and their heritage. It was his quest to combine both in the form of a perfect engagement ring for Elizabeth that briefly saw Philip's elusive mother take centre stage.

What's perhaps most remarkable about Princess Alice is not the severity of the breakdown she experienced in the late 1920s (including dubious treatments for schizophrenia received at two sanatoriums), but rather her extraordinary bounce back and resilience in later life. In 1946–7, like Philip, Alice often stayed in London with her mother, Victoria, the dowager Marchioness of Milford Haven, who resided in Kensington Palace* (an important reminder that, on one level, Philip's engagement to Elizabeth was a home-from-home affair, although apparently his sleeping quarters were in servants' attics).[18] While Alice had taken a backseat to her brother Mountbatten's extensive efforts to install Philip inside the British Royal Family, Dickie's departure to India as the subcontinent's last British Viceroy in March 1947 left space for her to briefly shine.

Missing treasures have long bedevilled exiled and overturned royalty, but Philip's father had carefully placed their family's valuables in a Parisian bank, at least so Alice thought. When she went to retrieve the jewels, some items were

---

* Princess Victoria of Hesse and by Rhine (later Victoria Mountbatten, Marchioness of Milford Haven) was Queen Victoria's granddaughter.

missing, and paste diamonds occasionally replaced the real deal (Andreas was a man with debts), but all was not lost. The imperial Romanov tiara, which she intended to dismantle for Elizabeth's ring, was in good condition and she reassured Philip about the quality of the diamonds within the collection.'[19] It mattered. After all, this ring would be analysed by the world's media and worn by a princess just back from South Africa. There, Elizabeth had been festooned with jewels in the country famous for De Beers diamonds.* The company's pre-war marketing campaigns were so aggressive that diamonds had become almost the only stone for an engagement ring. (Margaret delighted in her South African jewels, drawing sketches, designing a bracelet and toying with two large surplus gems.)[20] Philip needed something eye catching. But he also needed something meaningful.

'In the war you couldn't get 22-carat-gold wedding rings. They weren't manufactured at all. So re-crafted rings and heirlooms became very fashionable.' Barbara's fiancé, Stan, was determined that his wife would have a brand new ring – rubies, diamonds, 18 carat gold – but Barbara is right (Barbara usually is), refashioning jewels was all the rage in the 1940s. Alice and Philip were bang on trend, and their star-studded heirlooms far better than most. But only Alice liaised directly with the jeweller in Bond Street. That summer press interest had reached fever pitch, and Philip did not want to be spotted. By all accounts even the man who made the ring had no idea who it was for.[21]

---

* Elizabeth was gifted twenty-one diamonds for her twenty-first birthday, which she celebrated in Cape Town in 1947. Forty-eight years later in 1995, she wore them at a Cape banquet during her first visit to democratic South Africa under President Nelson Mandela.

Wednesday 9 July 1947 was a mild English summer's day. Philip had visited the Palace the night before and an official announcement would come later that same evening. The mood was joyful. 'I have never seen her look lovelier than she did on that day. Not even on her wedding morning,' Crawfie recalled.[22] Elizabeth wore an amber-yellow dress and, on her finger, shone a large 3-carat diamond flanked by clusters of smaller pavé diamonds. Alice would later refer to her own efforts as 'a great success'.[23] Her assessment was correct.* Worn by Elizabeth for the rest of her long life, the engagement ring suited the Princess perfectly: historic like its owner, here was a piece of bespoke jewellery that was as stylish as it was unostentatious.

Philip understood the woman he was marrying. Perhaps more so than most bridegrooms in an era when the age of the average bride tumbled to twenty-two and engagements were rarely more than a few weeks long. He came from the same stock as Elizabeth and he had known of her from childhood – royal weddings and coronations were part of their DNA. Crucially, although they were only distantly related, they spoke the same coded language of royalty.

Childhood friends rarely got beyond Elizabeth's natural reserve, likewise many found Philip a hard man to get close to. One acquaintance remembered him as 'a cold fish', another found him 'a bit "Naval"', with the scowl of a true royal. [24] They did not see the Elizabeth and Philip who are caught for ever in an unguarded moment in one of their many engagement photos. Still bearing a quaint utilitarian-style from the war years, the shot is of two people who belong together. Elizabeth, wearing one of her many tea frock-and-pearl combinations (it didn't

---

* Although the ring was slightly too large and had to be altered to fit Elizabeth's finger.

94

matter, all attention was on the ring), looks gleefully into the middle distance; she can't quite believe her luck. Philip is finally standing by her side in a naval uniform, smiling carefully, lovingly at his bride-to-be. But there is something more to his expression than affection. He looks visibly proud of her and he said as much to Crawfie.[25] Like no one else, Philip understood the pressure Elizabeth had been under. Finally it was out in the open.

> *Daily Mail*, 10 May 1947: It is with the greatest pleasure that the King and Queen announce the betrothal of their dearly beloved daughter the Princess Elizabeth to Lieut. Philip Mountbatten, R.N., son of the late Prince Andrew of Greece and Princess Andrew (Princess Alice of Battenberg), to which union the King has gladly given his consent.[26]

The court circular had been released the evening before but, if the press was hoping to catch the young pair together, they had to wait. On 9 July Philip dined with the King (there was much to discuss) and Elizabeth danced among friends at Apsley House in an emerald-green picture dress and no ring.[27] That wasn't on public display until the next day, when the couple were the main attraction at a 7,000-strong Buckingham Palace garden party, and later a balcony appearance.[28]

Alice witnessed a rapid transformation in her son. Two days earlier she'd helped him pack, and then his levels of excitement had been reminiscent of Philip's 'eager tail-wagging' days as a schoolboy, when he moved from pillar to post. But not anymore. Overnight her son made the transition and it was with a note of satisfaction that Alice wrote to her brother Dickie in India: 'It amused me very much to be waiting with the rest of the family, for Philip to come down grandly with Bertie, Elizabeth and Lilibet.' [29]

In the palace gardens the couple separated from the King and Queen and, under a light drizzle, made their rounds alone. The guests broke into spontaneous applause, elderly royal relations murmured their approval (doubtful Queen Mary couldn't resist pointing out 'Philip is very lucky to have won her love')[30], and the press towed the line. The *Daily Mail* did its best to suggest the pair were in love: they 'share the same interests and outlook. They have been friends and companions for years. This is the human aspect of the engagement.' As for Philip, he was 'British by education, upbringing and choice', and, as a future consort, a man whose 'character may be a factor of great importance in the years to come'.[31] But not now. In mid-1947, there was a more pressing matter to worry about than Philip's personality.

Exactly how much was the wedding going to cost? Ditto the maintenance of HRH Princess Elizabeth and her impoverished bridegroom?

—◆—

'An Austerity Wedding for Elizabeth' screamed the *Daily Express*'s headline on the very day of the engagement. Amid descriptions of a large diamond ring and a royal love match, its rival the *Daily Mail* pondered: 'What will their income be?', noting the Princess's allowance had already jumped to £15,000.[32] The *Daily Mirror* went further. Readers wanted to know if the Princess really needed extra coupons for her wedding dress (it required 300). Was an expensive celebration justifiable?[33] With years of speculation, photographs and second-guessing, Britain's press had deliberately hooked the nation into Elizabeth and Philip's romantic narrative and, finally, when news of their engagement broke, it brought forward a brand new set of problems. The country was in the economic doldrums (rations, debts, fuel shortages, a housing crisis and foreign loans), run by a government of radical socialists, but the braying masses needed a celebration to remember – didn't they?

Big puffy fairytale nuptials that establish a royal name overnight – Diana, Fergie, Kate, Meghan – are now considered standard fare, but a large celebrity-style wedding is a relatively recent confection. Pomp and pageantry had been identified as the life blood of popular British monarchy in the late nineteenth century, but it was rarely associated with weddings. Jubilees (Victoria's were Golden and Diamond, George V's Silver) and coronations (three in the first half of the twentieth century) provided the show-stopping displays of imperial wonder that made the world gasp at Britain's regal mystique, not the more modest betrothals of princes and princesses. Although sovereign over much of Britain's vast and growing empire, Victoria got married to Albert in pokey little St James's Chapel. But a lot had changed since then. As the Royal Family's political powers contracted, their role as national figureheads had taken centre stage. We know that George VI, the family man, was a new cosy royal construct, but, post-war, the media wanted more. A real love affair combined with ever evolving, high-tech mass media offered fresh opportunities for reframing a story with Hollywood-style dimensions.

On the evening of 10 July, when Elizabeth and Philip obligingly stepped out to share their engagement with the hordes below, *Pathé News* boasted it had the 'film industry's biggest lens trained on the palace balcony'.[34] The implications were clear: the press wanted to get as close-up-and-personal as they could to this couple. Austerity Britain was proving pretty dull; was it really necessary to have an austerity wedding? Concerned that a country run by technocrats, businessmen and trade unions might ruin the fun, the *Daily Express* ran their own poll: should the Princess's wedding have the 'traditional gaiety of a gala public event' or be an austerity wedding? Perhaps unsurprisingly, the results were conclusively in favour of a large celebration.[35]

In the end, the number crunching was a government affair, in liaison with the King. It's widely accepted that the Establishment took a knock post-45 – short of staff, money and political support, the landed gentry never fully recovered from World War II. Many stately homes were mothballed, handed over to the National Trust or (heaven forefend) opened to the public. Meanwhile, a policy of mass nationalisation and the introduction of the welfare state hardly sat comfortably with a social hierarchy, atop of which reigned an Emperor King. Especially one who was about to lose his crown jewel – India. But the anomaly of the Royal Family in the midst of a social revolution had a quirky familiar appeal; George VI was hardly flash, and Princess Elizabeth (despite her royal hobbies and toffy social set) looked very girl-next-door.

By August, when Clement Attlee signed off Westminster Abbey as the wedding venue, the message was clear. This would be the biggest 'austerity' wedding possible – no special stands for the crowd, and no national holiday granted, but it was important that everybody saw it. The plan was for the giant Abbey to be peppered with twenty-one microphones and for a Technicolor film crew to be in position to capture the royal procession to and from Buckingham Palace. Britain needed to remind the world it still knew how to put on a spectacle, and even better, the King was to pay for almost all of it.[36] Hurrah.*

---

* Only the decorations in and around Whitehall and in front of Buckingham Palace were paid for from the public purse. The Labour government got away virtually scot-free when it came to the wedding expenses.

By all accounts, Philip and Elizabeth were mindful to remain in step with the public mood (and stringent finances), but ultimately they were pawns in a greater game. Behind the scenes arguments rumbled on over their respective allowances, but all they could do was look the part and hope that people believed in what they saw. It is perhaps unsurprising that by now the public, fed a barrage of (predominantly) positive imaging, felt warmer towards the future consort than those in royal circles. Philip was held up in the press as a 'sailor from the sea', a down-to-earth lieutenant who played 'skittles' in his local and drank with fellow officers in the wardroom.[37] Even better, when the couple appeared arm-in-arm in public, Philip had the good grace to look 'a little shy'.[38] A disposition that implied the lieutenant understood the magnitude of what he had taken on. But if respect, awe even, for the Britain's monarchy was a prerequisite for winning hearts and minds, given the constant media glare his 'shy' appearance was probably something more akin to shellshock. 'It's rather like throwing him to the lions', tusked the ex-King of Yugoslavia over his morning papers.[39].

Elizabeth, on the other hand, simply looked 'radiant' – a word repeated ad infinitum across the press. She had been transformed from a 'shy, rather awkwardly smiling girl' into a 'radiant princess', someone with 'an added dignity, a consciousness of her new status.'[40] The numerous pictures from this engagement period tell the same tale. Elizabeth, never blessed with a naturally upturned face (as Daphne puts it, 'she often looked pretty glum') is beaming from ear to ear in almost every picture. The Princess had won her man and was well placed to handle the fall out. Unlike Philip, she'd lived in a goldfish bowl all her life.

An ATS recruit from the same wartime training camp remembered a restrained princess around her peers but someone entirely at home in front of the cameras.[41] In contrast, although Philip was from royal stock, until his connection to Elizabeth became public, very few people had shown interest in this Prince of Greece and Denmark. The pre-engagement rumours had given him a foretaste of what became a fixture for life from 10 July 1947. Heading north that summer to be formally introduced to their Scottish realm, he was caught scowling with his arms crossed in Edinburgh (tut) and, on the evening of his stag do, Philip got his revenge – approaching the photographers in question, convincing them to hand over their cameras by offering to take their picture, then calmly removing and destroying their flash bulbs.[42] He eventually learnt to tolerate the scrutiny, but unlike Elizabeth, it was never second nature. That required training from birth.

None of it was easy and nothing was private. Indeed, at 'private Balmoral' for a second summer, arguably the surveillance was more intense; it was certainly more personal. Decades later, recalling her late husband's many qualities, Elizabeth talked fondly of Philip's capacity to 'squeeze fun out of any situation.'[43] But that famous sense of humour did not have the same impact on the Highland court in 1947. Apparently the King was none too amused when a kilted Philip bobbed a mock curtsey at His Majesty; meanwhile men nearer to his own age were still second guessing just how in love with the Princess he really was.[44] Probably not as in love as Elizabeth, was Jock Colville's inferred assessment. Biographer Ben Pimlott suggests the Princess's new private secretary may have had a touch of the green-eyed monster. Either way, he certainly wasn't alone in trying to discover the depths of Philip's feelings.[45] But 'feelings' belie an emotional disposition that repressed male aristocrats are notoriously ill equipped to discern, and one which Philip, like most other upper-class men, spent a lifetime suppressing. Nonetheless, the court was undeterred and their interest perhaps most wonderfully illustrated in an anecdote from the game 'murder-in-the-dark'.

This evening entertainment is a staple in large Scottish piles, where stairwells, antler-studded halls and drawing rooms bedecked in tartan are plunged into darkness so the 'murderer' can commit his crime. A screaming victim alerts the detective, who sweeps in to find the body usually writhing on the floor in the final throws of a mock-death (the Queen loved parlour games). According to one courtier, irrespective of what Philip really felt for the Princess, the pair 'always seemed to find each other when the lights went out'. But the suspense continued. 'Whether he was [in love] with her, I couldn't say', mused (another) eyewitness, but 'she was in love with him'.[46]

The whiff of suspicion that comes from these half comments is indicative of a class of men who were resistant to the idea of a young buck entering the fray and running off with Britain's foremost prize. No matter that Philip was her choice, Elizabeth belonged to all of them: she was public property, she was their kith and kin, she was the future monarch. One suspects whoever had dared win her hand would have never been quite good enough. Philip was a brave man.

He was also broke. Who exactly was going to pay for the valet, security brief and secretary assigned to Philip straight after his engagement? He might have been about to sign away the entire subcontinent, but Uncle Dickie still found time to fire off a missive in response to mealy-mouthed Labour MPs' resistance regarding his nephew's future living costs. It was one thing not awarding Philip a lavish allowance, but quite another to expect him to live off his naval salary of less than £1 a day. As usual Mountbatten didn't hold back: 'You have either got to give up on Monarchy or give the wretched people who have to carry out the functions of the Crown enough money to be able to do it with the same dignity . . . as the Prime Minister.'[47] Touché. (Socialist Clement Attlee had settled on supplementing his modest income with generous expenses.)

How much money Elizabeth and Philip were to receive remained a thorny issue. Initially, there was pressure on the King to maintain Elizabeth and Philip *and* pay for their wedding out of his own finances. A statement was released in the press to that effect.* It was only after the ceremony, and with the fall of Chancellor Dalton (never a royal favourite), that matters were resolved more generously: Philip's initial annuity, settled in December 1947, was raised from a mooted £5,000 to £10,000 a year.[48] The subject had caused acrimony; according to (Conservative) ambassador Duff Cooper, the King was very outspoken over a pre-nuptials banquet: 'he seems to hate and despise' his Labour ministers.[49] In this tense atmosphere, the position of Philip was unenviable; the prospect of being kept by his father-in-law cannot have enhanced his ease in court circles. But ultimately it was the Labour government who missed a trick by foot-dragging and refusing to properly fund the wedding of a decade and its leading protagonists. After all, no other formula would so comprehensively revamp two cultural phenomena that had taken a massive wartime hit. It was Elizabeth and Philip's international love story that gifted both the institution of marriage and the Great British brand an Indian summer in late 1947.

---

* It was initially announced in the press that the King, keen not to 'impose a burden on his people', would source the finances for both from 'savings on the Civil List made during the war years' when there had been far less ceremonial and state banqueting.

SEVEN

◆◇◆

To Love, Cherish and to Obey

> The young generation who went through the war looked at things differently. We felt lucky to be alive and we wanted to crack on with life. Yes, I suppose we did get married young. But, how can I put this? Back then a girl belonged to her father, you couldn't do anything unless you were married.

Philip Jarman, still a tall upstanding man, is one hundred years old. To prevent confusion, I will call him Philip J. He'd fought in the British Army, not the navy, but, like the Prince, Philip J. returned from the Far East in 1946 to find Britain a changed place. It felt grey after his final posting in Singapore, and the food was terrible – 'cauliflower cheese every night'. Back home in Bournemouth, life wasn't the same: his brother John had been killed by the Japanese in 1942. 'I got a hero's welcome, I suppose you could say.' But there was a hole in the household, nothing would bring John back.

It was in 1947, the year of wedding fever, that Philip J., a trainee accountant, met Cora, an attractive, polished, privately educated girl who had spent the final year of war in a Wren's uniform at Bletchley Park.[1] They started 'courting'. It was modest affair, fitted intermittently around their respective jobs and the limitations of living with parents. Philip J. keenly recalls the swirl of news that surrounded Princess Elizabeth and her fiancé. 'We were stuffy in those days and very class conscious. People did say unkind things about him. But he had served in the Royal Navy and been commended for bravery. That was good enough for me.'

By autumn 1947, most people felt the same. The incessant coverage of Elizabeth and Philip epitomised an idealised version of love and marriage in a country looking for a new way forward. Here was a handsome sailor who had returned from sea to eventually clinch the deal and win the hand of his intended, a blemish-free bride. The waiting game the royal couple endured resonated for many young people. Philip J. delicately explains: 'Parents had a much greater say in the matter, or certainly interest in the matter, in those days. You were expected to ask permission from the father of the bride.'

He remembers marriage as the decent thing to do 'if you wanted to have sex with the girl you loved', but it was also a fraught decision: 'We took marriage very seriously. Divorce laws were much tighter, the whole thing was expensive and difficult. It was considered shameful to get divorced.' The high domestic stakes that marriage entailed were reflected in public debate, with considerable moral anxiety expressed at a rising divorce rate. MPs raged that 'marriage is too easy' and lax behaviour was blamed for undermining a 'healthy community'.[2] Newspapers and the church were quick to reiterate messaging that set fair the moral tone for the next fifteen years:

Marriage: the dangerous state of our times . . . '50,000 divorces to be granted or heard in British courts in 1947' . . . 'Disloyalty, unfaithfulness and disregard of social responsibilities in present day marriages are unparalleled in our history.'[3]

The war had unleashed unprecedented sexual license; this behaviour had to stop if Britain was to reclaim the moral high ground. Heaven forbid that the country might follow in the footsteps of America, where predictions suggested half of marriages would end in divorce within eighteen years. Over there, 'many bars and cocktail lounges jammed full of foolish wives' were seen as part of a bigger 'problem'.[4] Against this backdrop of young frisky love and high moral tenor, Philip and Elizabeth provided a multi-faceted tableau – they were the inspiration for couples preparing to risk it all down the aisle and an ideal for a church and state hoping to reassert the benefits of committed, sacrificial marriage.

At the symbolic heart of this ambitious emotional cocktail was the bride. What would she wear? What would she say'? How did she feel? People really cared – letters arrived for the bride-to-be 'from every kind of place and person. Girls wrote her that they planned to marry on the same day. Sailors who had served with Philip wrote her from ships at sea.'[5] Diminutive Elizabeth, with hair still rolled in a wartime wave, a girl never prone to big gestures, controversial thought or high fashion, was at the epicentre of a 1940s cultural phenomenon. Her response was to do what she had always done – follow the lead of her parents.

◆◇◆

Graphite pen in hand, wearing gym shoes and with a hellish cold (it was November), Norman Hartnell, the south London boy-cum-haute couture designer, tussled over the design of a fifteen-foot veil in his Mayfair workshop. Of course, the tea making, embroidering and buttonholing was all done by women, but he was the man in charge of dressing Britain's most famous female in white. (For the record, he did not sew: he designed.) Hartnell's selection for the big gig had been pretty much a fait accompli. The Queen, renowned for ostrich feathers, powder-blue ensembles and boxy two-piece suits with matching hats, was his most important patron. They were contemporaries and considered themselves above fashion – Hartnell was a man who dressed women for an occasion, the more ceremonial the better. Still, even he was somewhat taxed by the timeline (three months), the scrutiny (thank goodness his neighbour had resisted renting out the adjacent property to peeping toms) and the logistics (importing 10,000 American pearls for a floral fantasy was just the first international hurdle).[6]

Only the gown's 'lovely young owner' caused no problems. Gloriously uninterested in fashion, Elizabeth followed where her mother led and let Hartnell to do his thing. Her sole wish was for secrecy: dress intel must not get out to the wider world (constant leaks had seen the Queen abandon a Hartnell creation in 1938[7]). In the end, Elizabeth's dress enjoyed 24/7 security, and still there was a small indiscretion, courtesy of an early press preview. 'Never before has the "rag trade" fought so hard to find the secret of a single wedding-dress.'[8] The gown became a metaphor for the couple's lives, but, like them, it was impossible to replicate, enmeshed in its own magical 'complicated embroidery' of blossoms, wheat sheaves and white roses. [9]

It's perhaps unsurprising that Hartnell took his inspiration from a Botticelli angel: after all, divinely appointed Princess Elizabeth was just couple of steps removed from God. And the more virginal she looked, the better. There was 'poetry' worked within the rich palate of colourless white: 'Wherever there was space or weakness of design, I drew more wheat, more leaves, more blossom of orange, syringe or jasmine.'[10] The fertility metaphor was pronounced. Fortunately Hartnell was a man who worked well under pressure (there were also 'eight beautiful young girls' to turn into bridesmaids and two queens to dress). The four foot 'black shiny crush proof box' would be delivered to the palace on time, meanwhile the press had to content themselves with details of the Princess's accessories: 'no-ladder stockings' dyed beige (a royal first by all accounts) with a special two-way stretch when she kneeled, a deep 'Balmoral red' lipstick for the cameras, and translucent nail polish.[11]

Elizabeth was the archetypal bride but also an exceptional one. In 1947, archetypal brides obeyed. But what about exceptions? Even Hartnell, not a particularly political man, was struck by the fuss over one word: 'obey'.[12] Ditto the press: 'Never in the history of our royal family have bride and bridegroom had to endure such a barrage of rumour and counter-rumour . . . even down to the intimate question of whether the Princess should say "I obey." '[13] The Palace released a statement (a sure sign of trouble): 'Princess Elizabeth will vow "To love, cherish and to obey" Lieut. Philip Mountbatten'. Obfuscation was attempted with an excuse about different editions of the Book of Common Prayer but it was difficult to disguise the direction of the debate. A future British Queen obeying her foreign consort? (Lest anyone had forgotten, the *Daily Mirror* ran a picture of Philip in a Greek costume on the day of the wedding.)[14]

Elizabeth was a stickler for form; her mother vowed to obey her father, of course she was going to obey. She loved Philip and what better way to show the world than to 'obey'. It was a gesture that would be partially trumped by her eventual coronation, but it was also an indication of how she intended to go forward between the pillars of two ancient institutions; in the private domain seeking to be the conventional wife and in the public domain conforming to the strictures of her regal position, just as Philip would also have to conform to them. No one understood that better than her future husband.

Immediately before the wedding, he was invested with a flurry of royal titles. The newly appointed His Royal Highness, Philip walked down the aisle as the Duke of Edinburgh, Earl of Merioneth and Baron Greenwich. It was a timely gift from the King and a necessary one. The Duke needed the armoury of an institution to stand tall next to his decorated bride (Elizabeth received the Order of the Garter a week before him). There was still plenty ammunition out there if people wanted to belittle Philip, but the more embedded he became in the labyrinthine excesses of titles and ranks, the harder he was to reach. Or knock.

Much has been made of the couple's extensive wedding gifts: 1,200 of them were displayed at St James Palace. For a small fee, the public could join a mile-long queue and look at a picnic set in plastic cream (from Margaret), an 'ice blue' mink coat from the Canadian government (import tax: £3,000), a piece of cloth (not a loin cloth) hand woven by Mahatma Gandhi (Queen Mary was not amused) and a cover for keeping boiled eggs warm. Living creatures (a turkey and an eight-month-old chestnut filly, Elizabeth's first flat race winner) were housed elsewhere. It was a display that favoured the Princess; she received an entire wardrobe's worth of clothes to Philip's three silk shirts. But it was the Duke who gave the collection its *je ne sais quoi*. The *Daily Mirror* picked up on the statues (Elizabeth I, Philip of Spain) sent from actress Cobina Wright. Philip's glamorous friend from that hot summer in Venice, a woman, the newspaper noted, he visited in New York, was the only Hollywood guest at the wedding.[15] Philip's past had not been dull. The brand new Duke of Edinburgh was set to gain hugely by marrying Elizabeth, but he had lost something very precious. His freedom. The night before his wedding, he looked pale: 'I suppose I won't be having fun anymore,' Philip anxiously confided to a friend.[16]

◆

In 2012, twenty-seven kings, queens and representatives of monarchy gathered in the Grand Reception Room at Windsor Castle for a Diamond Jubilee photograph with the British Queen. Elizabeth took pride of place in hallmark powder blue (she remained her mother's daughter to the end) and, sitting right beside her, was King Michael of Romania. Just shy of his ninety-first birthday, he was the oldest royal in the picture and the Queen's third cousin, but it was his relationship with Philip that marked him out as special. First cousins once removed, the two boys played together as children. There are photographs of them swimming and riding by the Black Sea in 1928; Philip with a shock of blond hair and Michael in white canvas sandshoes. Aged six, Michael was already King of Romania. His grandmother, Queen Marie of Romania, once the most famous woman in the world, entertained the cousins in her castle beneath the Carpathian Mountains. They rode in her carriage, ate crystallised violets and listened to stories from the land of make-believe in the Queen's luxurious dressing room.[17]

That same Michael, tall and handsome like his cousin, with a similar dare-devil streak, 'landed his own plane at London airport' to arrive at Philip's wedding in November 1947.[18] All the newspapers picked up on his presence. 'Twenty-five-year old bachelor King Michael of Rumania is coming . . . from behind the "Iron Curtain" for the wedding.'[19] How times had changed in twenty short years. Post-war Romania was riddled with Soviet apparatchiks; Russia's 'liberating' Red Army had never left. When Michael went home that Christmas, he was forced to abdicate at gunpoint; his flight out of Romania in December 1947 marked the end of Eastern Europe's royal story. The Romanian King's presence in London that November was a salutary reminder of monarchy's fragility and Bolshevism's dark menace. Philip, the son of an exiled Greek prince, later helped Michael establish a new life in England. The ex-Romanian King became a chicken farmer and enjoyed holidays at Balmoral and Sandringham, thanks to his cousin, the one-time Balkan Prince who had fulfilled his childhood ambition to 'make a good marriage'.[20]

Biographers love to remind us that Princess Alice, Philip's mother, was his only close family in Westminster Abbey on that dank November morn. It's not true. Philip's maternal grandmother, the formidable dowager Marchioness of Milford Haven, was present, ditto his Uncle Dickie, now Earl Mountbatten of Burma. Philip's best man was his first cousin, David, the 3rd Marquess of Milford Haven, a decorated naval officer, and lining the pews were a number of other relatives: some, like Michael, clinging precariously on to thrones, others, including Alexandra, ex-Queen of Yugoslavia, had already been given their marching orders. A concession to the British Royal Family's paranoia about its own German stock as well as Philip's, his remaining sisters (all married to Germans) were excluded from the celebration, otherwise the Abbey was a festival of Queen Victoria's thoroughly European DNA.

But, in November 1947, only one royal family really mattered. Among the Dominion leaders, it was South Africa's Marshall Smuts who called it out when he told the bride's grandmother, Queen Mary: 'You are a big potato, the other queens are all small potatoes.' 'Shimmering in the iciest of ice blue, nodding away like a contended potentate', Mary pretended to be shocked, but she knew exactly what he meant.[21] Out on London's cold pavements, the public patiently waited for the proceedings to begin. It had been a long night – ground sheets, flasks, hot chestnuts – but worth it for a glimpse of royal flesh. Imagine the disappointment, then, when the state carriages went passed too fast, with a raggle-taggle bunch of unrecognisable royalty.

> These painted cabs, as somebody dubbed them, showed nothing as they bowled by but an occasional silhouette or saluting hand. Fingering its programmes as it might, the crowd could never be certain who was which.[22]

It was the appearance of Queen Mary that heralded the beginning of A-list royalty: her car travelled 'at the proper speed of a slow coach and she could be seen making her usual gesture, and erect as she was on Jubilee day'.[23] And then the arrival of the tour de force: at 11.15 am, advancing from the far end of Whitehall, the first military horsemen, moving at a well-controlled trot, came into sight, their helmets gleaming through the morning mist, their red plumes penetrating the gloom. There she was, encased in glass, suspended on wheels, drawn by horses, 'crystalline, gorgeous and revealing', the Princess with her Father-King.[24] 'I have to be seen to be believed.'* The crowd (seven women to one man) attempted a roar, it sounded more like a scream, and bells sang in the sky: how everyone loved their innocent British bride. And, in that moment, touched by their attentions, Elizabeth loved them right back.[25]

Framed in a sea of white satin, she peeked out of the window; that very morning this vision of purity had run the usual gauntlet of pre-wedding nerves, only on a grander scale than most. Amid the excitement and apprehension, Elizabeth couldn't find the string of pearls gifted from her father. They were still on display at St James Palace. And a footman lost her bouquet, without which the hourglass dress was incomplete. But staff have their perks; the missing items were retrieved

---

*   Elizabeth II's later famous refrain.

and soon the pair were on their way. 'I bet she ain't arf 'olding 'er fahver's 'and,' shouted a 'Cockney women with a Jubilee rosette in her lapel.'[26] Who doesn't love a good wedding?

Inside the Abbey, Philip walked up the aisle. Apparently he had a cold. Perhaps he was just tired (he'd overslept: the stag do went on after midnight), and nervous.[27] It was a big day, his moonshot moment: at last Philip was marrying up into the Premier League of royalty. With his lint-coloured hair and his father's sword, he appeared dignified, composed even, and the new Duke's timing was impeccable: when the fanfare trumpeted the arrival of his fairy bride, he looked up and smiled at the Queen – 'an inflated tangerine, her hat resembling a Don's perked up with ill-gotten plumage'.[28] His future mother-in-law was unmissable.*

Praise, My Soul, the King of Heaven sang out the choristers – a hymn that had pushed up into the eaves of the Abbey twenty-four years earlier. Elizabeth was again following in the footsteps of her parents, and there walking beside her was the King, in his Admiral of the Fleet uniform, looking 'unbelievably beautiful, like a French Prince'.[29] An exemplar of a perfect marriage, nothing was allowed to sully the picture. Certainly not the presence of the Duke of Windsor; he hadn't been invited, a snub which belied a certain insecurity. Surely a more confident Britain and a mightier royal family would have included German sisters and errant brothers with 'wicked' wives? No matter, 'big potatoes' could do what they liked.

Meanwhile Elizabeth, veiled, and Philip were reminded of their role in marriage by the Archbishop of York. In the Godly act of matrimony, apparently they were no different from any

---

* There are a significant number of unkind comments about Queen Elizabeth's weight, mostly written by men. Conservative Duff Cooper saw her just before the wedding and decided she had 'grown very large'.

cottager in the Dales (a sermon written for a home audience). Marriage was an unselfish union: 'Love must always be unselfish and unselfishness is the true secret of a happy marriage.' The Anglican Church saw their opportunity and seized it with both hands. Marriage means 'thoughtfulness and patience, ready sympathy and forbearance, talking over and sharing together'. This was heavy stuff; religious quasi-counsellor messaging that reminded a country where half a million houses had been destroyed that the British were a 'people who have a deep and instinctive love of their homes'.[30] One quarter of married couples still lived with their parents. But did it matter what the Archbishop said? Was anyone listening to the actual words? Or were they just focused on the sentiment, the soap opera, this wedding and their own future weddings, on royal hopes and their own dreams?

A 'dream couple' – the Princess with her 'wonderful complexion' and the Prince 'so devastatingly handsome', Elizabeth and Philip were the perfect symbols of marital bliss.[31] Their only lines were scripted, the only kiss they shared was private (in the Confessor's Chapel, where the Register was signed),[32] even their handwriting conformed to gender norms. His signature 'looped and tall and princely' and hers so 'girlish' in comparison. The register, beneath a glass top, was later guarded by a police sergeant. The bouquet went on display as well (a little wilted but then everyone was tired).[33] London had just thrown its first proper royal party since the coronation in 1937.

It had been an glorious understated victory. Two-hundred million listeners heard the ceremony on the wireless, new bride Barbara among them. She nods, 'Yes, yes very moving.' The BBC gave additional feeds to Latin America, to the Empire service and to their European service. Reporters (predominantly male except those roped in to talk about the dress) came from the US, the Dominions and Europe. Thousands of cinema goers and television viewers, including Daphne and Philip J., watched the procession exiting the Abbey ('at least I think it was the wedding, sometimes I get it muddled with the coronation'),[34] and wedding details were headline news in every European paper. The romantic moment was shared by millions. Michael of Romania even managed to find his future wife among the guests, just before he lost his throne.* For the *Daily Mail*, the message was loud and clear.

> Some have said that Britain is finished. It is not true – and none who felt the great heartbeats of this people yesterday could believe it . . . in such moments we are aware of our deep, essential unity – the KING, his family and his people; the people, their families and the KING![35]

Despite the start of a cold war and hot politics, winter gloom and a paucity of beer and plenty, shabby London with its insecure empire in tow could still put on a show to celebrate the House of Windsor and the world's most famous love match: Princess Elizabeth and His Royal Highness, Philip, the Duke of Edinburgh.

◆

'I never never spent such an evening! . . . He clasped me in his arms and we kissed each other again and again!' No, not the words of Elizabeth on her wedding night (certainly not!) but those of her great great grandmother, Queen Victoria. Already Queen in 1840, the twenty-year-old bride was uninhibited on the page: 'My dearest dearest dear Albert sat on a footstool by my side, and his excessive love and affection gave

---

* King Michael of Romania met Princess Anne de Bourbon-Palma at Elizabeth's and Philip's wedding. They got married in Athens, Greece, in June 1948.

me feelings of heavenly love and happiness I never could have
hoped to have felt before!'[36] Victoria was willingly, joyously
deflowered by a consort she chose and a man she loved. It was
that love, and subsequent dependence, she would mourn for
the rest of her life when Albert died prematurely in 1861, aged
forty-two.

On 20 November 1947, frequent comparisons were made
between Elizabeth and Philip's marriage and that of their
illustrious forebears. It was hoped the 'domestic tranquillity of
Victoria and Albert', which had 'a far reaching influence on
Victorian age', would be replicated with equal effect by the
Princess and her Duke. After all, like Victoria, Elizabeth had
chosen her bridegroom, a point that even non-royalists took
succour from and one frequently reinforced by the press. As
the Horse Guards' cavalry trotted towards the Abbey, the BBC
proudly declaimed that 'once only in 1,100 years of British history has there been such a day: an heiress presumptive to the
throne marries the man of her choice'.[37] Surely there was no
better indicator of true love?

The battered post-war world wanted to believe they
were witnessing a love match: long lens and fine analysis
confirmed that 'the affection between Elizabeth and Philip
cannot be concealed. Every picture, every snap shot has
proclaimed it'.[38] The pair's 'human touches' were expounded
in numerous publications: 'very young and very small in the
vastness of the Abbey, she walked down the aisle to marry
the man she loved'; 'his little protective gesture when he
took his wife's arm and smiled down into her eyes as they
turned to leave the altar' and 'her lovely train of silk tulle
and her veil . . . his anxiety over his wife's magnificent
train'.[39] This 'true' love, helped along with an historic comparison, served to reassure the older generation: 'mothers of

families and grandmothers who remember the happy relationship between Victoria and Prince Albert.[40]

Certainly Elizabeth's wedding was something of a transition and the King knew it. During the service he stared straight ahead; onlookers in the Abbey believed the twitching, flickering muscle in his cheek belied his emotional state (or perhaps he just needed a cigarette). The Princess anticipated her father's pain. She stopped in the aisle, hand-in-hand with her new husband, and gave George and his apricot-clad Queen a deep, respectful curtsey. But still it was difficult. Later he would write to his darling daughter: 'I was so proud of you & thrilled at having you so close to me on our long walk in Westminster Abbey, but when I handed you to the Archbishop I felt that I had lost something very precious.'[41] What father doesn't feel conflicted, especially then, in 1947, when a wedding was invariably the gateway to a whole other world at the hands of another man?

Let's return to great great grandmother Victoria – never one to mince her words – and that wedding night in Windsor Castle, February 1840. After supper (Victoria struggled to eat), her new husband did not have the pleasure of disrobing his bride. There was a break in their affections and the task was performed by her dressers. The apprehensive Queen vomited but made a quick recovery and the marriage was consummated that first night, Victoria confiding in her diary how 'we both went to bed; (of course in one bed) to lie by his side, and in his arms, and on his dear bosom.' Lest you are in any doubt, dear reader, they 'did not sleep much' that night and what passed between them had a 'purity and religion in it all'.[42] Nine months later fecund, felicitous Victoria gave birth to baby Victoria, the first of nine children.

Although a lot had changed in the intervening century, in

1947 the hype around the wedding night had not diminished. Sexual interest and discussion had increased despite the vast majority of brides still walking down the aisle virgins, often with astonishingly little knowledge of their own biology. As Philip J. sagely recalls: 'It was never enquired too much about the sexual past of the bridegroom, but if the bride was notoriously free and easy, well, that was a different matter.' Later he put it in laymen's term: 'For most of us decent young men, we didn't have sex with the girl we loved unless we got married.' That placed considerable pressure on the wedding night as the symbolic threshold into a previously forbidden, physical realm. And Elizabeth, the virginal Princess, and Philip, her 'shy' sailor bridegroom, were no exceptions, but rather the idealised poster-couple upon which a frustrated nation could unleash the vivid print of their imagination.

'For millions and millions of people . . . this honeymoon was the apotheosis of twentieth-century romance, the honeymoon of all honeymoons', so wrote Philip's cousin, (ex) Queen Alexandra of Yugoslavia (she cried during the service – naturally).[43] It is in this euphoric light that the extensive coverage of Philip and Elizabeth's honeymoon must be interpreted. The press were hungry for every morsel of information and scrap of colour they could muster to fan the embers of the nation's great love story on a cold winter's night. No, we don't have Victoria-style diaries to take us across the private threshold (our late Queen was far too discreet for that), but we do have Mills-and-Boon-style storytelling from the minute the couple set off for Uncle Dickie's Broadlands estate in an open-top carriage.

Ostensibly it all went to plan. A modest honeymoon in keeping with the time had seen generous offers of overseas locations politely turned down (Canada was keen to host;

travelling to India with the Mountbattens was also sug-
gested; and there was an offer to stay in America's White
House – presumably without the incumbent President).
Instead the couple opted for a brief sojourn in Mountbatten's Georgian home in Hampshire's proximate New Forest
before retreating to Balmoral. That evening, in another
Hartnell number (powder blue with matching feather beret),
Princess Elizabeth rolled through the gates of Buckingham
Palace (the people must have maximum visibility) in the
company of one corgi (Susan), four hot water bottles and a
husband.

The King did his bit and chased down the landau with
paper rose-petal confetti, the crowds roared afresh and the
newlyweds waved. Elizabeth was 'looking a little tired.'[44]
Small wonder. After the Abbey, there had been a breakfast
party with reams of hard-to-identify relatives and loud bag-
pipes, a cake (one of many) cut with a sword and endless
photographs and balcony appearances in a satin dress in
November (absolutely no kiss – a 'tradition' that came decades
later). 'Elizabeth clutched close to the arm of Philip as she
waved goodbye to well wishers gathered on the platform',[45] but
if the couple thought they were saying goodbye to the public at
Waterloo for a day or two alone, they were much mistaken.
The nation was on the edge of its seat, the story had only just
begun.

Daily Mail, 24 November 1947: 'Women scrambled
over tombstones and knocked down a wall to see
Princess Elizabeth and Prince Philip attending matins
at Romsey Abbey this morning. Some climbed up outside the church and clung on, looking through the
window.'

The BBC had let slip the honeymoon venue, with the result that India, America, Canada – any other option – would have offered more privacy. Most biographies recount the scrum that met Elizabeth and her freshly pressed Anglican Duke when they attended a church service on the third day of their honeymoon.* It was a bun fight. Ten thousand people tried their luck at an abbey with a one thousand capacity. Despite warnings from an overwhelmed vicar, 'hymn books and sheets disappeared'.[46] Thursday's sermon about 'selfless love' had been quickly forgotten by a smitten crowd. The scenes were disturbing and upsetting for Philip and Elizabeth, who craved the relative quietude of Balmoral. That it affected the Princess is in no doubt; she wrote to her cousin: 'we were terribly pestered by the press, and, of course, our going to church at Romsey Abbey was a most vulgar and disgraceful affair.'[47] Dressed in a standard tweed two-piece, honeymoon pictures show a muzzy-haired, slightly dazed Elizabeth. Was it the unwelcome crowds who 'lurked behind trees' and 'in the long grass?'[48] Or the impact of those first few days with her new husband?

We don't know. I can't tell you if, like his great great grandfather Albert, Philip was attentive on their first wedding night, but I can almost tell you almost everything else, or at least what the tabloids imagined was everything else. In Broadlands, apparently, the 'honeymoon house' was 'aglow with flowers' and the first evening's menu was simple: soup,

---

* In September 1947, Ben Pimlott refers to the completion of 'Philip's transmogrification into an Englishman' when he shed the Greek Orthodox religion and was given a formal reception into the Anglican Church by the Archbishop of Canterbury. The historian points out that this conversion took place at the same time as Philip's mother was establishing her own Greek Orthodox order of nuns (Ben Pimlott, The Queen, p. 176).

roast chicken and ice cream. Soft, orange-shaded lighting enhanced the romantic atmosphere and music was on a radiogram. There were two piles of records, options included: 'Cuddle Up a Little Closer' or perhaps a swing tune? 'Bess, you is my woman'.[49]

From the get-go, the press were across every last detail of the honeymoon. The *Daily Mail* went the furthest: inviting readers to walk with the couple as they entered their new private realm: 'Hand-in-hand they ran up the five stone steps to the open glazed doors . . . As they crossed the threshold the Princess squeezed the Duke's hand. "It's been a wonderful wedding but it's lovely to be here at last."'[50] Historian Edward Owens points out this was a new, quasi-fictional form of journalism.[51] Readers were encouraged to inhabit the mind, if not the body, of the Princess. Her first night was their first night, their love was everybody's love.

Under George VI, the Windsors had successfully rebranded themselves as the nation's dutiful first family: the epitome of rectitude and home and hearth supported by a respectful conservative press. But, in 1947, the rules of the game were changing.* Now the ration-stricken, patronised public were offered something more than an idealised symbolic royal family. They were invited to cross the domestic threshold and penetrate the emotional realm of their Princess. If some readers were appalled at the media's 'vulgar curiosity' and the publication of 'sordid detail', yet more were profoundly affected by a national love story where lines

---

* Edward Owens writes that 'in 1934 courtiers had managed to limit press coverage of George and Marina's [Duke and Duchess of Kent's] honeymoon through negotiations with the chairman of the Newspaper Proprietors' Association, but this was not an option in the less deferential world of 1947' (Edward Owens, *The Family Firm*, p. 325).

between public and private were blurred.[52] A Rubicon had been crossed. 'The Wedding that belongs to the World', screamed the *Daily Mirror*, but where did that ownership end?[53] It is a question the Royal Family have been trying to find the answer to ever since.

(*left*) George VI and Queen Elizabeth with their daughters, Princesses Elizabeth and Margaret, Windsor, 1940. The two sisters are dressed almost identically, as was often the case.

(*bottom, left*) Fifteen-year-old Philip, the dare-devil Prince of Greece and Denmark, in Hopeman Harbour near his Scottish school, Gordonstoun.

(*bottom, right*) Princess Elizabeth pictured on the cover of *Tatler* for her 13th birthday. Three months after the publication of this photograph the Princess had her first meaningful meeting with Prince Philip.

H.R.H. THE PRINCESS ELIZABETH — A BIRTHDAY PORTRAIT

The heir to the throne, their Majesties' elder daughter was born on April 21, 1926, and the Empire at large unites in wishing her many happy returns of this anniversary. The Princess Elizabeth and her sister the Princess Margaret, who is four years younger, are the most unspoilt and natural little girls in this world. Hence their supreme popularity wherever they go. The small dog, the Corgi, seen in the picture is a devoted friend of his young mistresses

Princess Elizabeth aboard battleship HMS *Vanguard* during the Windsors' tour to South Africa in early 1947. Unofficially engaged, Elizabeth and Philip wrote to each other frequently during this trip.

Princess Elizabeth marked her 21st birthday with one of her most famous speeches, in which she pledged herself to a life of service, Cape Town, April 1947.

Before their official engagement, pictures of Philip and Elizabeth together were rare. This image from the wedding of Louis Mountbatten's daughter, Patricia, at which Philip was an usher and Elizabeth a bridesmaid, was an exception, October, 1946.

The first engagement photograph of the royal couple, taken at Buckingham Palace, 10 July 1947. If you look closely, you can see Elizabeth's engagement ring.

Louis Mountbatten (also known as Uncle Dickie and by 1947 an earl) with his nephew Philip at the latter's stag do the night before the royal wedding.

A Balkan prince. Philip, aged seven, riding on the Black Sea coast in 1928 with his cousin Michael, who was already King of Romania. Nineteen years later Michael arrived at Philip's wedding 'from behind the "Iron Curtain."'

Prince Philip as a young boy in traditional Greek costume. To underline his 'foreignness' the *Daily Mirror* ran this picture on the day of his wedding to Princess Elizabeth.

(*top, left*) The newly appointed Duke of Edinburgh with Princess Elizabeth in her top-secret Norman Hartnell dress on their wedding day, 20 November 1947. It was a record-breaking year for tying the knot, with over 400,000 couples walking down the aisle. But marriage and monarchy came with its own set of challenges. (*top, right*) Lieutenant Philip Mountbatten stationed in Corsham, Wiltshire, post-war. He later admitted that he regretted having to relinquish his naval career prematurely.

Looking every inch the Queen, Elizabeth waves from the Danish State Coach on a visit to Copenhagen, May 1957, but not everyone was impressed. Three months later she was criticised by Lord Altrincham in *The National and English Review*.

The Edinburghs on tour: (*above*) Paris, 1948, where Philip contracted food poisoning and the Princess was three months pregnant. (*below*) In autumn 1951 they went on a longer Canadian tour with a 'pop-over' to America where the Duke wowed the crowds and outshone his apprehensive wife, Elizabeth.

(*right*) Two-and-a-half-year-old Prince Charles meets his father – 'a man's man' – at London airport on the Duke's return from Malta, 1951.

(*bottom*) Elizabeth in her coronation gown steps out of the Golden State Coach, Westminster Abbey, 2 June 1953. She is assisted by her maids-of-honour and an anxious Duke of Edinburgh in his Admiral of the Fleet uniform.

(*top*) Elizabeth and the Duke receive a rapturous welcome in Queensland, 1954. They visited 57 Australian towns and cities, allowing nearly 75% of the population to see the Queen.

(*left*) The Duke of Edinburgh bids farewell to his private secretary and friend Mike Parker, Gibraltar, February 1957. Scandal engulfed the tail-end of Philip's solo world tour when news of Parker's divorce broke in the press.

EIGHT

◆◇◆

Married Life

'Weddings and honeymoons were a very big deal in those days.' Ninety-seven-year-old Barbara is matter-of-fact and, to underline the point, tells her own story.

Stan and I got married in July 1947 and there was an announcement in the local paper. I still have the cutting. The *Yorkshire Post* had a page of brides and bridegrooms with the names of the bridesmaids, the church – ours was Bingley Parish church – and the bride's going away outfit. I wore a mustard suit with chocolate-brown accessories, including brown leather shoes. And of course the honeymoon destination – we went to Devon.

Even unknown Stan, a trainee policeman, and his bride, Barbara, got a mention in the local press. They went to the seaside village of Ilfracombe and enjoyed getting to know each other in a hotel for ten days. 'I suppose, before the wedding, we couldn't have been alone more than twelve times, so it was very nice. We went swimming and walking. Yes, it very nice, getting to know my Stan. No, I shan't tell you anymore. Stan was a very private man.'

Barbara was just twenty-two when she got married, – the average age of a bride in the late 1940s – and Elizabeth was twenty-one. Hundreds of thousands of dear girls who had dutifully served in the war read the economic and social mood music, and refocused their ambitions on marriage and family. In this context, it is easy to see why Elizabeth's story plucked at the nation's heart strings. But if her own baptism of fire in Broadlands with the press in tow was 'shocking',[1] the honeymoon's second leg had an intimacy more reminiscent of Barbara's Devonshire sojourn. The royal couple swapped southern England for a snow-clad Balmoral, where they stayed in Birkhall, an eighteenth-century manor house the Princess's family had used as a holiday home until George VI became King. The 'big little house',* just three stories tall with snug rooms, wood fires and back passages full of Wellington boots and stalking bonnets, provided the newlyweds with a bolt hole. They loved it and one another. In a letter to her mother, Elizabeth said she felt 'as though we had belonged to each other for years! Philip is an angel – he is so kind and thoughtful, and living with him and having him around all the time is just perfect'.[2]

Always an unsophisticated girl, Elizabeth felt most at home wrapped in the remoteness of that Scottish estate, surrounded by timeless staff, a familiar landscape and outdoor pursuits. Bobo MacDonald, her long-term maid and dresser, was a Scot; Crawfie, her childhood mainstay and governess, was a Scot; and her mother had been partially crafted in old, unrelenting aristocratic Scotland. Elizabeth was a pretty young thing, but hers was never a style that shone brightest at gala balls amid girls with long

---

* As the Queen Mother christened Birkhall, when she reacquired it after the death of her husband George VI.

tapered nails and yards of taffeta.* The Princess was at her most attractive when roughing it in Scotland. She said as much to cousin Margaret, in a letter sent during her honeymoon. To match the stalkers accompanying the couple's shooting expeditions, the Princess looked out her army boots and leather jerkin. It was a 'ruffian' disguise Elizabeth felt so good in that she

> couldn't help wishing that a photographer would come along, just for once, as he would never have believed what he saw! I imagined that I might be like a female Russian commando leader followed by her faithful cutthroats, all armed to the teeth with rifles.[3]

As for Philip, with his penchant for action and achievement, this proved the ideal holiday. He had received two guns from the King (a wedding gift) and wanted to improve his shot to impress the inner royal circle. Fortified with a hearty cooked breakfast and his new wife by his side, the Prince spent long days in the snow matched by evenings stretched out in front of a blazing fire. The Princess sent more adoring words south: 'It is so lovely and peaceful just now – Philip is reading full length on the sofa, Susan is stretched out before the fire, Rummy is fast asleep in his box beside the fire and I am busy writing this in one of the arm chairs near the fire (you see how important fire is!). It's heaven up here.'[4]

The scene is a charming one; the Princess was totally relaxed with her new husband, who was enjoying their downtime together. But Elizabeth had an antenna for what came next and it made her anxious. After all, a snatched two weeks

---

* Philip's valet, John Dean, observed that Princess Margaret had long painted nails, in contrast to her sister Elizabeth's simple manicures and absence of jewellery (except her wedding and engagement rings).

in Scotland was hardly representative of the royal life Philip
had married into: Elizabeth wanted to protect her handsome
duke who liked swearing and joking, gadgets and going out.
The give-away clue appeared (as always) in a letter to her
mother, where she confided: 'Philip is terribly independent,
and I quite understand the poor darling wanting to start off
properly, without everything being <u>done</u> for us.'

As for the Queen, she had her own worries. 'This is the
first time I have written to you as my son-in-law and it is
only to send you my love.' Except, in December 1947, Her
Majesty did not stop at the love she now professed to feel for
a newly minted Duke of Edinburgh. Fallout from the wedding and the first leg of the honeymoon saw the Queen press
on:

> I <u>do</u> hope that you won't find public life too trying; for
> people <u>are</u> demanding when they like you, but you will
> have the comfort of knowing that you are giving so much
> towards the happiness and stability of the country.

Philip was discreetly informed by Britain's most socially graceful woman that the new levels of interest in his marriage and
life were par for the royal course. The Queen was not known as
a 'marshmallow made on a welding machine' (by photographer
Cecil Beaton) without good reason. As a woman who had
entered the top tier of royalty unexpectedly, the Queen understood the sudden impact of press attention. Getting used to it,
indeed courting it, was part of her job and one she did well. She
expected the same of Philip. In that first letter to her son-in-law,
the message was uncompromising: managing 'interest' and
intrusion was part of his job – he was no longer 'a lone hand' but
rather belonged to a 'common pool', someone to help ease the
King's 'many and great burdens'.[5]

If these two women, more inextricably engaged in his life than any others, prophesied difficulties ahead, Philip, with his new role as husband, wasn't ready to see problems. Instead he and Elizabeth issued a statement to the press and Philip sent a letter to his mother-in-law. The first, released before their retreat to Scotland, was heavily laced with irony:

> The loving interest shown by our fellow-countrymen and well-wishers left an impression which will never grow faint. We can find no words to express what we feel but we can at least offer our grateful thanks . . .[6]

In contrast, the letter to the Queen was uncompromisingly grateful and full of promise.

> Lilibet is the only 'thing' in the world which is absolutely real to me and my ambition is to weld the two of us into a new and combined existence that will not only be able to withstand the shocks directed at us but will also have a positive existence for the good.[7]

Marriage to Lilibet had revolutionised Philip's life. He had gone from being an also-ran prince and naval lieutenant to occupying potentially one of the most influential positions in Britain, a country still just about clinging to its great power status. Untrammelled by the vagaries of an electorate, if Philip played his cards carefully, he could manoeuvre himself into a long-term position with significant soft power. It was not just the press who found parallels between one-time consort Prince Albert and Philip. The latter's valet recalled his boss perusing the pages of Albert's biographies.[8] If recent historians have since revised their opinion of this meddlesome controlling consort, in the 1940s Albert was still held up as a man of science and learning, an individual who emboldened the stock and cultural capital of Great Britain. That was the dream, the way forward, but, unlike Albert, Philip was not yet consort, his wife was not yet Queen and, like so many married couples in 1947, their domestic bliss was heavily compromised by a housing crisis.

◆

In 1945, at the end of World War II, Britain faced its worst housing crisis in the twentieth century. With Labour's promise to provide homes for heroes and a shortfall of nearly one million properties across the UK, the rhetoric did not match the reality. Barbara remembers being very grateful when her husband's landlady allowed them to share digs once they were married. 'She normally just took policemen, but she said, in my case, she would take a policeman's wife.' Barbara and Stan had one room and the communal use of an outdoor loo. When she fell pregnant later that year, they were kicked out. 'She didn't want a baby in the house.'

Philip J., who met Cora in the year of the royal wedding, decided to wait. 'We were both in Bournemouth. I was a trainee accountant and wanted to be qualified before I got married, and we were both living with our parents.' For three long years Philip and Cora tried to meet up once a week for a couple of snatched hours somewhere neutral. Privacy was hard to come by. 'Eventually, in 1950, we got married from our parental homes.' Philip laughs. 'Then we had the greatest bit of good luck. We found a self-contained furnished flat at the top of Brixton Hill.' After three years, the couple finally had their own front door.

It is important to bear these contemporary accounts in mind when considering the start of Elizabeth and Philip's married life. They had much more than most, but although living in a different economic stratosphere, like so many others, the Prince's dream of being 'boss in his own home' would have to wait.[9] There was a significant gulf between the beguiling picture of Elizabeth and Philip and their first two children later captured by Edward Halliday's pitch-perfect paintbrush in 1952 and what came immediately before. In Clarence House's sitting room, the artist recreated a relaxed Duke in naval blue sitting beside a roaring fire, his wife – by now Queen – is neatly tucked, legs crossed, into the nook of a generous green sofa next to her first born, Charles. Blonde baby Anne is playing on the floor and a blend of royal embellishments – chandeliers and a queenly portrait – are offset with all the trappings of a contemporary 1950s' family – dogs, toys, and the latest in wireless technology. But this domestic vision was created after the accession; Halliday painted the picture prior to the couple's first engagement of Elizabeth's reign – the Maundy Service at Westminster Abbey in April 1952. It was a far cry from the newlyweds' set up in 1947, when Clarence House still had a bombed-out roof and there was press speculation over where the royal couple would live. The *Daily Mail* surmised that the issue 'might even delay the wedding'.[10]

Elizabeth was having none of that, and at least they had secured a beautiful 'grace and favour' country home in the Windsor Park Estate for weekend escapades and love-ins.[11] The engaged couple took Philip's MG out to view Sunninghill Park in their free evenings. Together they had strolled 'around empty, echoing rooms', planning and arranging the house, thrilled with their new home.[12] The Georgian two-storey property with stucco embellishments was a perfect bolt-hole and very near to all Elizabeth held dear. But, suddenly, shockingly, three months before the wedding, the house was burnt down.

'Elizabeth's Home – a day of rumours, then denial . . .
Extensive damage, including to Elizabeth's personal

suite . . . The marital home for Elizabeth and Philip has been gutted by fire.'[13]

The *Sunday Pictorial* led the speculation, suggesting that the destroyed house was an act of arson. Even Philip's cousin mused that Sunninghill had been earmarked for conversion into workers' flats before the King gifted it to his daughter. Elizabeth was genuinely upset by an attack that might have been deliberate. 'Do you really think someone did it on purpose? I can't believe it. People are always so kind.'[14] Philip appeared more sanguine – but perhaps it was this incident that encouraged him to broaden the royals' reading base. After his marriage, he added the left leaning *Daily Mirror* and *Sunday Pictorial* on to Buckingham Palace's newspaper list.[15] Modern royals needed to stay abreast of their opponents.

Nonetheless, it is unlikely that Philip relished the prospect of beginning his married life at 'Hotel Buckingham' (as his mother-in-law delicately put it) while they waited for the refurbishment of Clarence House. The King and Queen's claustrophobic devotion to their daughter required greater space than even a palace could provide. No matter, 'us four' briefly became 'us five', and although there was no shortage of rooms, privacy was at a premium.

Canoodling with his new bride was challenging. Bobo MacDonald, who had nursed Elizabeth from infancy, still had access to all areas, including bath times. It is small wonder that Philip returned from their honeymoon slightly on edge, or 'a shade querulous', as Private Secretary Jock Coville ungenerously put it.[16] Despite his royal blood, Philip wasn't used to constant surveillance, condescension or bloated court etiquette. His valet John Dean also struggled to adjust.

Dean had been gifted to Philip on his engagement. Staff was something that the Prince would have to get used to.

The two men were the same age and both shared a devotion to the Mountbattens. Dean had been a butler in the family's pre-war London penthouse, where he overlapped with the fair-haired boy Prince, and again after the war, when the family downsized to Chester Street. Philip occasionally dropped by and Dean would rustle up a meal and wash his limited wardrobe. Enjoying a long-term connection, the pairing made sense, but their more glamorous jocular past in the Mountbatten household proved inadequate training for the 'cold and unfriendly' atmosphere of Buckingham Palace.[17]

Whipper-snapper Dean was received 'coolly' by the older brigade of staff at Buckingham Palace. Elizabeth's Bobo, a stickler for form, insisted on calling him Mr Dean, despite his request to be John. Many were jealous of the new valet's position and some felt overlooked. But Philip 'had his own ideas and . . . insisted on somebody of his own choice'.[18] Which was the precisely the problem, with Dean's frosty reception replicated on a higher and more intense level for the Duke, who tartly reminded a patronising courtier at Windsor Castle that his grandmother had been born there.[19] Sympathetic eye witnesses recall that life was 'very very frustrating for him'. Alan Lascelles, the King's long-in-the-tooth private secretary, was 'impossible' and courtiers, generally, 'were absolutely bloody to him. They patronised him. They treated him as an outsider.'[20] Philip was up against what James Pope-Hennessey identified in the 1950s as the 'numerous and obeisant throng of royal snobs which flourish like fungi in the shadow of royalty.'[21] Elizabeth was their prize possession, and having grown up among them, she had high tolerance levels for palace stiffs. Philip did not, and his brand of royalty – brash, foreign, youthful – was an affront to their very existence.

'Behind the scenes: Philip is 'warned' about his driving . . .
He has a zest for speed which has upset even the Royal
chauffeurs, men with accident-free records who are now
chary of driving with him'.[22]

Before Elizabeth and Philip were even married, the press had
got wind of a daredevil duke and an unsettled Palace. Spotting
Philip in his black MG sports car was a new national hobby; to
avoid recognition, he would pull an old slouch cap over his
head and don a pair of sunglasses.[23] But he didn't moderate his
speed. The call came late one autumnal evening. Philip had
been picked up kerbside by a female driver, shaken with a
twisted knee, his car flipped and badly damaged after an alter-
cation with a tree on the road back from Corsham.[24] The
Princess, just weeks away from her wedding, was horrified.
Was he ok? She must speak to him at once. But beyond his
wellbeing, Elizabeth knew the accident was a red meat to the
sticklers and suits in court circles. It provided them with
another reason to doubt her future husband. 'Certain officials
in the household . . . did not feel that Philip should be allowed
to drive the heir to the throne about London as he had been
doing.'[25]

They could carp all they liked, but Philip had no intention
of reining himself in behind the wheel. The King had a quiet
word, and the future duke continued to drive his princess.
Much to the chagrin of the Palace, vehicles were often returned
with unsightly dents and buckled fenders. In truth, Philip was
short-sighted and should have worn glasses – but such a concession to physical weakness, especially in the public gaze
when departing Buckingham Palace, was not in character.
This was a man from a generation and class that had a strong
aversion to appearing 'cissy'.[26]

Before the wedding, the newspapers recorded that the

petrol-head Prince set the Corsham to London record among naval friends; after the wedding, he was regularly topping 100mph. Police occasionally pulled him over but invariably turned a blind eye when they discovered it was the Duke.[27] Driving remained a lifelong passion. In 2019, aged ninety-seven, he hit the headlines once more – his Land Rover turned over in an accident that left the driver and passenger of a second car with minor injuries. The Prince (unharmed and this time wearing glasses) was remorseful, writing an apology note and relinquishing his driver's licence. But old habits die hard; he continued to drive on Sandringham estate.[28] With a hefty dollop of optimistic bias (a hallmark of the upper classes), Philip had a lifelong aversion to concerns about his own health and safety. It is no coincidence he married a woman who could handle a Bedford 1500 truck and famously rode horses without a helmet all her life.

Coming from the same class and stock, Philip and Elizabeth were well matched, and as the *Sunday Pictorial* correctly predicted in November 1947, just like his driving, Lieutenant Mountbatten was 'unlikely to curb his independence of mind in most other directions'.[29]

◆

Whilst writing I would like to mention that I am considering getting some staff together and would like you to join this as a general nanny and factotum.

Yours, Philip.[30]

It was in an off-hand flourish at the bottom of a thank you note that the Duke set out his stall to Lieutenant Mike Parker – he wanted his old naval chum and wartime sparring partner as equerry. Stuck in a dead-end salesman job in London, with weekend cricket the only levity, straight-talking Australian Mike accepted with relish. From the outset, in 1947, theirs was a working relationship based on firm friendship. There were no airs and graces about Mike, a man from a salt-of-the-earth Australian home with a Catholic education and an unpretentious military background. The Prince–Parker partnership couldn't have been more different from the modus operandi that defined Elizabeth's relations with her first private secretary, Jock Colville.

The Princess and Colville shared no early or casual repertoire; rather he was tapped up in the Foreign Office by Private Secretary Sir Alan Lascelles, who identified the civil servant as 'one of their own'. Jock had been a former page of honour to George V and his mother was a Woman of the Bedchamber to Queen Mary. Part of that 'magic circle of courtiers and aristocrats' surrounding the Royal Family, Colville had passed through two major public schools (Winchester and Harrow), and Trinity College, Cambridge, before cutting his teeth in the corridors of Whitehall. A man with high self regard, who had been assistant private secretary to three Prime Ministers, he was keen not to dilly dally too long at court. Unlike Parker, for whom a job with Philip was the opportunity of a lifetime, one senses Colville's reticence when first approached. He relented on the basis of a two-year secondment, with Churchill egging him on – 'it is your duty to accept!' – and used cut-glass (condescending) tones to describe the experience: 'It was in the event a greater pleasure than a duty, for I served a young lady as wise as she was attractive.'[31] He added no word about Prince Philip, but in his unpublished journals there's plenty of scepticism about a prince six years his junior and without a hinterland forged in the British Establishment.

It was Colville who decided that the Edinburghs' first overseas tour should be Paris bound. On the surface the suggestion was a sensible one: the Cold War was ramping up (the Berlin air lift just one month away) and deteriorating relations with

Russia saw America and Britain keen to establish a viable Germany, a move that necessitated close relations with France. Crucially they wanted the French to dump grandiose ideas about acting as an East–West intermediary and help create a West German state. A 'love bomb' was needed and what better way to win Gallic hearts than with a touch of royal glamour?

Republican France had long been susceptible to Britain's modest but mythical version of monarchy. Louche, dapper Bertie, otherwise known as Edward VII, had won Parisians with his style and bonhomie in 1903 prior to the Entente Cordiale in 1904, and Elizabeth's own parents had burnished relations across the Channel before World War II when the Queen shimmered in Hartnell crinolines. A warm reception for the Edinburghs was almost guaranteed from a Paris plagued with industrial action (electricity cuts had been suspended so the population could listen to the royal wedding). Colville read the moment well and his idea built on established precedent, but the channels he worked to confirm the visit – first the Foreign Office and then the King – overlooked a key player: the Duke.

Prone to mood swings, trying to balance a naval career with a marriage that doubled as a job, Philip was irascible about the prospect of traipsing around Paris. That it was presented as a fait accompli by supercilious Colville did not help. Together with his right hand man Mike Parker, Philip devised a revolutionary idea that would save time and minimise his absence at Greenwich Naval College, where he was stationed – the Princess and the Duke would fly to Paris.

Philip, like his Uncle Dickie, was an early adopter of technology and flying had always held mesmeric appeal. Convention dictated that he followed the Mountbattens' naval footsteps in the war, but an unsated yen to join the RAF morphed into a desire to learn to fly post-1945. No matter that his sister Cécile and her family had been wiped out in an aeroplane accident in 1937, ditto his brother-in-law Prince Christoph of Hesse in 1943. But, in 1948 the Duke's flying dream had to wait, meanwhile even the thought of the heir to the throne as a flight passenger gave courtiers collywobbles. If Philip didn't see the danger, they did: aviation was still a high risk game and the death of the King's brother, the Duke of Kent, in 1942 made the matter personal. It was a petulant Philip who left for France by boat in May 1948.

Across the Channel in Faubourg St Honoré, aristocratic Duff and Lady Diana Cooper had put on a dazzling display as Britain's ambassador and wife. Conservative, jovial and unrepentantly royalist Duff was, however, dismayed to discover that his tenure in Paris wouldn't overlap with the visit from a girl he had last seen on the eve of her wedding, when she was 'really charming' and 'everything that a princess in a fairytale ought to look like'. He felt sure that, in the hands of the Harveys, his more po-faced successors, the event would be a less colourful affair. 'They are parsimonious, have no imagination and, above all, are so terrified of doing the wrong thing that they can seldom do the right one.'[32] His judgement was partial and partially true. If not parsimonious, the visit was over choreographed, both by the French and the new ambassador – resulting in a tension that didn't improve the Duke's mood.

Expectations ran high: even the sceptical *Daily Mirror* was excited about the 4th French Republic going 'gay' for the Princess. 'The streets will be decorated with flowers' and 'French Republican Guards in their famous plumed helmets will form a guard of honour', but ceremonial regiments were not the only uniforms flanking the streets of Paris.[33] Insecure France, still suffering from a compromised Vichy legacy and worried about communists at home and aboard, took no risks. There were police everywhere – they 'have kept us from our adored', screamed the French press. Gendarmerie blocked the roads in processions of cars, lined the streets at two feet intervals and brandished batons and 'flying cloaks ready to force people back'. The young couple spun around an otherwise empty Le Carrere night club avoiding waltzing police duets, and officers even staked out the empty Tour d'Argent restaurant opposite Notre Dame, where Elizabeth and Philip were exclusively invited to dine. But thirty police inspectors gorging on French cuisine did not stop a sneaky photographer infiltrating the luxurious eatery, drilling a hole in the wall and spying on the British visitors with his protruding lens. It was Philip, not the police, who spotted the invader. In a 'frightful rage', the Duke confronted the journalist in the kitchen.[34]

Fractious and sweating under unseasonably hot sunshine, Philip's poor form was exacerbated by a bout of food poisoning courtesy of a British embassy party where the royal visitors struggled to do the rounds. Pea green, Philip soldiered on. Even Colville commended his stoicism, but the tension rattled Elizabeth.[35] Prophecies about her husband's lack of grace still lurked beneath the surface; he had to learn to manage the press (and his temper). Above all, she loved Philip and she wanted him to be happy, but over that Whitsun weekend there was only one star – HRH Princess Elizabeth.

In beautifully scripted (Colville had his uses) near-perfect French, the Princess wowed the crowds with warm words. It did not go unnoticed that she spoke better French than her husband – a man who'd lived in Paris.[36] Elizabeth accepted bouquets and medals, kissed presidents and politicians, smiled as she glided up the Seine, lunched at a shimmering Versailles and glittered in a diamond tiara. Everywhere she went, Christian Dior's wasp-waisted New Look lined the stylish streets; elegant Parisian ladies in full skirts showed off their

ultra-feminine fashions and showed their respects to royalty –
the ultimate symbol of state they no longer had.[37]

According to Colville, in just four days the Princess with
'beautiful blue eyes and a superb natural complexion' 'con-
quered Paris'. The press noted that she changed her hat
(sometimes floral, sometimes veiled) three times a day to keep
up with French fashions.[38] But there was no New Look from
Elizabeth; the British Princess was resolutely dressed in British
attire, with Hartnell once more the royal choice. The couturier
dismissively noted in his memoir that he provided 'nearly all
the clothes' for the trip. As usual, ceremonial dress was his pre-
occupation – the Princess's evening gowns needed straps 'on
which to affix'[39] orders and honours and sashes.* Unlike her
French equivalents, Elizabeth's skirts were neither full enough
nor long enough and the waist hardly clinched. Hartnell was
no Dior, but in France that May, he had an excuse for not showing off his princess's naturally neat form. Elizabeth was three
months pregnant.

Philip was not the only one feeling sick in Paris, but in true
Elizabethan style, the show went on and was deemed a great
success. Irrespective of their own personal discomfort, the
Edinburghs knew how to put on a performance in public.

---

* The couple left Paris with additional decorations – President Auriel presented
Elizabeth with the Grand Order of the Legion of Honour and Philip received the
Croix de Guerre.

NINE

◆◇◆

Domestic Bliss?

In July 1981, Barbara Cartland disingenuously claimed she had turned down a seat in St Pauls Cathedral in order to watch the Royal Wedding on television from her Hertfordshire home.* Elizabeth II's eldest son, Charles, was marrying Lady Diana Spencer (Cartland's step-granddaughter) and the romantic novelist told the press she did not want to miss one moment of the show-stopping spectacle. Enjoying the ceremony from a gold rococo four-poster bed in the company of her Pekinese, she exclaimed: 'Diana looked exactly like one of my heroines – even more romantic. My daughter looked beautiful and my son-in-law looked wonderful.'[1] It is deliciously ironic that the woman who wrote 7,000 love-themed words a day proprietarily showed off about the world's most famous bride when her connection to Diana was only made possible courtesy of two divorces. (Cartland's daughter, Raine, and 'Johnny', 8th Earl Spencer, Diana's father, were both embarking on their second marriage when they tied the knot in 1976.)

Cartland rarely allowed reality to impinge on her syrupy prose or traditional world view. A prolific novelist in her own

---

* Apparently Diana read Cartland's romantic novels, but Barbara wasn't invited to the wedding.

right, and twice married, with a string of men attached to her name, she nonetheless declared in the 1950s that 'however much women believe in emancipation, however much they talk of careers and professions, they all of them know that unless they can capture a husband and have a child they have failed – as a woman'.[2] Her words chimed with the unforgiving times. Baby boomer Britain was unrepentant in its enthusiastic embrace of the 'vital work' women had to do 'ensuring the adequate continuance of the British race'. The Beveridge Report upon which so much of Attlee's Labour government was based, spelled it out – the post-war world was about distribution not equality. 'The attitude of the housewife to gainful employment outside the home is not and should not be the same as the single woman.'[3] By 1946, the number of women in work had fallen by two million; meanwhile, inside the home, housewives had two unpaid jobs to be getting on with – a husband to look after and babies to rear.

Barbara (not to be confused with Barbara Cartland), who got married in Bingley Parish Church the same year as Princess Elizabeth, was relieved when she fell pregnant immediately. 'It was what you were supposed to do. In my case it just happened.' But, not permitted to have children in their police digs, Barbara urgently needed to find a home that would accommodate her little family.

Mrs Lake was our new landlady, she loved babies. I gave birth in her house. After three days in labour, Roger was born. The doctor came, and a midwife, and it was a forceps delivery. Yes, I've always liked the idea that I got married the same year as Elizabeth and had a baby the same year. Mind you, I was a few months ahead of her both times.

Princess Elizabeth longed to be as matter-of-fact about her first pregnancy as girls like Barbara. Just weeks away from giving birth, she complained: 'Why does everyone make such a fuss ... I am not the only woman who is going to have a baby.'[4] But no other girl was carrying the future head of state (gender depending) in her womb. Like Barbara, Elizabeth was pregnant within the first few months of marriage – young and fecund, these two girls and hundreds of thousands like them were fulfilling the Beveridge dream, but for Elizabeth the stakes were uniquely high.

The Princess knew that no matter how wholesome and well meaning she appeared, and irrespective of whether her 'foreign' husband had proved himself sufficiently British, what really mattered was the arrival of a royal baby, and the sooner the better. It is no coincidence that the Princess told Crawfie she wanted to be a mother before her first wedding anniversary.[5] History is littered with denigrated, barren queens. Even today, Anne, the last Stuart monarch, is often defined not by the unification of Great Britain but rather her succession of miscarriages and the absence of a surviving heir. Conversely, Queen Victoria's fertility established her brand. She had nine children all in a row; despite their sometimes dubious qualities, the sheer quantity of offspring helped reshape the royal house for a new Victorian era invested with bourgeois family values.

Crawfie, whose childless marriage was doubtless a propeller behind the indiscreet publication of her memoir *The Little Princesses* in 1949, understood the pain of an empty womb. Did she flinch when her heavily pregnant former pupil Elizabeth insisted that having babies 'is what we are made for'?[6] Nowadays critics refer to Crawfie's book as sugary and harmless, and some infer that perhaps her employer, the Queen, was a little harsh to cut her off so completely when she spilled the beans on royal life, first in America (with a serialisation in *Ladies Home Journal*) and then Britain (*Woman's Own*).[7] But I don't find Crawfie's prose harmless. She identified the Queen's private pain and wrote about it, telling readers that, after Margaret was born, 'No new baby appeared – I sometimes thought this was a sorrow – and the pram was sadly put away where it remained in purdah for some years.'[8] Yes, you have to clamber through the euphemisms, but there is no doubting what the erstwhile governess is trying to tell us. Sorrow. Sadness. Purdah. The delivery of two little girls hardly demonstrated aristocratic levels of breeding. Where was the son and heir? The Queen didn't have another baby. The medical term used today is secondary infertility.

The Duke and Duchess of York married in 1923; at that point they weren't directly in line for the throne, but the rakish Prince of Wales looked a long way off parenthood, and dynastic pressure was mounting. Royal biographer Hugo Vickers believes conception concerns were a motivation behind the big-game hunting emphasis of the couple's 1924 East African tour.[9] Perhaps a safari would help jog things along. Others have suggested the Duchess didn't like sex (preferring to mother a husband prone to anxiety and bouts of gnashing and anger), and there were rumours she saw a fertility doctor between the wars.[10] Baby Elizabeth took three long years to arrive, and then she was 'only' a girl. It was another four year wait before Margaret was born, after which there were no further children. Post Edward's 1936 abdication, eldest daughter Elizabeth was gradually and artfully reframed as a precious asset, destined to save the monarchy. It was clever optics but, as a mother with just two girls, the Queen must have felt the blow Crawfie landed. The retired governess had targeted Her Majesty's weak spot. As for Princess Elizabeth, she was determined to do thing differently. The heir to the throne wanted a baby before her first wedding anniversary and that is exactly what she got. Charles arrived with one week to spare on 14 November 1948.

'Prince for Elizabeth.' 'A lovely boy, a really splendid boy.' 'Born at 9.14[pm]: Both are doing well.'[11] The press were unequivocal and so was the palace. Everyone was overjoyed the baby was a boy. According to the *Daily Mail*, the King's private secretary, Alan Lascelles, 'hurriedly filled in one word – "Prince"– in the cablegrams waiting to be sent to Governor-Generals throughout the Commonwealth' before the Champagne appeared. Meanwhile, outside the palace, people gathered in front of the railings. A courtier 'waved to the crowd, now 6,000 strong, who, mistaking him for the Duke roared "Is it a boy?" He nodded and the crowd cheered and sang: "for he's a jolly good fellow!"'[12]

The arrival of baby Charles enhanced the alluring femininity of his mother at the same time as it promised the future return of masculine monarchical security for the longer term. Britain's next king enhanced the standing of the entire family, but it was Philip for whom the backwash of good will was most transformative. The pregnancy alone was enough to convert stickler Lascelles, who now decided the Duke was 'such a nice young man, such a sense of duty – not a fool in any way – so much in love poor boy', before qualifying his praise with the tell-tale line, that Philip has 'put the heir to the throne in the family way all according to plan'.[13] Didn't he just. As Britain's edged into the retro 1950s, here was the nation's ideal celebrity family.

Siring a son so early on in his marriage underlined Philip's male prowess. In a souvenir publication to celebrate Charles's arrival, the Duke was referred to as 'very much a man's man'. The birth that 'blessed his union with the Princess' unleashed 'public good will and admiration for his manly qualities'.

While Elizabeth was pregnant, Philip 'manfully' took on additional learning to get abreast of constitutional affairs.[14] This obsession with masculinity (a hangover from World War II) bled into ideas of Philip as a father. According to the press, the Duke was determined that Prince Charles would be a 'real "man's man".' While Charles was still a toddler, Philip had clear ideas about parenting: 'let's be men together', he would say, before taking the reluctant child for a game of cricket or football.[15] No wonder Anne was the Duke's favourite: second-born and a girl, the pressure to impress was considerably less.

If becoming a father conformed to post-war gender stereotypes, it was less clear exactly how a man should behave when his wife was in labour. Barbara takes up the story.

> Oh, yes, Stan was thrilled I had a boy. No, no! He wasn't there for the birth. Men didn't attend the birth! But he came afterwards and took Roger for a walk in our new Silvercross pram. I was still in my confinement and was most annoyed I couldn't join them.

Men were neatly extricated from the messy birthing process and Philip was no exception, taking his equerry, Mike Parker, off for a hearty game of squash – the 'hardest' match of his life – when the going got tough, and neatly reappearing with a large bunch of flowers just after Charles's arrival. The press carefully curated the story: 'wearing informal open collar, sweater and flannel slacks . . . it was the Duke . . . as husband and father, who saw the Princess first'. When she woke from the anaesthetic, there he was: 'her tall, fair-haired handsome husband with deep blue eyes'.[16]

The inconvenience of the Princess's weighty inheritance

was briefly over looked – now she was 'Elizabeth, Wife and Mother' – and carefully choreographed pictures were chosen to celebrate her maternal instinct, most famously the future Queen staring dotingly down at a lacy crib days before the christening. The evocation of Mariology* in the photography is striking; Elizabeth's face bleached white, almost beyond recognition, and the baby's fixed dark gaze, looking towards a mythical future.

Here was Elizabeth, the perfect housewife, in an era when mothers were encouraged to develop close attachments to their children. Apparently the Princess insisted: 'I am going to mother my baby – not the nurse', and plaintively told Mike Parker's Scottish housewife that she would like her children 'to be able to live ordinary lives', adding 'I wish I could be more like you, Eileen'. 'Normal' is apparently what the Princess coveted, and 'normal' is how the press briefly tried to depict her. They even pretended one of her hobbies was cooking. To be fair, she did manage to breastfeed for a couple of months. But Parker's wife was not convinced: 'I pondered, how much of a price would a princess truly be willing to pay in order to bring her children up like "ordinary people".'[17] Two top-drawer nannies were appointed before the birth.

Emotionally reserved and the heir to the throne, Elizabeth was not destined to be a hands-on mother. And 'man's man Philip' was never going to compromise his masculinity to look after the children. As the couple quickly discovered, there was much more to being the Edinburghs than met the eye.

◆◇◆

'If you are writing about Philip and Elizabeth, you will need to include Pat.' And with that a five-minute black-and-white

---

* The theological study and celebration of Mary, the mother of Jesus.

Pathé News clip pings into my Whatsapp. Simon Robinson is a 1940s–1950s' aficionado and the newsreel is bona fide. It is November 1953 and the Queen and the Duke are visiting BBC Television Centre. An evening event, BBC suits including director of television Sir George Barnes greet the royal car and out steps a beautiful Queen. Elizabeth looks unusually sexy in dark taffeta covered with a fur stole. Her Prince remains two steps behind and, as his valet noted, Philip's hair is thinning, and he's over done the pomade, which shines in the television lights.[18]

Pathé play a montage of behind-the-scenes shots (from the hit series *Animal, Vegetable or Mineral?*) a demonstration of a new high-tech world, which just months earlier had brought the Queen's coronation into millions of sitting rooms. Elizabeth is still riding the wave of post-coronation fever; the timing of this visit is surely deliberate? The Queen comes back into shot, glad-handing numerous artists, many of whom are household names. She wears long, elegant black gloves, her luminous bare arms and neck are offset with abundant creamy pearls, and daring black sequins dive down to a neat royal waist. She nods and chats; there are comedians Al Read and Norman Wisdom, radio star Jimmy Edwards, actress Sally Barnes and a rather incongruous Terry Thomas, who conducts a stilted conversation with Her Majesty while trussed up in a Beefeater costume. And there she is! Bobbing down into a deep respectful curtsey, the camera changes angles but, yes, it does appear that actress Pat Kirkwood is the only performer not graced with Her Majesty's small talk. Elizabeth moves swiftly on, drawing her lips down over her teeth and engaging the next in line, actor Bill Fraser, with a delightful smile.[19]

Pat Kirkwood had been given short shrift by a woman drilled in unparalleled social etiquette. What was going on? What was it about this actress that saw Elizabeth's exceptional discipline briefly desert her? With dark waved hair and a neat figure, at first glance Pat looks disarmingly like her Queen, but the two women couldn't have been more different. Five years Elizabeth's senior, Kirkwood had cut her teeth in the rough and tumble of variety halls both in London and up north. With a large abundant mouth and distinctive Lancashire accent, she oozed charisma. On stage Pat excelled in thigh-slapping principal roles and quickly became the star in a golden age of British musical comedy. Off stage she was married four times; few could resist this 'seasoned trouper' with legs that famously 'went up to her arm pits'. But it was not her multiple divorces that dogged Pat's reputation, rather the persistent rumours that, in late 1948, she had an affair with Prince Philip, HRH Elizabeth's new husband.[20]

The Princess was heavily pregnant, the couple were still living in Buckingham Palace, where the Queen called the shots (apparently Elizabeth always deferred to her mother's opinion), and Philip found his naval career compromised by a need to step in for his pregnant wife. A degree of sympathy is required for the brash young Duke. Penned in by courtiers and vicious camp followers, Philip sought to build up his own entourage: Mike Parker was the just one of a series of like-minded individuals who did things differently. Thanks to a recommendation from Mountbatten, Lieutenant General Frederick 'Boy' Browning was appointed as Comptroller and Treasurer of the couple's joint household. A former Guards officer, he bridged any royal divides by bringing with him a waft of glamour. It was Browning who first introduced Philip to Cowes Regatta and his delectable wife, author Daphne du Maurier.

But while Browning was an official recommendation from Uncle Dickie, there were other, less formal Mountbatten introductions. Photographer Baron Nahum was the playful, charming son of Jewish-Italian immigrants. He made his name photographing ballet and beautiful women in the 1930s and, by the time Philip met him at Broadlands, Baron had become a leading society photographer. The friendship worked both ways – Philip commissioned Baron to take pictures at his wedding and Baron introduced Philip to a London life totally divorced from the patrolled corridors of Buckingham Palace.

Philip had married into the pinnacle of British aristocratic society; actress and Bletchley Park veteran Pamela Rose, featured earlier in this book, was struck by how traditional and English he appeared when they finally met. By 1948, the Duke had most things in life, except the tantalising transitory magic of showbiz, a celebrity that was always infinitely racer than royalty. No wonder Philip's head was turned by Baron's Thursday Club, where an assortment of like-minded actors, editors and other men of the moment met in Wheeler's Fish restaurant under the cover of darkness on Soho's Old Compton Street.[21] Soon Philip could count David Niven and James Robertson Justice among his friends. Theirs was a masculine post-war world: it was expected that men should have a form of release, a means of letting off steam. Especially celebrities and aristocrats who had always played by different rules.

The particular night in question was in 1948, when Philip had a backstage introduction to Pat Kirkwood, a personal friend of Baron's. There was chit-chat in her dressing room followed by dinner at Les Ambassadeurs in Mayfair and a night cap in Milroy's supper club, where Philip invited the actress on to the dance floor. Just a couple of miles down the road, his young wife was gently expanding, a future king in her belly; meanwhile the Duke (whom courtiers had cautioned was unlikely to 'be faithful') waltzed the night away with a show girl. Faces fell in disapproval at Milroy's, and Philip, caught up in the moment, mocked the shocked onlookers before leaving with Pat and Baron for a late-night breakfast at the latter's flat.[22]

Word did not leak out in the press (that would come much later), but it did get back to the King, who was furious and gave his son-in-law a dressing down.[23] In public, as always, the Princess remained silent. The only clue as to any pain she felt about what may (or may not) have happened was in that awkward meeting caught by Pathé's cameras five years after the event, and the uncomfortable fact that, despite her stellar career, Pat Kirkwood was never honoured for her services to theatre and the arts.

In later life the actress went out of her way to deny the rumours of a story that always felt one-sided. She complained that 'a lady is not normally expected to defend her honour publicly. It is the gentleman who should do that.'[24] But Philip, a duke and husband of the Queen, enjoyed exceptional status. Pat was not the only girl that he was identified with during this period. There was a mystery woman that the Duke apparently drove to Windlesham Moor, near Ascot, the first real home the Edinburghs shared together. Again it was years later that a footman, Norman Barson, spilled the beans. The woman in question was beautiful, nameless and discreet (her head covered with a scarf). By all accounts Philip's manners were impeccable; he was attentive, flirtatious and careful. You can't accuse someone of adultery for sharing a two-seater, refilling a gin and orange and sitting beside a pretty woman in front of a roaring fire. Why, then, did Philip caution his footman: 'Don't forget, Norman, you haven't seen me!'?[25] If indeed he said that at all. To borrow the Queen's neat phrase of 2021, 'recollections may vary'.

Philip has proved a tough subject for biographers to pin down. Gossip sells books but there is no hard evidence, and, until very recently Her Majesty was still alive, which heightened sensitivities. The conundrum may explain the strange detour in Gyles Brandreth's otherwise illuminating portrait of the Prince. For a man who is unreservedly royalist (I last saw him broadcasting at the Platinum Jubilee in a sweater with a corgi on the front), and most definitely a fan of Philip's (whom he knew), there is a curious section in Brandreth's book. Promising (as all biographers tend to) an interrogation of Philip's reputation as a womaniser, Brandreth jumps down a Princess Marie Bonaparte rabbit hole. Marie, loosely married to Philip's paternal uncle, Big George (Prince George of Greece), was a sexual libertarian with a deep and active interest in the works of Dr Sigmund Freud. Brandreth uses this tenuous connection to 'investigate' what Freudian Marie might have made of Philip's female-heavy early childhood (he was a longed-for son arriving late in a family of four older girls) and the impact this may have had on his later relationships with women.

Brandreth taps up a Freudian psychologist; the pair discuss the hypothetical chance of Philip having 'penis awe', perhaps even 'phallic swagger' (conditions that stem from disproportionate female attention and devotion when young). Brandreth tells us what we already know, that Philip liked the company of young, attractive women, but his discussion with the Freudian psychologist is inconclusive. Apparently men with 'phallic swagger' aren't always serial adulterers.[26] Had Brandreth really wanted to land a psychobabble blow, he would have looked into the male role models in Philip's life. There were his father's failed marriage and glamorous lady friends in the Riviera and Uncle Dickie's notoriously 'open' marriage, not to mention Big George and Marie Bonaparte's 'unconventional' relationship.[27] Monogamy did not have a high currency in Philip's wider family.

Instead, Brandreth's effort feels like a jolly excuse to write the word 'penis' into a royal biography and it does little to move on a discussion long undermined by an obsession with trying to prove the impossible: whether Philip had adulterous affairs. Yes, the Duke's relations with women are part of the story of his marriage (no couple is an island), but as important is Elizabeth and *her* role in this furore. It takes two to define the unwritten rules of matrimony. All too often Philip's wife is absent in the circular debates focused on the Duke's alleged 'penis awe'.

What we do know is that Elizabeth was undoubtedly in love with her prince. A girl who had been served and pandered to her entire life fell for a man renowned for his bolshie attitude, flirtatious manner and occasional flippant cruelty. Valet John Dean was frequently crushed by his boss, while aristocratic Lady Glenconner asserts that Philip 'made everybody nervous and he knew it', and by all accounts Elizabeth was no exception. She frequently incurred the wrath of her husband.[28] Colville's initial reticence towards the Duke in part stemmed from the 'off-hand way' he talked to his bride-to-be.[29] In some instances it almost amounted to bullying. Biographer Ben Pimlott recalls an incident when Philip was driving too fast – Elizabeth's breathing became tense, and this infuriated the Duke so much that he threatened: 'If you do that once more I shall put you out of the car.' His wife breathed normally and the car sped on. At the end of the journey, Mountbatten, a fellow passenger, asked why she had not insisted Philip drove more slowly, to which Elizabeth responded: 'But you heard what he said.'[30]

A complex picture of the Edinburghs' early marriage emerges: on the one hand the impatient and flirtatious Duke is slightly out of his wife's reach, tickling the fancy of glamorous women, and on the other he is someone capable of at least superficial unkindness. Traits that beg the question: why didn't the future heir to the throne put her foot down? The answer to which is simple: first and foremost, Elizabeth was a young girl in love. She was also a woman born into a deferential society where men were expected to take the lead, until, of course, they met Her Royal Highness and resorted to obsequious platitudes and suffocating pleasantries. In this context Elizabeth's tolerance of Philip's brusque diffidence and (unproven) infidelity is much easier to understand. The Duke was an exception and exceptions are often very attractive. Perversely, his ability to hurt her was part of the appeal. Here was a man who was not overawed by the status of the woman he married. And perhaps it was because of that status and his compromised lesser role that he felt the need to occasionally kick back, with other women, or unkind words. It turns out the handsome Prince with deep blue eyes was human after all, which is precisely why his princess loved him.

-◇-

In 2022, the Queen's Platinum Jubilee year, Kensington Palace staged a stunning exhibition: *Life Through a Royal Lens* was a visual romp through our most recent royals, tracing the family's relationship with photography from the medium's inception under Victoria through to the present day. There are various standout shots: Dorothy Wilding's hand-coloured stylised accession portraits of our late Queen; Margaret being Margaret, sitting in a bathtub, a tiara a top her head; and David Bailey's mesmeric side profile of the late Diana, Princess of Wales. 'I like to take away everything . . . and get closer and closer until you have the essence of the girl.'[31] Diana's face, especially those doe-eyes, were a window into her soul – she was a photographer's dream, with an expression that immediately engendered sympathy, even compassion. Not so the family into which she had married. Royalty, reared in their confined privilege, learned from birth how to keep the camera at bay, which is why, of all the photographs in that 2022 exhibition, the one I loved the best was Matt Holyoak's 'never-before-seen picture' of the Queen and Prince Philip.

It is a darling portrait of the pair, captured in deep old age to celebrate their 2017 Platinum Wedding anniversary. Elizabeth, in gentle cream, is seated looking up with incredulous devotion at a jovial Philip. The Duke's face is cracked in a wide spontaneous smile, he is laughing at the camera, a demobbed hand casually thrust into his pocket. Squint your eyes and there is something of the young sailor boy about him. As for the Queen, her expression is one of deep love, a sentiment more commonly associated with teenage girls than nonagenarian monarchs. But although there is no physical contact between the couple, the photograph was initially considered 'too personal' for wide distribution. Prince Philip was not a man who indulged in public displays of affection – the portrait's release came after his death in 2021.[32]

This careful editing of their marital image is a reminder that what we saw of Elizabeth and Philip's relationship was only ever part of their story. All too often the public were privy to abrupt Philip, the man forged by upper-class detachment and remote (virtually non-existent) parenting, someone whom even his equerry, straight-talking Mike Parker, tried to goad into being a little more affectionate with his young wife. 'I always wanted to see him put his arms around the Queen, and show her how much he adored her. What you'd do for any wife. But he always sort of stood to attention. I mentioned it a couple of times but he just gave me a hell of a look.'[33] Like any marriage, much of Elizabeth and Philip's relationship existed behind closed doors and yet, even when the royal couple were finally tucked up in Clarence House in 1949, their privacy was compromised. By the mid-1950s, valet John Dean, like governess Marion Crawford before him, divulged the Edinburgh's domestic secrets in an insipid little memoir.

Thirty years after the publication of Dean's book, an

intruder burst into the Queen's bedroom. Amid all the security consternation and outrage that followed, the tabloids still
found the space to feign mock shock upon the discovery that
Elizabeth and Philip slept in 'separate bedrooms'.[34] The *Daily
Mirror* had little truck with what it considered to be a 'royal
and aristocratic tradition'. How did the Queen manage without 'a cosy, going-to-sleep chat and a cuddle . . . and a good
morning kiss'? It was a faux debate and not a fair one to level
at a couple born in the early twentieth century. Back then
Marie Stopes, that champion of *Married Love*,* recommended
separate bedrooms because 'everyday association . . .tends to
reduce the keen pleasure each takes in the other'.[35] She had a
point. How many couples still sharing a bed after thirty-five
years of marriage have nightly chats, cuddles and morning
kisses? And, more pertinently, news of the royals' separate
sleeping arrangements was not new. Valet John Dean had
already spilled those particular beans. He'd told his readers
that, in 1950s' Clarence House, 'the bedrooms of the Princess
and Duke were communicating and their dressing-tables were
placed only a few feet from the door, so that they could chat
through the door while they were dressing'.[36]

This domestic set up spoke more about the couple's wealth
and class than it did about their relationship. Between the wars,
twin beds were sold as fashionable items for newlyweds who
could afford them in an era when 'a relative autonomy' was
anticipated between a husband and wife.[37] Certainly in the early
days, their sleeping arrangements do not appear to have
impinged on the couple's sex life. Biographers assure us Elizabeth and Philip were occasionally caught in bed together early
in the morning. An invidious predicament for the domestic staff

---

*   *Married Love* was the title of Stopes's 1918 book, which was one of the first to
openly discuss birth control and 'great sex' in the context of a happy marriage.

in question, made more so because the Duke insisted on sleeping naked.[38] It all feels a bit puerile. And arguably more revealing in terms of the possible fault lines in their marriage, were the interior design traces that the couple left behind in Clarence House and other royal residences. Or rather the lack of them.

Upon the death of the King in 1952, Clarence House, which had benefited from a £50,000 refurbishment under the Edinburghs, was given to a retitled Queen Mother. Despite the money and enthusiasm the couple had expended on the premises, it was the latter who left her aesthetic mark. The biographer Hugo Vickers explains that the newlyweds 'failed to impose any style on the place', relying on borrowed art from the Royal Collection and an assortment of wedding presents. The Princess's predilection for daffodil yellow was on display in a newly tiled kitchen and the dining room was painted Adam green to go with the carpet.[39] It was a similar story in Sandringham, the Windsors' private Norfolk retreat, stuffed full of family memorabilia and a place where the royals celebrate almost every Christmas. Queen Mary's arch biographer James Pope-Hennessy visited in 1956 and was given full access, including to the bedrooms of Elizabeth and Philip. The former's boudoir (previously Queen Mary's) was 'about the most depersonalised room I have ever seen outside a hotel: three pictures on the vast walls, hung not centrally nor symmetrically. Peter Scott, say, of duck flying and a vague picture apparently of Antibes.' Elizabeth objected to the dressing table's brass handles, 'which have now been replaced by porcelain ones with pink rose buds on them. It is now like the bedroom of an anonymous mouse.'[40]

An anonymous mouse. Elizabeth lacked confidence in the domestic arena. How could it have been otherwise? She had grown up enjoying a famously close relationship with her parents, but, despite the love, there had always been an absence of informality. Brought up inside museum pieces –Buckingham Palace and Windsor Castle – this was a girl who was 'neat and methodical beyond words' but had little clue how to make a home.[41]

Ironically a great patron of the arts and ultimately replicated on canvass more frequently than any other woman, the problem was compounded by the Princess's lack of artistic appreciation: she didn't have a good eye.[42] Years later, when Kenneth Clark's ground-breaking series, *Royal Palaces*, was shown to the Queen and Philip prior to transmission in 1966, Elizabeth was unimpressed.* The art historian noted: 'All she could say was "it's so sarcastic" . . . She didn't say a word about the photography which is excellent.' (Tellingly, 'the only member of the royal family who showed any interest in the film was Prince Charles'.)[43] In her early marriage, Elizabeth's absence of aesthetic ambition bled into the domestic sphere and is perhaps reflective of a natural reserve that existed in most of Elizabeth's relationships, including with her husband. This reticence left space for Philip to impose his personality in their most intimate surroundings.

Older than her, more worldly and long covetous of his own home, early on he showed the Princess how to better inhabit her own space. Before their wedding he brazenly rejigged Elizabeth's stuffy Buckingham Palace apartments: 'a large sofa was drawn in front of the fire with the chairs on either side

---

* Kenneth Clark was Britain's leading art historian, and is most famous for his 1969 *Civilisation* series. Clark's relationship with the Royal Family began early; he was appointed Surveyor of the King's Pictures in 1934, a post he held until 1944. George V was adamant he should accept the role, and his subsequent relationship with Queen Elizabeth (later the Queen Mother) was warm. However, he became increasingly impatient with court life, which may explain why Elizabeth and Philip found him and the tone of *Royal Palaces* 'sarcastic'. (See James Stourton, *Kenneth Clark*.)

instead of being isolated at the window . . . so already he had begun to have his influence, and instead of looking stiff and unlived in . . . it now had a homelike look.'[44]

Likewise in their first weekend home, Windlesham Moor, he discarded his jacket, hammered up pictures and moved furniture. The smallest house the couple ever lived in (with room for six resident staff), there is something almost pitiful about Philip's efforts to create domestic respite here. He would return from the Ideal Homes Exhibition with the latest 1950s gadgetry – electric mixers, tin food, washing machines – contraptions his valet quietly observed were designed to 'make life easier for a servantless couple living in a flat'.[45]

Philip's taste was unapologetically masculine. At Sandring-ham his sleeping ensemble showed evidence of

a positive but somewhat vulgar personality, sofas and arm chairs covered in virulent magenta chintz with huge medallions 'His Majesties Shippes in 1672' in full sail on them; always the same shippes, whether blue or magenta. Naval pictures and so on.[46]

This was a young man trying to establish himself within an ancient family. Minus any real domestic experience of his own, he fell back on his second home, the navy. The ward-room, the deck, the bridge: these were places where Philip had proved himself, irrespective of his wife and the titles that came with her. If Elizabeth didn't need to establish a domestic style because it had always (and would always) be done for her, Philip found one that gave him a distinct and separate identity. First and foremost, the man's man was a sailor boy who had earned his stripes in World War II.

◆

The sky was burning, as if on fire, and the water caught up its reflection as did the rocks on the harbour. Earth and heavens and sea were ablaze, a stupendous illumination Nature had arranged for this festive occasion . . . Oh the sweetness, the beauty, the enchantment . . . everywhere flowers, fragrance, sunshine and the buzzing of a myriad wings . . . Oh the joy, the joy, the joy![47]

A 'paradise' is how Queen Victoria's granddaughter, English-born Princess Marie, described the island of Malta when she lived there for three years as a teenager.* In 1886, her father, the then Duke of Edinburgh (Alfred, Victoria's second son), was posted to the British stronghold as the newly promoted Commander-in-Chief, Mediterranean Fleet. As HMS *Osbourne* advanced slowly into the fortified harbour of Valletta, Alfred came down to greet his family. 'Papa at the height of his career, at the height also of his good looks, Papa with his deeply tanned face in which his eyes shone extraordinarily, fascinatingly blue. A sailor in every sense of the word, a sailor, an Englishman, a prince!'[48]

Sixty-three years later, the next Duke of Edinburgh took his own place in Malta. A tanned blue-eyed sailor, an (almost) Englishman and a (former) prince,† Philip, after the birth of Charles, relinquished his desk job in Britain for an active naval posting on the island. The First Lieutenant of destroyer HMS *Chequers*, by 1950 he had been promoted to Lieutenant Commander in charge of his own frigate, HMS *Magpie*, in one of the most powerful naval forces in the world. Philip

---

* Later Queen Marie of Romania, renowned for her pro-Allied propaganda during World War I and numerous affairs.
† Although he was often referred to as Prince Philip, the Duke wasn't formally given the title Prince again until 1957.

remembers a 'very happy wardroom'.[49] Others were less sure. Under his stewardship, apparently men were worked 'like dogs' as 'Dukey'* stamped around, a little too keen to prove himself.[50] However, no one could deny that he cut a dash among his men – there were regattas (which his ship invariably won) and never-ending naval exercises. Whatever his faults, Philip was a man who liked to be physically involved, oar in hand, torso exposed, sunglasses shielding his eyes from the sea's glare. It is easy to imagine Princess Elizabeth, (a first cousin twice removed of Marie's) arriving in Malta to find her Duke as tanned and attractive in his crisp whites as Prince Alfred once looked. (Both women shared an appreciation for men in uniform.)

The script of Philip's life tells us that Malta represented the brief zenith of his naval career; this was certainly one of his 'happiest times'.[51] But it's important not to over egg the pudding. The Philip who arrived in Malta, a man temporarily free from the shackles of palace life, immediately found himself compromised by another family association. Having dutifully dispatched India, the subcontinent's last viceroy, Uncle Dickie had been posted to Malta commanding 1st Cruiser Squadron before becoming Second-in-Command of the Mediterranean Fleet. Philip had left the embrace of one set of relations to find himself embroiled in a second. Could he do nothing without family? (The question was an uncomfortable one.) Initially minus accommodation, he stayed with Mountbatten and his wife, Edwina, in Villa Guardamangia, where the Duke was immediately 'very busy showing his independence'. Philip was no longer prepared to tolerate his uncle's 'dominating influence and patronage'. There were

---

* Philip's crew nickname.

clashes that hurt Mountbatten, who privately longed for a son of his own.[52]

By the end of November, Princess Elizabeth had joined them. For all the talk of motherhood and Elizabeth's longing to be 'normal', baby Charles was left back in Britain, while the reality of the couple's 'happiest time' was disjointed and brief. The Princess arrived in Malta nearly two months after her husband. In England she had been shadowing her father, acquiring the working knowledge of an heiress apparent while trying to establish her own voice. There were regular readings of Foreign Office telegrams and an appearance in front of the Mother's Union in Central Hall, Westminster, where Elizabeth deplored the 'current age of growing self indulgence, or hardening materialism' before hopping on an aeroplane to join her husband.* Decades later she would quietly note of her reign, 'I didn't have an apprenticeship'.[53] But nor did she have much time alone with Philip in Malta, and that winter of 1949–50 was a case in point. Initially she, too, moved in with the Mountbattens, where Edwina obligingly gave up her sleeping quarters. The Princess enjoyed a few snatched weeks, extended to include the Christmas period, and didn't return again until the following spring. By then she was pregnant with Anne, which restricted future visits.†

When she was on the island, the 'radiant' Princess was undoubtedly happy. She visited hospitals and destroyers, drove her own car – a Daimler saloon – and unveiled plaques. The couple could eat alone in local restaurants without being disturbed and enjoyed swimming and fishing in the local creeks and bays. Here, Lady Mountbatten decided, Elizabeth led a

---

* Elizabeth's schedule meant she was finally permitted to take short haul flights.
† Elizabeth travelled to Malta to spend a second Christmas with Philip in 1950. Both children stayed with their grandparents in Sandringham.

'more or less human and normal existence for once'.[54] There was certainly less standing on ceremony in Malta and, an equine paradise, the lifestyle suited both the horse-obsessed Princess and Philip, who finally mastered how to play polo with his uncle (a relief for Elizabeth, she much preferred watching polo to hockey, another pastime of the Duke's). It was a place where naval japes and dances abounded. With his giant-sized ego, Mountbatten was keen that the 'enchanting' Princess, who loved to Samba, should like him.[55] It speaks volumes of Elizabeth's restrained personality that she didn't feel compelled to volubly reciprocate Mountbatten's affections.* But if the latter's head was easily turned by royalty, his wife Edwina had less truck with the trappings and (prosaic) tastes of the Windsors. This cultured, polyamorous millionaire was privately dismissive of the 'ridiculous games' and gangster movies that Elizabeth grew up learning to love.[56] But it was the Princess's lo-fi recreational palette that provided 'vulgar' Philip with a perfect foil – a shared sense of unpretentious fun would stand the couple in very good stead.

In January 1950, Edwina waved goodbye to their little house guest: putting Elizabeth 'into the Viking when she left was I thought rather like putting a bird back into a very small cage and I felt sad and nearly tearful myself'.[57] Unlike Edwina Mountbatten, who loved freedom, affairs and fine living, the Princess's life was constructed around clearly defined lines. She, too, shed a tear on departure, but Elizabeth had been brought up knowing what came next and at least she had a husband who understood her royal burden and was prepared to share it with her. What neither reckoned with was just how

---

* Mountbatten concluded, after her birthday celebrations in April 1950, that 'I think she is so sweet and attractive. At times I think she likes me too, though she is far too reserved to give any indication.' Philip Ziegler, *Mountbatten*, p. 492.

quickly that burden would become a reality. It is unsurprising that, retrospectively, their days in Malta have been invested with a halcyon glow. Conforming to 1950s conventions, it was here that Philip enjoyed a naval promotion and military status in his own right – HMS *Magpie* was 'Cock of the Fleet'* – while Elizabeth played the biddable naval wife. This was as near to normal as the couple got, but it wasn't destined to last. Instead Malta's transitory magic would for ever hold them in its spell.

---

*   Term applied to the leading ship in competitive exercises and regattas, etc.

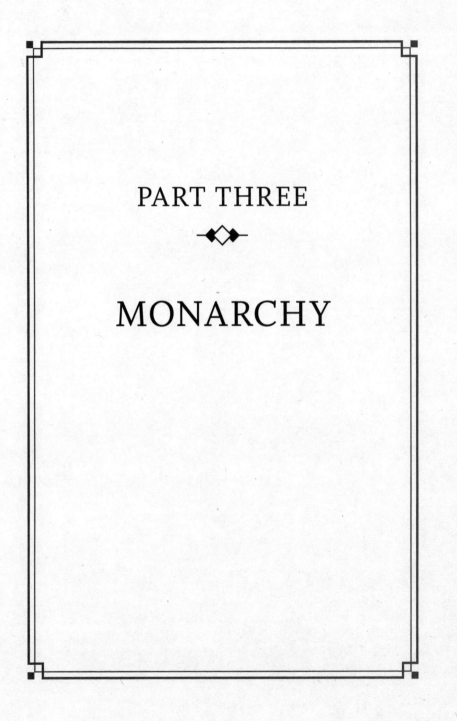

PART THREE

◆◇

MONARCHY

TEN

◆◇◆

'Good Health is a Precious Gift'

Pat Owtram is ninety-nine years old, her sister, Jean, is ninety-six. As children growing up between the wars, home was a large sandstone house in rural Lancashire during a period when people were acutely aware of their social standing. 'We were squirarchy – one below aristocracy – and we were brought up in a completely royalist family.'[1] To illustrate her point, Pat recalls that, like Princess Elizabeth, she too had a pony. 'Dolly was given to us by a rich aunt and Jean and I would take turns being led around the garden.' To reinforce their royalist fervour, the little sisters would run down to the crossroads with small Union Jack flags when the royal party swept north to Lord Sefton's private shooting lodge in the next village but one. The Owtram girls loved waving at George V almost as much as the King loved shooting.

It was many years later that Pat and Jean finally came face to face with a British monarch. By the spring of 1951, the same rich aunt decided that the Owtram sisters would benefit from presentation at court. Pat was less sure. After a successful war (a Wren with the rank of Petty Officer who had signed the Official Secrets Act and worked as a wireless inceptor and translator), Pat capitalised on several bursaries that saw her enjoy a tertiary education at Oxford, St Andrews and Harvard Universities. If this meteoric rise through the ranks of academia didn't quell her royal enthusiasm, it did encourage a reality check. Pat suggested that perhaps, at the age of twenty-four, she was a little old to be presented at court? But her aunt was undeterred.

Pat dutifully bought a mauve cocktail dress (far too short) and feathered hat and headed south to meet her sister. Much to their relief, the Exhibition of Britain planned that summer resulted in an early, pared-down presentation in a Buckingham Palace drawing room. Pat found herself bobbing in front of Princess Elizabeth, two years her junior, perched on a stool beside her father, George VI. 'I had a terrible job trying to get out of the room backwards.' And there is something else that snags in Pat's memory. 'The King looked terrible. Really terrible. I think he was wearing bronze makeup to hide how ill he was.'

Perspicacious Pat was on to something. Within months of the girls' presentation, doctors diagnosed the King with lung cancer. But he had no idea how ill he was. Alan Lascelles wrote to Churchill* in September 1951, explaining there would be an operation on the Monday, but 'poor fellow, he does not know what it means'.[2] The monarch was kept in a childlike state of ignorance. On the eve of an operation to remove his left lung, he was simply told the problem was caused by 'a blockage of one of the bronchial tubes'. George VI survived the surgery, but (unbeknown to him) the outlook was bleak. That his royal cocoon avoided the 'C' word at all costs was indicative of the times. One did not talk about health, especially not with the patient. One certainly did not tell George VI (prone to anxiety) he had cancer. Morale must be maintained. Kings lived for ever (until they died).

---

* Winston Churchill was still in opposition. The General Election was held on 25 October 1951, when, at seventy-six years old, he became Prime Minister for a final time.

Nor was the idea of knowledge on a need-to-know-basis confined to George VI. Heavily pregnant with her first baby, Elizabeth had not been privy to her father's earlier compromised physical state in late 1948. Days before she went into labour, results from a medical examination confirmed that the King was seriously ill – he had arteriosclerosis, which restricted blood flow to the lower part of the legs, with gangrene so severe that amputation of his right leg was considered. In fact, George VI had been in discomfort for nearly a year; he'd lost over a stone in weight and his courtiers frequently caught him banging his legs against the side of the desk to restore circulation.[3] Biographer Ben Pimlott suggests that Elizabeth must have had an inkling about her father's condition prior to the cancellation of his long-awaited Commonwealth tour of Australia and New Zealand, just days after she gave birth. But that is to suppose the Royal Family talked about health – generally they didn't. George procrastinated about seeking help and his wife went even further. 'The Queen never allowed you to contemplate the fact of the King's illness.'[4] She loved her husband, and it turns out she rather liked being married to the monarch. Mortality was not up for discussion.

It is worth drawing attention to this curious stasis regarding the King's health because his death in 1952 has long been identified not only as a personal tragedy for Elizabeth, Heir Apparent, but also something of a professional shock both for the girl destined to be Queen and her husband, the Duke of Edinburgh. Yet the clues were there early on. Premature death was much more commonplace seventy years ago than it is today, especially among men. Philip's own father had died aged sixty-two, and his Uncle Georgie, 2nd Marquis of Milford Haven, at just forty-five. George VI had never been physically robust, undergoing operations for appendicitis and a duodenal ulcer as a young man. One of the takeaway impressions, reading Crawfie's memoir (published before the King died) was her observation that even as Duke of York, he 'did not look very strong' and latterly appeared 'desperately tired' and 'ill'.[5] Like Pat, it was easier for Crawfie, an outsider, to acknowledge.

Of course 'tired' and 'ill' are a far cry from the finality of death, and the omnipresence of kings gives them an immortal sheen even when all the indicators suggest otherwise. Here it might be judicious to point to the recent obsession with our late ninety-six-year-old Queen's heath. No one lives for ever, but to suggest that Elizabeth II might die in her Platinum Jubilee year was unthinkable. 'Mobility issues' became a catch-all that allowed everyone to avoid contemplating the inevitable. This apparent lack of transparency regarding the monarch's health proved even more elusive in the 1950s when knowledge of medical conditions and causes was patchy. After a major operation to relieve the circulatory deficiency in the King's legs in March 1949 (a room at Buckingham Palace was converted into His Majesty's own operating theatre), George VI was never fully out of the woods. Churchill later described him as a man who 'walked with death', but the country was kept in the dark.[6] According to one surgeon, when pictures emerged of an ailing George VI in 1951, 'every doctor and nurse in the country realised he had a malignant disease, he looked terrible'. But his medical team released a statement saying the King had 'influenza with slight inflammation of the lung'. It was 'twaddle'.[7]

In 1949, prior to his operation, George VI was told he should cut back his notoriously heavy smoking, the habit that eventually killed him.* But in a culture where 81% of men

---

* George VI had severe vascular disease in his legs – 99% due to smoking; he had carcinoma of the lung – 99% due to smoking; and he died of coronary thrombosis – 90% due to smoking. Professor Harold Ellis, talking to the Royal College of Surgeons, 27 April 2015.

were addicted to tobacco, and the government was addicted to the tax revenues that tobacco generated, transparency regarding Britain's primary killer was a long time in coming.* It wasn't until 1956 that the then Tory health minister concluded there was probably a link between smoking and lung cancer, but he didn't stop smoking himself. Regarding the King, the idea that he sacrificed his health (and ultimately his life) when he ascended his brother's throne has proved enduring. It was a line vehemently sustained by his wife, who saw the impact the public role of kingship had on her stuttering husband. Stress may have increased his tobacco consumption, but it was the cigarettes that proved fatal.

It is noteworthy that, the night before Philip got married, he quit tobacco. Elizabeth had grown up around men she loved dearly who smoked continuously. Until that point the Prince also 'smoked quite a lot'. His ability to suddenly relinquish the habit suggests Philip was looking to please his bride and points to his self discipline.[8] The newspapers were impressed: 'He can crack a good joke . . . and he can cook a good dinner . . . and he can give up smoking!'[9] Philip's new clean living matched the style of his future Queen. In fact, as royal couples go, they were remarkably abstemious. George V, George VI, the Duke of Windsor and Princess Margaret all depended heavily on tobacco; Margaret also loved a drink and by all accounts, so does our new King, Charles III, (in keeping with his generation). Not so Philip. On the morning of his wedding, no doubt to temper nerves and compensate for absent tobacco, he had a gin and tonic.[10] But, like Elizabeth, he

---

* After the cancer-smoking link had been established, Prime Minister Harold MacMillan, worrying about the Treasury's revenues, hoped people would stick with tobacco and BBC's *Any Questions* provided a reassuring anecdote about Churchill smoking.

was not a big drinker – enjoying the odd beer and fine wine. The couple's diet when alone was hardly more indulgent, a simple savoury and the avoidance of pudding ensured that the world's most photographed duo always looked trim despite obligatory and frequent fine dining. And while Elizabeth loved her nursery high tea – sandwiches, toast, cakes – Philip made do with a cuppa.[11]

Latterly the Duke watched his intake of carbohydrates, preferring protein, and we know from his valet that, in the early years, to keep his weight down, he would go running wearing three or four sweaters.[12] These pretensions towards the body beautiful presumably helped Philip kick cigarettes with apparent ease. After all, by the late 1940s, although there was not yet a definitive cancer link, smoking hardly enhanced a man's appearance. Addled by tobacco, Alan Lascelles was not alone in recalling George V's 'physical repulsiveness' in old age – 'he was much worse than most *strictly ugly* people can ever be'.[13] Image was very important to Philip, as columnist Roderick Mann was at pains to point out when he saw the Duke at Cowdray Park after a polo match.

> When finished play he dismounted, went over to his car, stripped off his shirt and stood there – torso bared – taking a couple of swigs of water . . . then he towelled himself down, put on a fresh shirt, combed his hair and strode through the onlookers towards a special enclosure.[14]

It is perhaps not surprising that, in contrast to his sickly father-in-law, Philip would live for nearly a century, dying just two months shy of his hundredth birthday in 2021. Like his wife, he knew how to take care of himself. But despite the Duke's very long life, his naval career was short. By mid-1951, aged just thirty, he had been recalled from Malta to support Elizabeth and her ill father. If only the King hadn't smoked.

◆

Hugo Vickers is one of Britain's longest standing, most acclaimed royal biographers. In fact, the word biographer is inadequate for a man who has dedicated his life and considerable intellect to the detailed pursuit and celebration of Britain's royalty. His encyclopaedic knowledge of the Windsor family and its innumerable hangers-on is second to none, his list of erudite publications is extensive and his exquisite thatched Wiltshire home a veritable treasure trove of royal memorabilia, including gold embroidered blue velvet 1977 Silver Jubilee chairs and photographs galore. There is a young Hugo with the Queen Mother; the Queen in her Imperial State crown; and a life-sized cardboard cut-out of Harry and Meghan in the porch 'to terrify burglars'. (The man is a traditionalist.) He loved Her Majesty. For Hugo, the Platinum Jubilee celebrations were bitter-sweet and her subsequent death painful. The Queen was a woman he first met in St George's Chapel, Windsor, as a young boy; her life helped define his and he has always been very protective of her. And of them.

I ask him about Her Majesty's relationship with Philip and the rumours that billow around the latter's reputation. Even at the end of the Duke's life, he spent much of his time with a far younger glamorous blonde – Penny Romsey* – in Wood Farm, Sandringham. The story was an open secret, the tabloids were full of it.[15] But Hugo points out that the Queen frequently invited Penny to both Windsor Castle and Sandringham and, in the wake of the Duke's death, continued to ask her to the

---

* In 1979, Penny Knatchbull, now Countess Mountbatten of Burma, married Norton Knatchbull, Louis Mountbatten's grandson, then Lord Ramsey and now 3rd Earl Mountbatten of Burma.

Windsor Horse Show. Likewise Penny was one of a select few at the late Duke's Covid-19-restricted funeral. Unlike many who profess royal expertise, Hugo is someone who actually witnessed the Queen and Duke together on a number of occasions, when he was struck by 'how well they got on as a couple'. Theirs was an impressive relationship that worked, of that he is absolutely certain.[16]

His words chime with an anecdote from another royal biographer – Gyles Brandreth – who recalls the Duke and Queen working a room: he took one end, she the other. Midway through their interminable handshakes and smiles, the Duke raised his head and caught the Queen's eye with a reassuring smile before returning to his duty. Even in the latter stages of their marriage, Philip looked out for Elizabeth.[17] It is a touching story and one that explains the success of their union. Philip – no matter his gaffes and indiscrepancies – always took care of his wife in public. And nowhere was that support needed more than in the autumn of 1951, when together the young Edinburghs ventured out of Europe for the first time and criss-crossed the vast expanse of Canada.

The operation to remove the King's lung saw the couple's projected tour of the oldest country in the Commonwealth postponed until the beginning of October 1951. The build-up to the trip had been inauspicious. There was the long shadow cast by the King's illness, Philip's irascibility at the sudden imposition of civil, court (and married?) life,* and an anxious Elizabeth pinned between constitutional obligations and family tensions.

At just twenty-five, this was Elizabeth's first big test – an

---

* Initially Philip held out against the idea of a Canadian tour, citing his desire to start a family. However, he ran out of excuses, especially once he had retired from the navy in mid-1951.

international tour with her husband. On 8 October, in front of a disarmingly silent crowd at Quebec airport, 'a pale young woman in a short mink coat and teal blue dress stepped hesitantly down the gangway'. Canada's finest wordsmith described what he saw when she arrived in his country and her realm.

> It was observed that the small black handbag on her left arm was trembling and that as she greeted her welcomers she continually moistened her dry lips. Only by an iron self will did she conceal how anxious she really was. Thus, under the worst of conditions did Canadians catch their first glimpse of Elizabeth of England.[18]

Pierre Burton, one year Philip's senior and already an established journalist, identified the Princess as 'badly worried'. Not only did she have to contend with anxiety over her 'father who lay ill from a critical operation and was far sicker than the public knew', she was also feeling insecure about 'her own appearance which had been criticised. (She felt she was too heavy in the bosom.)'[19]

Daughter of a sick man, mother of two young children, wife of a discontented husband and the future head of Britain and its Commonwealth, it's easy to forget that Elizabeth was also a woman under the gaze of incessant flash bulbs. Any body image issues were compensated for (or exacerbated?) by the ninety-seven trunks that accompanied the Princess on tour – two-piece woollen suits and sturdy leather shoes, ball gowns that strapped in her royal chest, distracting white gloves, tiaras and broad blue garter sashes, raincoats, tartan rugs, silk scarves and pillar-box hats. ('Conservative and stylish', was how the press described her wardrobe.)[20] Elizabeth pumped arms in torrential rain, gale force winds, snow drifts and sunshine, she travelled ten thousand miles by aircraft, train, limousine and destroyer, inspected twenty-four guards of honour and listened to the national anthem a hundred and fifty times.[21] The five weeks were draining and it showed; initially she didn't smile enough for the Canadian press. Back in Britain, the papers pointed out how tired Elizabeth looked. And glum.

Offsetting the future Queen's gauche uncertainty was her lean, attractive Duke – whose manner, according to Berton, 'had an ease about it that was in sharp contrast to her own tension'.[22] Canada soon woke up to Prince Philip's appeal; girls lined the route, incessantly shouting 'Phil! Phil!' at the royal car. And here was a 'Phil' who knew how to handle himself. Naturally confident, the 'speeches he made were pithy and popular'.

> I am not impressed with how many miles we have travelled. What is important is the personal contact we have made with Canadians of all walks of life.[23]

Philip hit the right note and Canada was only the beginning. A two day 'pop-over' to America was belatedly tacked on to the schedule. World War II had woken the Stateside giant up from its isolationist slumber and the world's democratically elected new superpower could never resist the trappings of monarchy. Across the border they'd watched Canadian fervour for the royal couple slowly grow – the Commonwealth country took a while to work out how to embrace this young foreign girl as their future head of state – but, in the USA, there was no equivalent deliberation. They had booted out the British monarchy near two centuries earlier but never relinquished their love for the mythical and magical that came with it. Presidential America was its own elective kingship and now, once more, the real deal from 'little old England' was coming to town.

It was a full throttle celebrity welcome that greeted the couple when they arrived in Washington D.C. The ballroom in the Statler Hotel was jam-packed with cameras and reporters: 'Princess!', 'Liz!', 'Hey!', 'Stand still, walk about, move closer, smile, smile, smile!' She did her best, but Americans weren't convinced by her 'frightened little appearance under the television cameras'. 'The shy little princess appeared nervous and fatigued, obviously showing the strain of the long Canadian tour.'[24]

The Duke 'on the other hand was booming with vigor and wisecracks as befits a royal salesman for the beleaguered British empire'. The American press didn't hold back:

Philip, to tell the truth, almost stole the show from his wife during the couple's first hours in Washington. Thousands of women along the line of the motorcade shrieked 'there he is' as the big blonde boy with the big smile waved at the crowds.

It was a slam dunk for the dashing Duke in a country unencumbered by the rules of monarchy – here Elizabeth did not need to come first; it was Philip who had the star power.

Tossing out hearty handshakes, joking with some old World War II shipmates he spotted and accumulating names, places and business connections from all hands, the man who can never become king enjoyed himself immensely.[25]

Life magazine got straight to the point: Philip had a 'tang of sea salt' and 'looks startlingly alive', with a 'mobile face which refuses to wear the waxwork mask of professional royalty, alternatively glossy with condescension or glassy with bore-dom.'[26] The comparison with his wife, prone to 'unsmiling tenseness', was an uncomfortable one. Scroll forward thirty years to the adulation that greeted Princess Diana when she first arrived on the scene in the early 1980s (the extent of which upset her sidelined husband, Charles), and there is a temptation to presume that Philip's popularity during the 1951 tour adversely impacted on the Edinburghs' relationship. But that is to misunderstand them and the time they lived in.

The 1950s was a decade when husbands were unequivocally at the helm; Elizabeth's unique position too often sidelined her alpha Duke.[27] Post-navy, in his new fulltime constitutional role as her husband, Philip coveted a level of empowerment and recognition the British would never give him. Briefly in America, those tables were turned to the benefit of both husband and wife. Unlike her son, Charles, in his first marriage, Elizabeth understood that together she and Philip were greater than the sum of their parts. His success was her success. A happy Philip meant a happy Elizabeth. And there were other benefits to the tour. Here the Duke was entirely hers – together they worked the crowds, but he was beyond the reach of his screaming fans and there was no Thursday club or polo match fallout to compete with. He belonged to his wife and, facing a whole new continent together, she willingly accepted his support.

Canadian Berton waxed lyrical about Philip's care for Elizabeth. On their flight over, 'she could not sleep', so the Duke took his anxious wife to the bar, where he tried to teach her a game called 'liar dice'. 'He grinned and said "You'll never make a good liar with that empire on your shoulders." They went to bed.' The scene is an intimate one and it set the tenor for the trip.

When she was worried, 'the Duke patted her arm to reassure her and she gave him a grateful little look'. On board the train, he 'turned to her and said "Darling, you look simply smashing!" At this calculated compliment her face lit up in animation.' The impact of Philip's full attention worked its magic: 'as the tour progressed, Elizabeth began to relax. This was due in large measure to her husband . . . if the crowd around her began to press he would move in closer as if to protect her from it.' He never let her stand alone, he cracked jokes to 'take the weariness from her face', and he mopped up the crowd to give her wrist a rest. Gradually, 'as the tour moved on, the two learned to talk to each other in public without moving their lips or changing expression'.[28]

Berton's words must be treated with caution; they were retrospectively published in 1953, the coronation year, when Commonwealth affection for the new Queen was at its height. But poetic license notwithstanding, it's unlikely this esteemed writer who had great access invented the story. Like Philip, Berton was a part of a post-war world where men were expected to take care of their women. What he saw in Canada was a conventional young couple working as one, finding their way through, in extraordinary circumstances. Out of Britain, on the other side of the Atlantic, Philip's experience and confidence complemented Elizabeth's constitutional precedence and princess status. Briefly the Edinburghs could pretend they were evenly matched.

◆

Elizabeth stayed in close contact with her sick father. His September operation had seen the postponement of the Edinburghs' departure from England; to make up time, travel by sea was swapped for the Princess's first long haul flight. Criss-crossing between two continents were phone calls and letters, with the Queen often acting as the go-between, but ultimately nothing could get in the way of the Princess's love for the King.

Darling Papa, I do hope you are feeling really better again. On the telephone Mummy has told me that you are now in the Audience Room during the day.[29]

It is 2022, the year of the Queen's Platinum Jubilee and her subsequent death. Biographer Hugo Vickers pauses. What was it about Elizabeth II's commitment to monarchy? 'I think at the end of her long reign she wanted to be able to say to her father, "I did it. I did it for you."' George VI was in the last months of his life when his daughter, Elizabeth, was working away in Canada as the living embodiment of a symbol that held together a new Commonwealth.

There have been so many messages to you from every part of this country and from so many people I couldn't possibly tell you all of them.[30]

Rather than sitting with him in the Audience Room, she was out there, on the world stage, doing his job for him; the human receptacle for monarchical veneration in a free association of countries that bore the stamp of Britain's disintegrating empire. Small wonder the Queen clung to the Commonwealth for the rest of her life 'as one of the principal *raisons d'êtres* of the crown she inherited from her father'.[31] His outlook and his love defined her. As Lady Airlie, life-long friend of Queen Mary, wisely observed, Elizabeth was her father's 'constant companion in shooting, walking, riding – in fact in everything.'[32] In patriarchal Britain, the King's first born had always respected and relied on 'beloved papa', the monarch and her father rolled in one.

In this context, it is no coincidence that observers noted Elizabeth's sudden ease when President Harry Truman 'put a fatherly arm around her' in Washington. They surmised that, for this 'over-sheltered and governess trained' future Queen, 'it was the only occasion during the entire five weeks in which she found there was someone else to look to make all the decisions.'[33] But the President's appeal ran deeper than his control of the schedule. (Elizabeth had never had control of her own schedule.) In 1951, a woman benefitted from the optics of an older man, and *in loco parentis*, Elizabeth found Truman reassuring. This former peanut farmer with his avuncular manner was the American President; head of the country's first family, his status was in some way commensurate with the Princess's own and his fatherly vibe a familiar one. He called Elizabeth 'dear' and hoped she would have as nice a time in Washington as his daughter had enjoyed in London. Older men liked Elizabeth; they felt paternal towards her and protective, sentiments heightened by the knowledge her father was very ill. The Princess's private secretary decided the President 'fell in love with her'.[34]

Her track record with elderly gentlemen would stand Elizabeth in good stead; as the Edinburghs wowed Washington, Winston Churchill, one month off his seventy-seventh birthday, was voted back into office after a six years absence. Attlee's great socialist experiment had run out of steam and money. The Conservative leader added a deaf aid to his props, conceded that his post-war premiership would not occupy a hundredth of the interest his wartime one did, and was prone to long, distracting bouts of nostalgia. This was not his finest hour, but at least it wasn't his final one. The same could not be said of his friend the King, a man whom Britain's most ardent monarchist had lunched with every Tuesday during the war.

Woken on the morning of 6 February 1952, Churchill was told by the King's Assistant Private Secretary Edward Ford: 'Prime Minister, I've got bad news for you.'[35] When he heard

George VI had died, Churchill replied: 'Bad news? The worst.'
The same evening he addressed the nation, concluding: 'In the
end, death came as a friend; and after a happy day of sunshine
and sport, and after saying good night to those who loved him
best he fell asleep.'[36] The speech was well received, his line about
the King walking 'with death as if death were a companion', is
often cited, but Churchill's final comment was not accurate.
George VI did not say good night to all of those who loved him
best. How could he when he died in Sandringham and his daughter was once more thousands of miles away doing her royal duty?

The Edinburghs had returned from Canada in November
1951. Their send-off was a warm one – 'goodbye from all of us,
goodbye to a sailor and his wife homeward bound across the
sea'[37] – and back in London, superficially at least, the King's
condition had improved. He managed a birthday photograph
with three-year-old Prince Charles and, on the Edinburghs'
return, the whole family went to Sandringham for Christmas,
where the King pre-recorded his speech in hoarse sections.
The script was optimistic. Despite an ongoing shortage of
'meat and housing' (Churchill's twin obsessions), everyone
was to 'count their blessings'. Especially the King. 'I myself
have every cause for deeper thankfulness . . . by the grace of
God and through the faithful skill of the doctors, surgeons and
nurses have I come through my illness.'[38]

He had not come through his illness, but kingship is a job
for life; there's no good time to die. Writing letters and planning trips, George VI pretended he was better. The wheels
kept turning and, if the King couldn't go to Australia and New
Zealand, then the Edinburghs must. After all, they had just
been to Canada.

The turnaround was fast. Broadcasters said as much at the
time. 'Three months after their Canada tour, they are off on

their royal travels again.'[39] The weather was grey and cold but the King came to see his daughter off; it was George VI's first (and last) public appearance since the lung operation in September. The footage is of a gaunt but still good-looking man, shoulders hunched, eyes bulging. His visible weakness underscored his devotion to Elizabeth. Up close he looked much worse (the cameras were kept at a discreet distance). Heaven forbid that the watching world might discover what his daughter had surely guessed. Her father, 'ashen-faced and obviously very weak', might die any day. The King stood watching the aeroplane until it was a vanishing dot in the sky.[40] He was flanked by his Prime Minister; afterwards they drank a glass of Champagne together. Both were big believers in the Commonwealth, and the Edinburghs had proved so very adept at these bonding missions.

Inside the plane there was an air of anticipation. Elizabeth and Philip had a holiday in Kenya to look forward to before they arrived in the Antipodes. The venue was a remote hunting lodge in Sagana, including a platform in a giant fig tree for spying on the wildlife in the watering hole below.[41] The couple's footage, shot on a cine camera, is full of antelope, giraffe and buffalo. The dusky savannah, their little car, them – young, fit, each enjoying the other. In a different time, this could have been a gap year moment; students (privileged ones) at play, in brown slacks, enjoying the latest tech, miles from home. When they were alone, when the pressure was off, the distractions removed, the Edinburghs knew how to have fun together, how to be together. Their cine films tell us that.

It was Mike Parker, Philip's Australian equerry, who had to break the spell and tell his boss the news from London. The King had died. Philip informed his wife; alone, outside, they talked and talked. Back in London, Churchill sighed. He did not know the new Queen well and lamented that she 'was only a child'.[42] He underestimated Elizabeth II and her lifetime of training.* Irrespective of the personal tragedy, the young Queen had a job to do; soon she was at a desk, 'very composed, absolute master of her fate', drafting papers and letters of apology for the cancellation of their tour, 'a slight flush on her face' the only sign of emotion.[43] It was Philip who 'looked as if the whole world had dropped on his shoulders'.[44]

---

* Churchill first met the Princess at Balmoral when she was two years of age.

ELEVEN

◆◇◆

An Elizabethan 'Golden Age'

Wesley Kerr OBE is a much-in-demand and highly unusual royal commentator. Of Jamaican decent, (his mother, Birdella, was among a 250,000 strong crowd who came out to welcome the new Queen during her 1953 tour) and brought up by foster parents in England and later educated at Winchester College, he straddles two worlds – Her Majesty's Commonwealth and Foreign Realms, and her Great British Kingdom.[1] I last met Wesley in a television studio on the seventieth anniversary of Elizabeth's accession to the throne in February 2022.[2] He came bearing treasure – an incredible stash of newspapers that his foster mother, born in 1904, had collected in the wake of George VI's death.

According to Wesley, she had publications dating back as far as Queen Victoria's Golden Jubilee, but he was particularly struck by just how many she'd held on to from February 1952. They were a tribute to a king people 'really really loved'. He recalled how George VI, 'who had lived through two world wars . . . was regarded as having gone through so much, taking over after the abdication' and standing alongside Churchill during the war, 'which probably broke his health'. Wesley summed up the mood at the time across both Britain and the Commonwealth, in a reaffirmation of George as a revered committed sovereign.[3] Certainly much 'press hysteria' greeted his death and, at times, the atmosphere almost verged on a 'national obsession'.[4] 'In every town shop fronts were dressed in black, armbands worn and curtains drawn.'[5] Here was evidence of an emotive twentieth-century form of royal fandom, the full expression of which culminated much later with the death of Diana, Princess of Wales, and was evident again during Elizabeth II's own period of national mourning and state funeral in September 2022.

In 1952, national grief was cast through the prism of adoring newspaper coverage, which savoured small details often fabricated to embellish the sombre mood. According to the *Daily Express*, the new Queen had been up all night in brown slacks and a bush jacket watching wildlife through a lens when the Duke broke the tragic news to her.[6] Mirroring Prime Minister Winston Churchill's immediate presumption she was 'only a child', there was a tendency to infantilise Elizabeth and cast her as a lugubrious victim. The *Express* continued: 'she wept like a twenty-five-year-old girl who had lost her father'.* In fact, no record exists of the Queen crying until she got into her car after the Accession Council back in London, but a sobbing daughter hit the right note in a dutiful family narrative.† Here was Elizabeth relinquishing her youth and, in the middle of a personal tragedy, stepping up to serve for the rest of what would be a very long life. When Churchill addressed Parliament on 11 February 1952, he described Her Majesty as 'a fair and youthful figure, Princess, wife and mother'. He focused on the young Queen's vulnerability and femininity as the signal for

---

* Ironically it was Churchill (famous for his tears) who was overcome with emotion when he was the first to greet Elizabeth II upon her arrival back in Britain.

† Philip's valet observed that, during the flight, occasionally she would leave her seat and return looking as though she had shed a tear.

a 'brightening salvation of the human scene' and an Elizabethan 'golden age'.[7]

It was standard hyperbole from a verbose old monarchist. But other political commentators, younger and less sentimental, saw something else at play as Elizabeth swapped her safari outfit for mourning dress and flew four thousand miles home. 'Wake Up Women', screamed the headline in a *Sunday Graphic* article that hoped 'the accession of Elizabeth II can help remove the last shred of prejudice against women aspiring to the highest places'. It was written by one 'Margaret Thatcher who as Margaret Roberts, was the youngest woman candidate in the last two General Elections'. (The aspiring politician's byline explained that Thatcher had married three months earlier and was 'only a few months older than the Queen'.)[8] A precursor to her own career path, ambitious Margaret used Elizabeth's dual role as wife and monarch to berate housewives. 'I hope we shall see more and more women combining marriage AND a career. Prejudice against this dual role is not confined to men. Far too often, I regret to say it comes from our own sex.' As for girls who gave up work when they got married: 'THIS IN MY VIEW IS A GREAT PITY.'[9] The hectoring tone (block capitals in the original) was unfair in a post-war climate that encouraged wives to stay at home, but young Mrs Thatcher had flagged up an uncomfortable contradiction at the heart of Britain's adulation of Elizabeth II. What old men disguised as the new Queen's regrettable duty and sacrifice was high-profile proof that wives and mothers could also work.

The Queen was naturally very upset when her father died. Biographers love to recall the Accession Council, where a 'slight' Elizabeth, dressed in 'full mourning', committed herself to the constitutional task ahead, before admitting in a 'very small – high pitched, rather reedy' voice: 'My heart is too full for me to say more to you today than that I shall always work as my father did.'[10] Complementing that weak woman narrative, it was husband Philip who 'stepped forward and led her out'.[11] But beyond those early days when she also had to adjust to the Royal Family's obeisance (her grandmother's insistence on getting in that first curtsey and kiss was unnecessary but so very Queen Mary), there is much to suggest that Elizabeth took great consolation her new role.

'What would my father have done?' became her mantra in the early days, as she found her way amid a bustle of elderly gentlemen, led by an increasingly besotted Churchill, who quickly decided the Queen had an 'air of authority and reflectiveness astonishing in an infant' and Alan Lascelles, once the King's private secretary and now hers.[12] (Terrifying and prone to glaring, the latter was more than twice Elizabeth's age and not put out to grass for another year and a half.[13]) There was comfort to be had in an abundance of engagements and protocol. Biographer Sarah Bradford is quick to remind us just how busy the Queen was at the very start of her reign: before the funeral, she met ambassadors and foreign ministers, High Commissioners from the Commonwealth, the Prime Minister of New Zealand and received a deputation from the House of Commons. Here was a monarch 'at ease and self possessed', according to her former private secretary, Jock Colville (now Churchill's right hand man).[14] How times had changed; it is hard to believe this was the same woman who had anxiously lent on her attractive, confident husband in Canada just months before.

Even today, in our supposedly gender-neutral modish twenty-first-century society, most men still love to have the final say. Back then, in the alpha male 1950s, the bread-winning husband was the head of virtually every household with one almighty exception – the (otherwise bracingly traditional) Royal Family. Marrying the heir to the British throne, Philip always knew he would walk behind his younger wife, but the reality of his new position threw up indignities he had not anticipated. The problems started early. Immediately after George VI's death, there were so many old men taking charge around the Queen that the Duke was insensitively (sometimes deliberately?) muscled out of the picture. Retrospectively, this was a mistake, and at least some of the responsibility lies with Churchill.

There is no doubt that, when it came to Elizabeth, the sentimental Prime Minister, who arrived for his weekly audiences in frock coat and tails, saw himself playing Melbourne to Elizabeth's Victoria.[15] The nineteenth-century relationship between the great Whig leader and his very young Queen has been well chronicled: Melbourne grasped with both hands the opportunity 'to educate, instruct and form the most interesting mind and character in the world'. And, subsequently, accusations of an 'old man's *amitie amoureuse*' and Victoria's favouritism have been upheld with justification.[16] Churchill and Elizabeth's situation was very different. In 1952, the monarch no longer enjoyed the same constitutional prerogatives and Elizabeth was seven years older and also more experienced than her ancestor. Victoria declared of Melbourne: 'I love him like a Father!'[17] Elizabeth never admitted to being more than 'very fond' of Churchill, although by all accounts their weekly meetings went on, and on.[18] But the key difference, most crucially, was that, unlike Victoria, Elizabeth was already married.

Philip never received Albert's title of Prince Consort. He understood that times had changed, later dismissing any comparison with the line: 'Victoria was an executive monarch. Prince Albert was the Queen's secretary. He could do things. It's very different now.'[19] But with no concrete role to call his own, ranks and names mattered, and among royalty they always had. Lest we forget, Philip was the boy who always signed himself the Prince of Greece, a man who had given up both that title and a naval career to support his British wife and family in their constitutional duty. It is therefore understandable that the Duke was furious when, just three days after the King's funeral, he discovered his (new) name, Mountbatten, which Elizabeth had taken when she married him, was to be dumped in favour of Windsor. 'I'm nothing but a bloody amoeba' became one of his most famous epitaphs. Philip was a proud man and his wife's (deliberately discreet) pronouncement a wounding blow: 'I hereby declare My Will and Pleasure that I and My children shall be styled and known as the House of Windsor.'[20]

There had been bitter behind-the-scenes wrangling. Within the Royal Family, the latent anti-Philip sentiment fostered by Queen Mary (never a fan of Philip's) and, to a lesser extent, his mother-in-law, Queen Elizabeth, now had a focus. Struggling with their own diminishment in relation to the new Queen's promotion, the cocksure Duke was an obvious target. 'Agitated' Queen Mary triggered the alarm, alerting an ever sceptical Jock Colville of Mountbatten's presumptuous toasting of the accession of his own family name to the titular head of Great Britain. Churchill 'took the greatest exception to this idea' and brought up the matter in Cabinet; there was unanimous agreement that Windsor must stay. The Prime Minister duly approached the impressionable Queen, who did as she was told.[21]

Churchill's unequivocal stance was unhelpful. True, his once dazzling relationship with Mountbatten had been tarnished by Indian affairs post-war and the latter's affection for the Labour government, but the nomenclature 'Mountbatten' wasn't the only option. After all, Philip had already changed his name once. If bastardised 'Mountbatten' (no more than an anglicised Battenburg) was not acceptable, what about 'Edinburgh'? Or, more specifically, 'Family of Windsor of the House of Edinburgh'?[22] Apparently Philip wasn't fussed over which name, so long as it was his name. Given the good will that greeted the new Queen's accession and the firm tradition that regarded family names as a male prerogative, surely Edinburgh would have been an acceptable fudge? And a timely sop to Scotland, whose fervour for independence would take off in the post-war years. But Churchill did not budge. The Prime Minister's romantic attachment to the House of Windsor trumped any concern for the domestic tightrope his new Queen had to walk.

Churchill – well past his sell-by-date – added his name to a long list of stiffs who were wary of the irascible Duke, commenting that he 'neither liked him nor trusted him and only hoped that he would not do the country any harm'.[23] Philip might well have said the same about Churchill, whose meddling did not stop at the family's name. Instead the Duke had to play host to him at Balmoral, where the Prime Minister was treated with kid gloves and put to bed in style – a mug of hot Ovaltine and three different coloured pills.[24] But ailments (including a minor stroke) did not stop Churchill joining forces with Alan Lascelles for a second time in the immediate aftermath of the King's death. He agreed with the private secretary that the new Queen and Philip must relinquish Clarence House and return to Buckingham Palace as soon as possible. Within a matter weeks Philip discovered that, as the monarch's husband, he had no say over what his children were called, nor where they would live. The Elizabethan golden age had started inauspiciously for the isolated Duke.

◆◇◆

In his final year at Cheam Preparatory School, Prince Charles, forced to drudge up a line on 'The Advantages of Boarding

Schools', conceded that they were about 'preparing you for the outside world. Away from your homes for so long.'[25] The boy's contempt for his schooling is well known; what's interesting in this statement is Charles's pluralisation of the word home. Where was his home? Buckingham Palace had been the boy's official residence from the age of two, but the Prince always felt a much greater emotional attachment to Balmoral, with its dark marmalade interiors and bewitching grounds. Likewise Sandringham, where the family spent Christmas and Charles could nurture his love of the outdoors. In contrast, Buckingham Palace was less a home and more of an institution. That is certainly what his father, Philip, thought when he was flatly told a move back to Buckingham Palace was on the cards in early 1952. Against his will the Duke had to wrench his little family out of Clarence House, the residence where the heir to the throne, Charles, had learnt to walk and talk. It would be another five decades before Charles returned and made the house his London home. After the death of the Queen Mother, he shared the stylish Nash-designed mansion with his second wife, Camilla, then Duchess of Cornwall.*

One of the arguments Philip had used for staying put after the accession was that his son would eventually need his own London pad and Clarence House seemed the obvious choice. How right he was. But Churchill decided that Buckingham Palace was where the monarch had always lived and so it must continue. In fact, the historical precedent wasn't long established: in 1837, Queen Victoria moved her court to the Palace full time in order to escape her overbearing mother. Philip's suggestion that the family should remain in Clarence House

---

* According to reports, in their new capacity as King and Queen Consort, it is likely they will retain Clarence House as a London residence, particularly while Buckingham Palace is undergoing renovations.

and use Buckingham Palace as a royal office wasn't unreasonable. In her final years, the Queen lived at Windsor Castle and Buckingham Palace remained the Royal Family's primary office and symbolic headquarters. But Churchill and Lascelles, at the end of their respective careers, holding fast to the idea of monarchy as fading Britain's mythical (restorative?) heartbeat, wouldn't be moved. Not even when the grieving Queen Mother proved resistant to a reshuffle that would demote her and daughter Margaret to Clarence House.

The subsequent house swap was a reminder of the Royal Family's impotence in the face of untrammelled tradition, however recent. 'You can imagine what is going to happen now', lamented Philip to his sister just two days after the King died. The Accession was so much worse than he had imagined. His mood remained black.[26] Arguably the new Queen could have put her foot down, but that was not Elizabeth's style. A natural conserver and somewhat overawed by the bluff and reputations of dinosaurs like Churchill and Lascelles, who had worked so closely with her father, the monarch once more did what she was told. The result was the break-up of a working home that Philip had invested in with characteristic energy and vim. What he lacked in aesthetic vision, the Duke more than made up for in 'thorough-going pragmatism'. Rewired to the highest spec, with intercom phones between rooms and a modern filing system, Clarence House bore the Duke's stamp. He knocked a hole into the back wall and a bridge was constructed to join the residence with the offices in neighbouring St James's Palace. The Edinburghs' staff recalled a close-knit happy team.[27] This was a building where Philip was in charge. The move to Buckingham Palace changed all of that.

Philip's valet, John Dean, who had been with him since 1947, didn't last long back at 'the gloomy palace'. Like his master, he 'dreaded' returning because of all it symbolised.

Confirming his worst fears, the relocated furniture looked out of place, and the maudlin atmosphere was compounded when Philip contracted jaundice and convalesced in a 'depressing room' heavy with gilt and black interiors. Dean, prone to self pity, mourned his 'greatly changed' status among the servants. Philip suffered equivalent slippage, having to make do with morning, afternoon and evening visits from his wife while she struggled with her workload and he came to terms with a new regime.[28] According to one relation, 'for some time' there 'was quite a difficult situation' between the couple;[29] a tension replicated throughout the palace. 'Head shaking' was the common response to the Duke's forthright views; economising and modernisation were not concepts that an institution run by an enormous intransigent staff took kindly to.[30] The transition was a painful one; Private Secretary Parker was as gloomy as the Duke, and Dean had left the Palace before the coronation. Unlike Philip, his job didn't come with his family.[31]

Elizabeth and Philip, plus children and staff, moved to apartments on the Palace's first and second floors, with the nursery (another six rooms) directly above them. In November 1952, Prince Charles had his fourth birthday party in Buckingham Palace's Gold Music Room, when twelve children were invited for pass-the-parcel, races and musical chairs. The day stood out for another reason – this was the first time Charles had celebrated a birthday with his father.[32] Naval Commander Philip had been in Malta until 1951, he then escorted his working wife to Canada. Needless to say, the young boy was intimidated by his abrupt dad, whose renowned impatience and intolerance of 'cissys' weren't ideal for managing his timid son.

Back then, an absentee father was not unusual. But an absentee mother was. In the 1950s, thinking that discouraged fussing and mollycoddling over children between the wars, particularly among the upper classes, had been overturned. In line with the post-war idea of a homely wife as the symbolic repository for British optimism, child psychologist John Bowlby's pioneering attachment theory argued that 'the infant and the young child should experience a warm, intimate and continuous relationship with his mother'.[33] His work was hugely influential. A 'good' mother did not leave a child under three with anyone else, except perhaps granny for a few days' holiday.[34] Unless, of course, they were the Queen. In fact, even as princess, Elizabeth had rarely prioritised spending time with Charles (or Anne). Two Christmases in a row she joined Philip in Malta and left her children behind at Sandringham. (The Duke's reputation suggests perhaps he was the sort of man a wife needed to keep an eye on.) When they were all together in Britain, the monarch managed a half an hour stint with her children in the morning and another hour for 'a final romp' in the evening, but one suspects 'romping' was never the Queen's strong suit.[35] Nor cosy family time. Charles's biographer, Jonathan Dimbleby, certainly seems to suggest that, as a boy, the Prince missed out on vital parental attention,[36] and his own son, Prince Harry, would later caution against handing on 'the pain or suffering that perhaps my father' had experienced.[37]

Despite Margaret Thatcher's optimism about working mothers, the Queen quickly discovered that managing the demands of a family was almost as hard (harder?) than reigning over a rapidly contracting empire. (Easier than both was caring for her beloved corgis, which she fed personally every afternoon from a silver tray with a silver spoon.)[38] Born healthy and male, Charles slipped down the Queen's to-do list after her accession and decisions about his upbringing were delegated to Philip, with results that we now know were often counterproductive. The Duke always found gutsy, equine-loving Anne easier to handle and would probably have preferred to assist his overwhelmed little wife, but that was out of the question.

It turns out Elizabeth was a stickler for keeping the Red Boxes to herself. Matters of state were hers and hers alone and politicians certainly preferred it that way. Was Philip left wondering whether he had made the right decision? Perhaps. But neither marriage nor monarchy are part-time gigs. And the Windsors weren't any old family. The young couple had to keep the show on the road. Diminished post-war Britain needed them – the prospect of an almighty Elizabethan coronation beckoned. How else would Prime Minister Churchill deliver his long-promised 'sunlit uplands'?

◆

A formal little book, *The Queen's Coronation: The Inside Story*, published six decades after the event, boasts a foreword by 'His Royal Highness, The Duke of Edinburgh'. Philip, softened by time and no doubt the enduring success of his union, agreed to give the publication his stamp of approval. The foreword, predictably, gives away very little, but the Duke does remind us that while 'the Queen succeeded her father in 1952 . . . it is easy to forget that her Coronation only took place nearly eighteen months later'.[39] It was a long, expensive journey in a country still lumbering under a balance of payments crisis and rationing: Churchill batted away the question of cost with the line 'everyone likes to wear a flower when he goes to see his girl'.[40] He made no pretence: his government would lean heavily on the event, deliberately moved into the summer of 1953 to give Britain time to 'get the bailiffs out of the house' and fine tune the positive global impact so desperately coveted.[41] It was a period pregnant with expectation and tensions ran high. Even in Philip's careful foreword, he admits that there were 'inevitable discussions, even arguments' in the run up to the big day.[42]

Elizabeth appointed her husband as Chair of the Coronation Commission; it was a much needed concession for her sidelined Duke. A lot has subsequently been made of this role; in the final year of his life, we were told 'Philip had a huge part to play in the organisation of the historical event' and, in keeping with his reputation as a moderniser, that 'the Duke of Edinburgh immediately threw out a radical idea: he wanted the coronation to be televised for all Britain to see'.[43] It would be great if that were true. After all, the coronation has been written about more than any other royal event in recent history, and the decision to televise it credited as a key component in day's success: here was the magical alchemy that fused traditions of monarchy with high-tech accessibility. If only Philip had been the lead instigator – what better revenge against his doubters within the court? But in keeping with so much sloppy journalism concerning the royals, it isn't true. Putting the coronation on television was not Philip's brainchild. But the idea did cause 'arguments', which had the potential to pit Elizabeth against her public.

It's possible that Philip was credited with the suggestion because he was so much younger than the rest of the commission and apparently pushed for features 'relevant to the world today'.[44] After all, this was a ceremony dating back to William the Conqueror; a few updates couldn't do any harm. But every new-fangled idea had to get passed his vice-chair, the Earl Marshal and 16th Duke of Norfolk, a blimpish aristocrat with extensive form when it came to coordinating ceremonial.* He was unbending, as tends to be the case with men whose strengths are historic not academic, and was flanked by the Archbishop of Canterbury, Geoffrey Fisher, who looked like a corpulent egg and had the air of a headmaster.† Fisher would

---

* The Dukes of Norfolk have been responsible for organising the coronation since 1672. The 16th Duke of Norfolk was also responsible for organising the coronation of George VI (1937), the state funeral of Winston Churchill (1965) and the investiture of the Prince of Wales (1969).

† Fisher was ordained in 1913 and became headmaster of Repton the following year.

be crowning the Queen; it was important he had her confidence. Needless to say, Elizabeth did not like the thought of being televised live, a prospect first mooted by the eager BBC. Her Christmas messages were not yet televised and she refused to be shot 'close-up' during royal appearances (can you blame her?)[45] Why on earth would the Queen want to be filmed as she committed herself to God in a sacred and ancient ceremony?

On 20 October, Buckingham Palace announced that 'after very careful consideration and further consultation with the Prime Minister' television coverage would be restricted to the procession in and out of the Abbey. Churchill, ever devoted to his monarch, followed Elizabeth's lead and, like Fisher, he worried that televising the coronation would place the Queen under 'intolerable strain'.[46] The BBC, with its rash of new masts and transmitters, was very disappointed, but it was the newspapers that kept fighting. The *Daily Express* ran a poll (of course it did); four out of five readers wanted to see the whole ceremony on the television, and opposition MPs capitalised on the moment to attack Churchill.[47] Weren't the public, who were ultimately footing the bill, entitled to see the show? The Prime Minister reconvened a meeting of all sides. He had changed his mind. The Coronation would be televised, with the exception of the Anointing, the Consecration and Communion. And no close ups were allowed. The public had forced the crown's hand and (in a move that speaks volumes about the press's love of their Queen) Elizabeth got the credit. According to the *Express*, it was the Queen's desire to be 'crowned in the sight of all the people'.[48] 'Moderniser' Philip didn't have to do anything, but he *did* have to live with a nervous wife who hadn't got what she wanted.

In December 1952, Elizabeth made her first radio broadcast as monarch from Sandringham. Unmade-up in a dark tweed suit with her timeless sweep of hair neatly coiffed away from her face, she began: 'Each Christmas at this time, my beloved father broadcast a message to his people in all parts of the world. Today I am doing this to you.' It was standard fare – a fitting tribute to the late King, a nod to the 'British Commonwealth and Empire, that immense union of nations' and a hope that the 'tremendous forces of science and learning' might be used for 'the betterment of man's lot'. And then, at the end, a personal request from the woman due to be crowned that June in a ceremony everyone would see.

> I want to ask you all, whatever your religion may be, to pray for me on that day – to pray that God may give me wisdom and strength to carry out the solemn promises I shall be making.[49]

The old-fashioned Queen was determined that the television cameras would not detract from the solemnity of the day. She was and remained a devout if undemonstrative Christian as well as a born-and-bred monarchist. She believed in her divine right to be Queen. Without that belief, could she have withstood the course? Equally devout, and more theologically engaged, was her husband Philip.[50] And while his wife was apprehensive, looking for succour among her subjects, he was more courageous. If the idea that television cameras should enter the Abbey was not his, he certainly helped prepare his Queen for this brand new form of royal exposure.

Now part of the House of Windsor, Philip was trapped in an unyielding institution, hemmed in by customs and traditions. However, supporting the Queen was the job he signed up to when he got married, for better or for worse. Belief in monarchy requires faith, and Philip shared that faith in spades. But he was also an outsider who loved technology.

He loved innovation. Unlike his wife, he also loved pushing the envelope and he wasn't afraid to stick up for himself. He was going to ride with his Queen in her golden carriage as part of the coronation procession, irrespective of what Queen Mary or anyone else thought.[51] And he had plenty of other ideas too: about how to make the ceremony more inclusive – for the Church of Scotland, for the Commonwealth – and more efficient.[52]

Perhaps no story better encapsulates Philip's spirit in that first difficult year before the coronation than that of Churchill and the helicopter. The young Duke made no secret of his passion for flying. Post war, his ambition to be airborne still lingered. Permission to fly with his wife was a breakthrough, but not enough. He wanted to be in the cockpit and nothing deterred him. Not even the death of aviator John Derry, whom Philip had met at Farnborough Air Display. One day they were exchanging niceties in the pilots' tent, the very next Derry would break the sound barrier and pitifully, fatally, crash his plane into the watching crowd.[53] Flying was not safe, which is why Philip found it so appealing. His lessons began in the coronation year.

Churchill, himself a novice pilot, did not approve. The last thing he needed was a dead Duke just before his Queen was crowned. There was a meeting where Philip managed to convince the Prime Minister that, in his new role as head of the Coronation Commission, he had places to go and people to see.* A pilot's license was a vital skill for an up-and-at-it young duke. Churchill relented, but it wasn't the end of the story. Soon private secretary, Mike Parker, (also learning to fly) was summoned to Downing Street. The atmosphere was tense.

---

* The Duke had a full pilot's licence by the time of the coronation and flew himself to Germany to finalise some of the invitations in person.

The Prime Minister prolonged the Australian's agony, shuffling through papers, failing to acknowledge Philip's conspirator, before looking up with a 'long accusing stare' and demanding to know: 'Is your objective the destruction of the whole Royal Family?'[54]

Philip had graduated from aeroplanes to their considerably more dangerous rivals, helicopters, and Churchill had got wind of it. Choppers were ideal for popping down to welcome and inspect incoming troops for the pending coronation. They were also a great way of ensuring the Duke felt good about himself in his subsidiary role. There is a 'Biggles' quality to this story and so many others attached to Philip and his right hand man, Parker. They got the job done and they prioritised fun, a quality which was sorely lacking in the corridors of Buckingham Palace. Elizabeth knew this. She had married Philip for his spirit – that 'mischievous enquiring twinkle' she reminisced about in the last year of her life.[55] 'I do not think the Queen raised any objection', Philip's valet recalled of the flying episode.[56] Elizabeth very sensibly decided not to get involved. She had more than enough on her plate.*

---

* The Coronation Honours list delighted the left-wing press. The *Daily Mirror* decided they were in 'sparkling contrast to the usual drab political choices'. They included the actor John Gielgud and 'two of our geniuses in the field of aircraft design, Sydney Camm and Tom Sopwith'.

TWELVE

◇

'I Have My Husband to Support Me'

Prince Charles has a vivid childhood memory from the run up to Coronation day. The four-year-old ventured into his mother's study; she was sitting at her desk with a giant crown on top of her head. This imposing ermine-trimmed and jewel-encrusted treasure dated back to Charles II. The Queen delicately explained to her son that she was trying to get used to the weight before she was crowned.[1] Other monarchs – Victoria and Edward VII – reneged on wearing it, but Elizabeth was not a woman for half measures and practice makes perfect.

St Edwards crown is one of the heaviest and certainly the most iconic of all the coronation regalia, but 2 June 1953 would also be remembered as a family day, with Charles another of his mother's vital accessories. The public were enthralled, the press overjoyed; here was the people's Queen allowing her subjects to penetrate 'at last, even vicariously, into the solemn mysteriousness of the Abbey scene', where the little Prince was in sight, sitting next to his beloved grandmother on the balcony, hair plastered down with 'the most appalling gunge'.[2] It had all the ingredients of a great national event; everyone was involved, my own mother included.

Her father, Peter Blenkin, was a superintendent in the

Metropolitan Police; on coronation day he was tasked with lining the route and stationed at Hyde Park Corner, but things hadn't gone according to plan. 'They ran out of horses, so Father had to stand and his ceremonial sword dangled on the ground. He should have been mounted.' No matter, at least Mum had a seat and, aged eleven, a drawing slate to keep her occupied. 'I was envious of my cousin because she was in the Mall and saw the Queen, but I knew I was very lucky to be part of it and I was struck by all the military, especially the Gurkhas.' She pauses. 'King George had made such an amazing impression, so there was unconditional love for Elizabeth. I was brought up to be in awe of her, she was a fairy Queen.'

And it was a fairytale day. The Union Jack Mum waved is one of her favourite keepsakes, so too a teeny-tiny lead replica of Elizabeth's golden horse-drawn coach. But the highlight was still to come. 'We rushed back to Granny's house in Kent. She'd a bought a nine-inch television. It was set up in the billiards room and we watched what we'd missed on the little black-and-white screen.' My mother's love affair with the Royal Family was sealed. Their story was part of her story. Their family entwined with her family. Royal, Anglican and accessible, that Sunday in church she prayed for 'Mummy, Daddy and Queen Elizabeth'.[3] The scene was replicated up and down the country. In total nearly eight million watched the coronation at home, another ten million crowded into neighbours' houses. The average television set had seven people hunched around it.[4] Trestle tables were erected, paste sandwiches eaten and bunting hung. Despite the dismal weather, this was a national holiday and an unforgettable celebration. 'The archways and the banners will be taken down. But no one can take down the memories in the hearts of millions who have seen Coronation London.'[5]

Mum pauses. 'No, I don't think I was especially aware of

Prince Philip. I mean it was all about the Queen. Philip, well, he wasn't terribly interesting to a girl of eleven.' And judging by the coverage, most of the public agreed with her. Walking the 'side streets' of London, 'all more or less slums' on coronation day, a student noticed that in nearly every window there were pictures of 'the Queen and/or [her] children'.[6] Philip was far harder to find. This anecdote mirrored press coverage that focused on a maternal image of the Queen with Prince Charles, which historian Edward Owens argues was part a deliberate royal strategy to keep hearts and minds on the line of succession.[7] Edward, the Duke of Windsor, was still lurking in the background and the runaway success of his memoir, *A King's Story*, in 1951 didn't help. Elizabeth could not prohibit her disgraced uncle from appearing at his brother's and mother's respective funerals in 1952 and '53* but he was forbidden from attending the coronation. How dare he try and reclaim the limelight – 2 June 1953 was all about commitment, duty, and God-given divinity.

The future was Charles, not Edward. The latter hit back in a letter to his wife: 'what a smug, stinking lot my relations are'.[8] It's difficult being on the losing side. As one Dimbleby (Jonathan) noted of another's (Richard's) broadcast: 'Inside the Abbey, a television camera framed the young Prince at the moment when the Archbishop of Canterbury placed the crown on his mother's head. It was a fleeting glance, but it seemed to say "You, my child, will be next!"'[9] The House of Windsor was on display for all the world to see. The Queen was the main protagonist in her Hartnell gown. Still impeccably preserved today, up close the dress, with its tiny waist and dimensions, is a striking reminder of just how petite our late monarch was; unimpeachable, beautiful and

---

* Queen Mary died 24 March 1953.

unquestionably feminine. The coronation script couldn't keep up: 'Receive the ring of Kingly dignity . . . Reign with him who is the King of Kings.' Here was God's servant, our Queen, Charles's mother and Philip's wife, in that order.

Back in the 1950s, the tendency is to assume that vanity stopped with women. The Queen, wrapped in embroidered satin with 'sugar pink cheeks' and 'tightly curled hair', was 'absolutely ravishing' and her six 'white, lily-like ladies' in their prickly gowns (one must suffer for beauty) 'looked sublime'.[10] Fifty Wrens in the coronation procession were told by the navy to: 'Go easy on the lipstick', as girls must 'apply make-up with moderation'.[11] And yet, behind the scenes, there was a different story at play. Anne Glenconner, then Coke, daughter of the 5th Earl of Leicester and a maid of honour, recalls that the Duke of Norfolk 'had the foresight to work out that his bald patch would need to be powdered a few times . . . due to the aerial shots the television cameras would take.' Meanwhile, the 5th Marquess of Cholmondeley 'seemed very proud of his looks – he always sat bolt upright with his head slightly to one side'.[12] It was men like these – older, vain, posturing – who were in charge of the Queen. The Marquess oversaw the sovereign's costume changes, the Duke of Norfolk showed him what to do.* Philip, his naval uniform hidden beneath his gown and coronet, looked on as other men laid claim to his wife, the monarch.† Later, Anne Glenconner described the Duke of Edinburgh's behaviour when entering the Abbey as 'very fussy' and 'adding to tension'.[13] Can you blame him? Even

---

* According to Anne Glenconner, the Marquess struggled with the hooks and eyes on the back of the Queen's dress, so they were swapped for poppers. Apparently 'every time he did up a popper he pushed her rather violently'. (Anne Glenconner, *Lady in Waiting*, p. 61.)

† The Duke of Edinburgh was made [Honorary] Admiral of the Fleet in January 1953.

the press couldn't resist a comparison between 'the puffy pomp of the peers and the almost film-star handsomeness of the Duke of Edinburgh'.[14]

Vivat! Vivat! After the Archbishop of Canterbury, Philip was the first peer to kneel before his wife and pay homage:

> I, Philip Duke of Edinburgh, do become your liege man of life and limb, and of earthly worship, and faith and truth will I bear unto you, to live and die, against all manner of folks. So help me God.

Fanfares of trumpets, a blaze of violins and kiss on the cheek for his wife and her wobbly crown. It was a three-hour service, with more to come once the state-coach wended its way back to Buckingham Palace. The 'rain poured, the crowds still roared' and photographs still had to be taken. Lots and lots of them, images now so engrained in our national psyche that it's hard to imagine the crowned Queen in any pose that isn't faintly kitsch with a golden orb and fake 'blow up' Abbey in the background.[15] An empathetic woman, she had predicted that, by the time the photograph stage was reached, everyone would be exhausted. They were and her husband didn't hide it. With a 'ragging attitude', Philip abandoned pleasantries in front of photographer Cecil Beaton. 'His lips pursed in a smile that put the fear of God into me. I believe he doesn't like or approve of me.' Making a 'great deal of fuss', the 'frightfully bossy' Duke infuriated the photographer; there was a spat and indignant Beaton briefly downed tools. Apparently the Queen was horrified.[16] But such tension was predictable. Philip, 'disappointed that his friend Baron' hadn't got the coronation job, made life difficult for Beaton.[17] Baron was Philip's special Thursday Club conspirator and had taken the royal wedding pictures, but, six years on, the Queen Mother's photographer trumped her son-in-law's.

Brandreth has explored this slight at length in his biography, concluding that 'Baron was Philip's man and Philip was someone Queen Elizabeth [the Queen Mother] did not entirely trust'. He repeats Sir John Wheeler-Bennett's remark of her that there was a 'small drop of arsenic in the centre of that marshmallow'.[18] Perhaps. Either way, Beaton loved his bosomy patron; he thanked her for clinching him the gig and concluded at the end of the day that the only time he'd felt 'airborne' was when photographing 'the Queen Mother and her grandchildren'.[19] Needless to say, the photographs only tell half the tale.

Anecdotally, its clear Philip overplayed his hand on 2 June 1953 and his discomfort did not go unnoticed. But while the Queen Mother could take care of the grandchildren, only the Queen could placate the conundrum that was her husband. In the evening, she broadcast to the nation. First she thanked her subjects:

> I have sincerely pledged myself to your service, as so many of you are pledged to mine. Throughout all my life and with all my heart I shall strive to be worthy of your trust.

But only one person was singled out as travelling with her on that journey: 'In this resolve I have my husband to support me. He shares all my ideals and all my affection for you.'[20] In June 1953, the nation was almost exclusively focused on Elizabeth, but it was thanks to Philip that she was more than just a Queen, she was an exalted image of the ideal 1950s' woman: 'a radiant young wife and mother' and a monarch.[21] For a patriarchal society struggling to find itself post-war, the package was both reassuring and fresh, and, better than anyone else, Elizabeth understood its value. She confidently rebutted comparisons with her Tudor forbear, Elizabeth I, explaining that, unlike the Virgin Queen, she was not a despot 'blessed with neither husband nor children'.[22] The success of Britain's twentieth-century monarchy was premised on marriage; beyond the crowns and oaths and crowds, Elizabeth needed Philip. It helped that she loved him.

-◇-

In the wake of the Duke of Edinburgh's death in 2021, press coverage returned to those challenging early years; his dislocated childhood, relatively penury and reputation as 'Philip the Greek'. The temptation was to portray the Prince as a disadvantaged outsider who had to earn his place among the unforgiving ranks of British royalty. Coinciding with the departure of his grandson, Prince Harry, and his American celebrity wife, Meghan, from the same Royal Family in 2020, clumsy parallels were inevitable. But it is a mistake to frame Philip as a victim; his formative years were a vital training ground for sizing up the British monarchy.

Born in royal exile, with parents profoundly impacted by their loss of status, both material and social, Philip inherited an astute antenna for the value of both. Post-1947 and finally on the inside, his life's work became the maintenance of that which he had married into. Irrespective of the odd snide comment, the worst that he can be accused of on coronation day is caring too much. With 'his eyes almost constantly on his wife',[23] he wanted perfection, and in many ways that is what he got. The ceremony, the procession, the live broadcast, the balcony wave (four of them), the positive coverage – this was the high watermark of monarchy in the twentieth century.

It didn't last long – the pitch-perfect moment was shattered within a week.

'PRINCESS MARGARET; Scandalous stories of her 'romance'. <u>They</u> must deny it <u>now</u>.'[24]

In the immediate aftermath of the coronation, newspapers pounced on Margaret's intimate gesture when she picked a piece of fluff from Group Captain Peter Townsend's lapel in Westminster Abbey. A story that had already been circulating in the overseas press crashed across the British news agenda. The twenty-two-year-old Princess was in love with a thirty-eight-year-old divorcé. To compound the problem, Townsend was mere 'staff' – by 1952, George VI's former equerry had become Comptroller of the Household to the Queen Mother and Margaret.

Elizabeth and Philip were yesterday's news – here was a story that would run and run. It had all the ingredients of a storming soap opera. The handsome war hero, the beautiful Princess, the moral dilemma. Conservative Britain, high on righteous indignation and mawkish curiosity, was still a decade away from the swinging sixties. *The People* was unequivocal.

> The story is, of course, utterly untrue. It is quite unthinkable that a royal princess, third in the line of succession to the throne, should even contemplate a marriage with a man who has been through the divorce courts.[25]

But the story was true and the Royal Family had known about it for months. The Queen proved sympathetic if non-committal: she loved her sister and was fond of Townsend. But, as Philip had already discovered, his wife wasn't fully in control. The institution of monarchy, emboldened by Elizabeth and Philip's marriage, was about to be hoisted with its own petard. In theory, the Queen could have taken a stand. Just months before, the *Sunday Graphic* prophetically wrote: 'if the personalities of the Queen and her consort are a true guide, perhaps the greatest change in the new reign will lie in the humanising and the broadening of the monarchy'.[26] But during her exceptionally long reign, the Queen wasn't known for taking a stand, and certainly not a progressive one. Coming so soon after the accession, at a time when royal marriages were boxed in by legalities and religion, action was even more unlikely. As Defender of the Faith in a church that didn't recognise divorce, how could she support her sister? Even Churchill, once an exceptional champion of Edward VIII and Wallis Simpson, railed against another royal marriage that involved a divorcé.

'One motor accident and this young lady might be our Queen', he huffed, but the Prime Minister's comment was wide of the mark. The accident would also have to involve Prince Charles and Princess Anne.[27] Poor Margaret. What was the point of her if she couldn't even marry the man she wanted to in an era of true love and perfect housewives? The question wracked journalists, many of whom were sympathetic to her plight. Readers were offered a glimpse into 'the real Princess Margaret', the 'loneliest girl in Britain'.

Incisive commentary provided an uncomfortable reminder of how dependent one sibling was on the other. That wartime lockdown in Windsor had a lot to answer for.

> The greatest clue to Princess Margaret's character lies in the change which came over her life when her sister married. Until then she and her sister had always lived together and shared everything. Margaret was the first to know when Princess Elizabeth fell in love. She watched the progress of that romance right from the start.[28]

In pushed Philip. The relationship between this blond interloper and Margaret was never straightforward. She tagged along like a gooseberry and he quickly tired of her games and attempts to pull rank.[29] Nor was he above wounding sarcasm. Both of them circled the future Queen. But unlike Philip, who knew what it was like to live on the outside looking in, Margaret enjoyed entitled complacency. Daddy's little girl, she was born into Britain's first family without any of the responsibility and all of the expectation. One minute she wanted to be treated like a little princess, the next Cinderella.[30] Life was a game and she liked being at the centre of it. When gorgeous Group Captain Peter Townsend – dreamy, heroic and unhappy (conveniently his divorce was granted on the basis of his wife's adultery) – got a little too close, no one imagined anything would come of it. Apparently the Princess had forgotten about the 1936 abdication; she was only six at the time. The Queen Mother lined up a couple of unprepossessing aristocrats, but, like her sister, Margaret wanted to steer her own course. Looks and panache mattered to the Windsor sisters.

Philip had set his heart on entering the upper ranks of British royalty; desire took second place to martial ambitions. Not so Margaret. It is harder to appreciate what you've got when you've always had it. And as the newspapers observed, she was lonely. The King was dead, she had been shunted to Clarence House as an also-ran royal, and her sister was always busy. Philip thought she was spoiled. What did he expect? As early as 1953, the press had picked up on her habits. 'She generally has two cigarettes when dealing with her letters in the morning, others after coffee and meals. And like many highly-strung people, she tends to "light up" if she is feeling nervous about an important function ahead.' They consoled themselves that the Princess only drank squash.[31] There were also concerns about her weight. Anne Glenconner recognised a forlorn girl when she saw one at the coronation, but by then it was too late.[32] The dam was about to burst.

In true Elizabethan style, the distracted Queen recommended the couple wait a year, but press attention hardened opinion. Alan Lascelles, in consultation with Churchill, oversaw a separation. Townsend was posted to Brussels and Margaret went on a mini-tour of Rhodesia; the sting in the tail came when she wasn't allowed to see him on return. ('She collapsed as she does when things go terribly wrong.')[33] Monarchy wasn't about to take a risk. Elizabeth had been beamed across the world in a televised coronation extravaganza,* but, for the Commonwealth to actually mean something, its new head had to show herself to all her people. While Margaret lay on the floor and wept, eight tonnes of clothes, including the coronation gown, were being packed for a hugely ambitious Commonwealth tour. There were two sisters but only one Queen.

Philip was defensive at the suggestion he was unsympathetic towards his sister-in-law and her romantic plight. 'What have I done? I haven't done anything?' In 1953, his main gripe had been that Margaret's story capped the coronation hype.[34] In fact, one cast the other into sharp relief. The coronation was a tableau, a set piece where the main players had defined roles. It was devoid of raw emotion. There would always be public sympathy (and criticism) of Margaret. She was human; the flawed Princess, born in the wrong era and falling in love with the wrong man.

The compromise when it came two years later was cruel: even at the age of twenty-five, as a member of the Royal Family, Margaret's marriage had to be signed off by Parliament. Lord Salisbury, a senior member of the cabinet, threatened

---

* Even in the developed world, not everywhere had television; for instance, Australia didn't get television until 1956. For footage of their Queen, they relied on newsreel.

resignation if the Princess got her way and new Prime Minister (and divorcé) Anthony Eden, took the path of least resistance. How about Margaret married Townsend and gave up being a princess? Ideally they would live abroad. Well, there was a thought. When the Queen Mother wondered where her daughter would live, Philip was contemptuous. The man who grew up without a house sarcastically suggested that 'even nowadays it was still possible to buy a house'.[35] He who had married into Britain's biggest 'house'. Did he really expect Margaret to marry and give up hers? It took his sister-in-law two years to realise that being a princess was more valuable than a (happy?) marriage. Despite his good looks and war decorations, Townsend was a middle-aged commoner with a couple of children in tow. The come down would have been too great. Philip, born in exile, could have told her that.

THIRTEEN

◆◇◆

Keeping Up Appearances

Coronation day was just the beginning. As nineteenth-century constitutional expert Walter Bagehot sagely observed: 'to be a symbol, and an effective symbol, you must be vividly and often seen.'[1] The British empire was on its way out, but now there was a Commonwealth to maintain, imagined through the person of the young Queen. This was Britain's bold new future, at least so Churchill thought. The Royal Commonwealth Tour of 1953–54 was set to break records; Elizabeth would be the first monarch to circumnavigate the globe with her war hero husband, and if she didn't enjoy comparisons with her Tudor namesake, the Prime Minister couldn't resist them.

> Her Majesty's ship *Gothic* is more spacious and travels faster than the *Golden Hind*, but it may well be that the journey the Queen is about to take will be no less auspicious and the treasure she brings back no less bright than when Drake first sailed on an English ship around the world.

The modern treasure in question was surely the 'love and loyalty of her subjects overseas'.[2] Shelia Albrecht is one-hundred years old; in a lemon jersey and pretty polka-dot scarf, she's talking to me on Zoom from Melbourne with her son, Jon. 'I first arrived in Sydney, Australia, in 1947.' Shelia went to join her husband, who was working there; she was one of over two millions Britons who emigrated to Commonwealth countries post-1945.* 'The English were treated better than other immigrants. I suppose straightaway we had things in common; there was our language and the Royal Family.' Jon, born in Australia the same year as Prince Charles, interrupts his mother. 'And the war united you, Mum! You had all fought a common enemy.'[3]

In World War II, Sheila had been a Wren in the Women's Royal Naval Service, working on the now-famous Bombe machines attached to Bletchley Park, and later posted to Ceylon (today's Sri Lanka). On VE Day, 8 May 1945, she was back in London, clambering up the Victoria statue outside Buckingham Palace, shouting 'We want the King! We want the King!' 'Oh, yes, I've always been a royalist.' She smiles. She fought for King and country, and then migrated thousands of miles to Australia, where the then new Queen provided a consistent thread between Sheila and her new home. 'I've lived here for seventy-four years. People often ask me if I feel Australian; I do absolutely love this country but I'm still English. Your identity isn't something you can just take off like a coat.'

The knotty question that surrounds national identity was diffused across the Commonwealth in the form of young (British) Elizabeth – at least that was the idea. There were excessive quantities of commonwealth 'garnish' to assist with the task: respective countries' emblems picked out in satin threads on her coronation gown, an array of Commonwealth troops and

---

* Until the 1980s, Britain was a net exporter of people – more people left the country than came into it. So many emigrated in the years after World War I that Churchill put out an appeal: 'I say to those that wish to leave our country "stay here and fight it out – do not desert the old land."'

representatives in the coronation procession, and an abundance of Commonwealth-themed souvenirs on sale across the globe.[4]

> Ha, yes. The Australians are great collectors – spoons, plates, crockery, you name it. Today there's still a giant undercurrent of older women who have memorabilia from that first visit. Do I? No. It was enough that the Queen was coming. Australians really loved the Queen, in most public buildings there was a picture of her.

Never was that love more securely and demonstrably affirmed than during the royal tour of 1953–54. 'All night wait begins for thousands.' 'Sightseers Jam City.' 'Sydney in a Fever!' 'Serious overcrowding warning.'[5] From November 1953 to May 1954, Elizabeth and Philip were on tour in the West Indies, Australasia, Asia and Africa, with over three months spent in New Zealand and Australia. The trip, initially intended for George VI, had been a while coming: first postponed, then cancelled (the King's ill health) and finally aborted (the King's death). Anticipation was riding high and everywhere the couple went they got a rock star welcome. Millions turned out to greet them. Years later, Philip would look back at this high noon of modern monarchy – a small woman in the back of a Land Rover facing down a roaring sea of humanity – and explain 'it was the institution'. But it was more than that; the young Queen symbolised a moment in time when deference met democracy, war met peace, empire met independence and romance met marriage. Together the couple represented hope.

Shelia laughs. 'Oh, yes, I have always been an admirer of Philip. He was a strong young man, she needed him. She loved him and he loved her.' Shelia pauses. 'At least I think he did.' At home and abroad, the narrative did not waver. According to the press, this was a monarch whose 'gifted' husband, 'with ability and charm above the average, must be her principal support.'[6] Commonwealth countries were more conservative even than Britain; the opinions of Dominion leaders were cited as a reason for rejecting Margaret's marriage plans, with Elizabeth and Philip the robust counter to her tainted narrative. As a Canadian historian articulated of George V's earlier 1908 tour – 'By reaching out to the people of his far-flung empire he hoped to create a personal bond' and 'his people in turn, he hoped, would see an image of their better selves in him' – it was up to the Queen and her Duke to provide a 'better' image for the modern age.[7]

By 1954, Shelia had moved to the then Australian territory of Papua New Guinea. Each week the 'mail plane' landed with the mainland's papers and the locals got very excited about '"Mrs King! Mrs King!" That's what they called her, after her father.' The *Sydney Morning Herald* was full of carefully crafted stories from the tour. New Zealand had handed on the baton – it was Australia's turn to bask in royal glory. Amid specially constructed arches, beneath highly choreographed fly pasts and fireworks, and under baking summer sun, the royal couple passed their endurance test with flying colours. The Duke was a 'damned good fellow', his Queen 'seems to love talking to children' (she hadn't seen her own for months) and 'the variety of interests of the Queen and the Duke of Edinburgh is quite remarkable'. They were the perfect pair and, if their vehicle drove slowly enough, the view of Her Majesty up close was rewarding. She had acquired a slight tan.[8]

Of course there were tensions. Elizabeth could be curt: 'take your hands out of your pockets!', a reproach to a weary member of her entourage; and she still hadn't learnt to smile properly: rumours persisted of a 'tired and strained' Queen.[9] According to Sheila, in later years the Australians fell out of love with Philip. 'It was his gruff comments,' she diplomatically admits. Neither was perfect, but people were on their side. Royal historian Robert Hardman describes the 'carry on' scene that followed a lovers' tiff in a chalet. It was all caught on camera. The exhausted pair let rip (this was five weeks into the Australian leg of a six-month tour). Philip bowled out of the door, followed by flying tennis shoes and a tennis racket. And a 'very angry Queen shouting for him to return'. They were meant to be on holiday (who doesn't argue on holiday?) and had forgotten a prior engagement. Cameraman Loch Townsend was in position and started rolling as soon as the door opened. Needless to say, the reel never saw the light of day. Press secretary Richard Colville came striding over and Townsend 'opened the back of the camera, removed the film and told Colville, "Commander, I have a present for you. You might like to give it to Her Majesty." The cameraman was rewarded with a tray of beer and sandwiches and a message from the Queen. "I'm sorry for that little interlude . . . but as you know, it happens in every marriage." '[10]

Well, quite. But Philip and Elizabeth were not every couple. And their marriage not every marriage. Their union was presented as an example to a loose federation of countries anxious to make the transition between Empire and independence. Elizabeth became a metaphor for family, both literally and in the context of the Commonwealth. Here was their feminine, sympathetic figurehead. Australian magazine *Woman's Day* ran former governess Crawfie's *The Little Princesses* extracts during the Queen's visit and, as historian Ruth Feingold has argued, this tour 'explicitly appealed to women.'[11] Elizabeth ended her trip to Australia with a farewell speech:

I hope that it [our visit] has demonstrated that the Crown is a human link between all the peoples who owe allegiance to me – an allegiance of mutual love and respect and never of compulsion.[12]

The only figures in a relationship that was compelled to work were Elizabeth and Philip. Their love story had just been taken on a global tour and, by 1954, it looked like they had mastered the art of togetherness, in public at least. It was going to prove a tough act to follow. Sheila always loved the late Queen; Elizabeth was her enduring connection with a homeland that she rarely returned to. But son Jon is not so sure about future generations of Australians. 'There's a big Republican movement over here now and Charles, well, he hasn't done so well, has he?'

❖

In December 1997, the royal yacht *Britannia* was decommissioned. The farewell came at the end of a particularly difficult year for the Queen and during the parting ceremony she appeared to shed a tear – for a mere boat.[13] The timing was unfortunate. Just months earlier, the press (or was it Tony Blair?) had prized the Queen out of Balmoral and insisted she went on what playwright Alan Bennett famously described as a 'mournabout' in the wake of Diana, the Princess of Wales's shocking death.[14] Public displays of affection have never come easily to our monarch – an incontinent face (which is what the media wanted when Diana died) ran counter to an aristocratic upbringing in the early twentieth century. One must not be a cry baby. Undemonstrative, the Queen found it easier to express emotion towards dogs, horses and apparently boats. But *Britannia* was not any old boat. It was a time piece that tied the monarch back to the beginning of her reign.

The contract to build the royal yacht was signed off just two days before George VI's death in February 1952. The Windsors' 1947 South African tour in an old battleship had focused minds on the need for a suitably regal vessel to transport modern monarchy around the world. There were hopes it might aid the King's recuperation, and worries about cost were off set with a design that would allow *Britannia* to double as a hospital ship if there was another war. But by 1953 the King was dead; it was the new Queen who travelled to Scotland and launched *Britannia*. The name spoke volumes; Britain had no intention of leaving the world stage quietly and this sleek navy-blue luxury liner, although not ready for the beginning of the Commonwealth tour, sailed to Libya in April 1954 to pick up the royal couple on the final leg of their trip. Famously it was here that Charles and Anne, the first to sail on *Britannia*, were reunited with their parents after six long months. The meeting (of course) lacked any public display of affection. Five-year-old Charles got a handshake and had to wait his turn while Mummy took tea with King Idris of Libya and visited a cemetery.[15]

Formalities aside (it is notable the British press never questioned Elizabeth and Philip's absence from their children, despite the prevailing hands-on parenting culture[16]), *Britannia* proved a smash hit in the early days. A visual feast, in May 1954 it sailed up the Thames with the royal couple standing on the bridge next to an ecstatic Churchill: 'I assign no limits to the reinforcement which this royal journey may have brought to the health, the wisdom, the sanity and hopefulness of mankind.' The riverbanks roared their delight and quayside cranes respectfully lowered their jibs.[17] It was another hit for monarchy and a far cry from the latter-day reputation *Britannia* acquired.

What had started out as an emblem of post-war optimism and Britishness had become a victim of the Royal Family's plummeting popularity by the end of the century. Princess Margaret got married in 1960 to photographer Anthony

Armstrong-Jones and took *Britannia* on a two-month tour of the Caribbean. So began the yacht's slow fall from grace. There were four expensive royal honeymoons – Anne and Mark followed Margaret to the Caribbean, Charles and Diana floated around the Mediterranean and Andrew took Fergie to the Azores, where she was stung by jellyfish.[18] All four marriages failed, and by the end of its life *Britannia* was mired with high running costs and a reputation for seedy opulence and jinxed relationships. No wonder the Queen shed a tear. She must have wondered where it all went wrong.

Elizabeth and Philip came from a unique generation and class. Born royal, they were both entitled and privileged, but that abundant advantage was fused with distinct ideas of duty and obligation forged in two world wars. Brought up between those wars, the couple's brusque exteriors bore the hallmarks of an offish upper-class society. It was a model they replicated as parents and one which was informed by their relationship with each other. This matter-of-fact style helped facilitate an extraordinary working relationship and *Britannia* was part of that story. Despite its later reputation as a 'Love Boat' with gold taps and spoiled princes, the yacht's primary function was as a working vessel, for hosting foreign dignitaries and housing the monarch on diplomatic missions. Elizabeth and Philip understood that: it suited their exceptional work ethic.

On their return journey up the Thames in 1954, while Churchill entertained the crew, Philip and Elizabeth talked to Sir Hugh Casson, the yacht's interior designer, about any alternations they wanted. Casson had been hired to fulfil the couple's desire that Britannia's interior should be elegant, but unostentatious, and in line with Britain's on-going austerity. The couple's rooms on opposite sides of the yacht allowed them to develop an effective working relationship on a vessel that made more than 700 overseas visits.[19] (Honeymoons were the only occasion a double bed was taken onboard.)[20] Frequently Philip would pad across the corridor and amend his Queen's speeches. Here they were very much their own masters, each assisting the other, before they stepped ashore and represented Britain and the Commonwealth. Their shared goal was unambiguous – the maintenance of Britain's monarchy for the common good.

This modus operandi partly explains the enduring success of the royal couple's marriage, despite their differences. Much has been made of their contrasting personalities and friendship groups. Deeply conventional, the Queen was most comfortable with a conservative, upper-class set, best exemplified by Sir Michael Adeane, her private secretary from 1953. His family had long roots at court and Adeane fulfilled all the markers of a classic royal appointment – an officer in the Coldstream Guards, then a student of history at Cambridge, he remained in the Queen's service until 1972. Meanwhile, Philip's natural inclination was towards a more unconventional type, and the contrast between Adeane and Parker, Philip's private secretary and loyal friend, are striking. Hailing from Australia, Parker had no court stamp and was ideally placed to help Philip push back against the suits and stalwarts who inhabited the palace.[21]

There is a temptation, partly fuelled by Philip's reputation as both obstreperous and something of a ladies' man, to focus on that difference. Eileen, Parker's wife – Scottish, unhappily married and resentful about her husband's long absences from home – wrote at length about 'Philip's funny friends'. This was apparently the term Elizabeth coined for her husband's social set away from court.[22] At the centre of the nucleus was 'Boy' Browning, by 1952 the treasurer of the Office of the Duke of Edinburgh, and someone who worked hard, played hard and loved all things nautical. The inscrutable novelist Daphne Du Maurier, 'a most attractive woman with piercing eyes', was his 'part-time' wife (according to Eileen, they'd worked out an 'eminently sane and civilised compromise between two life-styles').[23] Du Maurier's name is frequently associated with the Duke's – apparently Philip expressed doubts to her on the eve of his wedding – but the latter always protested his innocence.[24]

Beyond the Browning pair, was Baron, the society photographer, and Uffa Fox, an eccentric playboy who made his name designing boats, courting controversy and marrying beautiful women. When Philip met Uffa, the latter was somewhere between his second and third wife. If Baron was the heart of the Thursday Club, which gathered in London every week, Uffa provided a more rural style of release, which culminated in Cowes Week on the Solent. There the Duke and he made headlines racing together in one of his 20 ft keel boats.[25] Eileen stiffly tells us that Philip required 'an antidote to the strict public life and public scrutiny to which he was more and more exposed' and Uffa, who led 'a double life', provided it.[26] Much of Eileen's book is written in coded inferences (published in the 1980s, she did not want to tread on toes), but it is clear she felt sidelined by her husband and implicitly drew parallels between her treatment as a spurned wife and that of the Queen's.[27]

But there were key differences. Crucially, the Parker marriage didn't last and the Queen's did. Eileen, who got married during the war to her ambitious Australian sailor, had idealised notions of a companionate marriage, much in vogue at the time, in which it was anticipated that a spouse would meet all of their partner's emotional and physical needs. Or as a panellist on the 1954 Royal Commission of Marriage and Divorce put it: 'we are coming to expect more and more of our marriages'. It was these expectations that meant 'marriages today are at risk to a greater extent than formerly'.[28] Eileen, stuck at home with two children, a long way from her native Scotland, was in that high-risk category. When she tried to tag along with Mike, she was invariably made to feel unwelcome. He 'arranged for me to spend Cowes week on a friend's boat' – it was 'beached on the mudflats, and forever at an angle'. Parker made it clear he didn't want her there. In stark contrast, Elizabeth 'never came to Uffa's house', and she avoided Cowes week 'like the plague'.[29] That was Philip's domain. The royal couple did not attempt a companionate marriage. Theirs conformed to a more old-fashioned model.

In *The English in Love*, historian Claire Langhamer explains that the mid-twentieth century proved something of an emotional crossroads for marriage. If post-war 'husbands and wives were conceptualised as inhabiting emotionally and sexually exclusive worlds', this was a recent trend and the fall out would be considerable, (the divorce law was eventually reformed in 1969). In contrast, earlier twentieth-century commentators 'had not been so afraid to recommend emotional and spatial independence . . . Maintaining separate interests and a degree of emotional distance was the basic tenor of marital advice.' In 1935, co-founder of the National Marriage Guidance Council, Edward Griffith, recommended 'the independence of each must be guaranteed'. Others were more explicit. 'A woman may love her husband with all her heart, but even love needs an occasional rest.'[30]

Elizabeth loved her husband, and she also knew how to keep her distance. Doubtless it was not always easy, but she would eventually become a past master at 'maintaining separate interests'. If Philip had his 'funny friends' and playboy sporting pursuits, Elizabeth's counter balance was centred around the ultimate royal hobby – horses – and those who helped her facilitate that recreational world. In later decades, as the Queen's confidence grew, so too did her interest in riding, racing and breeding, and her reliance on an old war-time chum, Lord Porchester (Porchey).* Yes, he too had danced with the young Princess on that unforgettable VE Day night, and, yes, steady Porchey, trusted by her father, was by Elizabeth's side at Newmarket on October 1945 and numerous subsequent derbies. Theirs was an enduring friendship and, by 1970, Porchey had become the Queen's racing manager. Elizabeth 'was very fond of him' and he 'devoted to her'.[31] They spoke an equine language Philip did not share, and the Netflix series, *The Crown*, insinuates they shared something more than that.[32] Sexual intimacy between two such old married friends seems highly unlikely, and, if anything did occur, our discreet Queen would never have divulged it. However, Elizabeth did leave us a textbook example of how to maintain a 'degree of emotional distance' in marriage. Unlike so many other wives in post-war Britain (Elieen included), the Queen was a very busy, financially independent working woman as well as a highly practical one. Her marriage would outlast her sister's, two of her sons' and her daughter's. It would also outlast Eileen's.

◆

In July 2022, the British Court of Appeal dismissed a challenge from the *Guardian* newspaper. The publication had contested the legality of a private court hearing that banned public access to Prince Philip's will for ninety years. In a piece of stunning legal gobbledygook, two appeal court judges argued: 'it is true that the law applies equally to the royal family but that does not mean that the law produces the same outcomes in all situations'. They concluded that to publicise decisions concerning the will 'would have compromised the need to preserve the dignity of the Queen and her family's privacy'.[33] If ever proof

---

* Henry Herbert, later 7th Earl of Carnarvon.

was needed of what it means to be a monarch in twenty-first-century Britain, there it is. Of course, beneath this contested case is the presumption that Prince Philip's will contains something worth hiding. As the *Guardian* coolly explained, with the exception of the monarch,* the first member of the Royal Family whose will was kept secret was Prince Francis of Teck, brother of Queen Mary, in order to 'hush up a sex scandal'. Apparently the errant Prince had bequeathed 'prized family jewels to a mistress' before his death in 1910.[34]

It doesn't take a genius to work out what the *Guardian* is inferring. This issue of Philip's hidden will scratches an itch that bothered the late Duke ever since his alleged rendezvous with actress Pat Kirkwood – she whose legs were the 'eighth wonder of the world'† – in 1948. But back then, when the royal pair were still in the early throes of marriage, the story did not break in the press, and later, in the wake of the coronation, Princess Margaret and her doomed relationship with Townsend kept the gossip columns occupied for two years. The Princess proved a far easier target; the story was in the public domain, Townsend made no effort to hide away and, crucially, Margaret was one step removed from the monarch. Allowing a scandal to engulf a lesser royal was one thing; targeting the husband of the Queen quite another. It was not in the press's interest to endanger monarchy. And apparently they didn't have any proof.

Proof of what? Well may you ask, but, unless you're planning to live another ninety years, in all likelihood you won't find out. The Establishment are pretty good at looking after their own. As a friend of royalty said to me, 'I can't tell you anything because then I would stop being invited to parties.' For clarity (or lack of it), lets briefly return to Daphne Attridge,

---

* The monarch's will is hidden from the public by law.

† According to theatre critic and writer Kenneth Tynan.

who we met earlier in the book. She is ninety-nine years old; like the Queen, Daphne served in the ATS during the war and shared a birthday with Philip. She finally met them both on a walk-about in Ipswich; it was the highlight in a long life of royal watching. 'I think he did make a wonderful husband in the end. But there were lots of stories about him. I mean, aristocrats had a bit of reputation. There were certain people who they employed who knew, I am sure.' Daphne is referring to Philip and rumours that came to a head in 1956–7. Her response is cryptic, because the case was never clear cut. 'I remember it was in all the newspapers, lots of innuendo and something about a party girl. Was it Pat Kirkwood? She was a wonderful actress, a lovely girl, I thought. And he did too apparently.'

It is no coincidence that Philip hit the headlines shortly after the (first) Margaret scandal had been put to bed. In the wake of their staggering coronation and commonwealth tour achievements, Britain's number one couple were experiencing an inevitable come down. Royalty and royal fans love births, weddings, jubilees and, of course, coronations – big landmark events that allow the British to dress up their ancient institution in all manner of paraphernalia and pomp and parade it around as if human perfection exists after all. But having been identified as the world's perfect fairytale, the reality of royal living was always going to be a bit of a grind. Elizabeth had to get her head around a flailing Conservative administration under a temperamental Sir Anthony Eden, while Philip established himself as a commendable guardian of the royal estates as well as a man in possession of an enquiring scientific mind and numerous patronages. He didn't have a proper job but he was very good at keeping himself busy.

That busyness was to involve another trip on *Britannia*, this time without his preoccupied wife, (the Suez Crisis did not bode well for Her Majesty's Government and almost delayed Philip's tour on the royal yacht – a hospital ship might have been needed off the coast of Egypt). In the end, war was averted and the Duke readied to go on his travels, with the Melbourne Olympics the main, but certainly not the only, focus of a trip that clocked up 23,000 miles in HMY *Britannia* and 15,000 by air.[35] Inevitably, Philip was not alone; accompanying him on what proved to be a landmark tour* was his private secretary, Mike Parker, and several of their 'funny friends'. However, unlike Philip, Parker was not travelling with his wife's blessing. Eileen Parker had already given up on their marriage; by now the couple were living separately – Parker's infidelity the final straw – and she wanted a divorce.[36]

On two fronts the timing could not have been worse. Months earlier, in March 1956, the Royal Commission on Marriage and Divorce published its long-awaited report. The panel had failed to agree on the question of divorce law reform, but they were unanimous on the importance of matrimony. 'It is obvious that life-long marriage is the basis of a secure and stable family life and that to ensure their well-being children must have that background.' Despite spiralling divorce applications, the marital ideal remained the foundation of modern civil society.[37] Compounding this problem from the Parkers' point of view was his quasi-celebrity status as head of a family unit that flanked the Royal Family. With his wife and children, adulterous Parker had posed for *Tatler* in 1951. His son and daughter attended the birthday parties of Charles and

---

* The 1956–7 trip included Kenya, the Seychelles, Ceylon, Malaysia, Papua New Guinea, Australia, New Zealand, Antarctica and the Gambia. In the Atlantic, the British Overseas Territories of the South Shetland Islands were visited for the first time by a senior member of the Royal Family (Clarke and Goodsir, *Prince Philip*, p. 72).

Anne.[38] Good behaviour was expected from the main support act to the world's most famous married couple.

But, by 1956, Eileen had little truck for the needs of a family that she identified as compounding her marital woes. Richard Colville, the Queen's press secretary, was sympathetic when she went to see him, but he did ask that Eileen might wait until the end of the tour before she announced her plans to divorce.[39] No such luck. *Britannia* was en route home, somewhere between West Africa and Gibraltar, when the news broke.

> Michael Parker, the Duke of Edinburgh's personal friend and private secretary and his wife Eileen have parted . . . it ends rumours that circles close to the Palace have hushed up for months. <u>The parting will come as a shock to the royal family because Michael Parker is held in such high regard.</u>[40]

BOOM. A touch paper had been lit. Parker was forced to bow out in Gibraltar, where he was bid a touching farewell by the Duke, a man not usually known for demonstrable affection.

> Mike . . . forced a smile and held out his hand as he and the Duke stood on the tarmac. The Duke, looking sad, grasped it – and then impulsively clasped his left hand over it, too. AND FOR SECONDS THE TWO MEN FACED EACH OTHER IN A DOUBLE HANDCLASP FAREWELL AND SAID NOTHING.[41]

The pair were very close, but despite this (or maybe because of it) Mike resigned. Richard Colville made sure of that.[42] However, rather than quelling the flames, the story grew legs. As Eileen obliquely suggested, 'my first instinct was to blame sheer panic for Mike's abrupt decision, but then upon reflection I started to wonder if his resignation was a smokescreen for something, or somebody else.'[43] The British press was initially too cautious to suggest such things of the man married to the monarch, but American newspapers didn't hesitate. The *Baltimore Sun* insisted that 'there is a "rift" between the Queen and the Duke of Edinburgh' and, as the *Daily Mirror*, admitted – 'This stuff was DYNAMITE.'[44] The story ran and ran on both sides of the Atlantic. Royal fan Daphne was gripped. 'Well, you didn't know what to make of it, really. Let's face it, no marriage is easy, including my own. But you did wonder.'

Was the world's most famous couple in trouble? Why had the Queen stopped at two children? What did it say about Philip when the man he was closest to was having an affair? Suddenly the gulf between royal rhetoric and reality didn't appear to stack up. In 1949 Elizabeth had been adamant: 'We can have no doubt that divorce and separation are responsible for some of the darkest evils in our society today', and now 'in any bar room in the world' there were 'malicious rumours' 'embroidered beyond recognition – about the Queen and the Duke.'[45]

Philip was infuriated that his ground-breaking tour of Antarctica and beyond had been hijacked by an unsubstantiated soap opera; it was a story that intermittently repeated on him for the rest of his long life. On several levels the scandal was significant. In Britain, a country crying out for divorce reform, Parker's resignation sent a clear message that once again the monarchy remained a stubbornly conservative force. Or was it just a smokescreen, as Eileen suspected? Seemingly imperturbable, Philip and Elizabeth did not bend their schedules to the headline demand that the Duke should 'fly home'. Instead a 'nine days wonder' ensued between the scandal breaking and the couples' reunification in Lisbon. The delay – much to the chagrin of the press – was indicative of a household that believed it was still in control and that it could afford to ignore the press. And, for the time being, it was and did.[46]

When Elizabeth and her entourage finally met Philip, they were wearing fake whiskers in homage to those he and Parker had grown when sailing through the remotest regions of the Commonwealth.[47] The jokey message was clear: the Queen and Philip were just fine, thank you very much. The couple remained firmly united, a denial was issued,* no mud stuck and, months later, the new Conservative Prime Minister, Harold MacMillan, proposed that the Duke should be rewarded with the 'style and dignity of a prince of the United Kingdom'.[48] The Queen acquiesced.† Prince Philip was back on track. But was the title a well-deserved reward for a maligned man? Or another example of the Establishment looking after its own? Or both, perhaps?

---

* The British press were furious that the Palace issued their denial of a rift to the American press and not, initially, to them.

† This was originally Churchill's idea; he proposed it to the Queen informally in 1955.

FOURTEEN

◆◇◆

A 'Tolerant and Understanding' Marriage

A typical dreich November day in 2021 and the world's leaders were descending on Glasgow for the UN Climate Change Conference (COP26). Not well enough to attend (those mobility issues), the Queen was deeply disappointed. The gigantic gathering, long in the planning and convened with the invidious task of trying to face down a global climate crisis, would have to manage without her, and more was the pity. After all, the environment, a hot potato democracies deliberately ducked for decades, had become the major cause célèbre of Elizabeth's unelected family.

It felt personal and, perhaps because of that, the ninety-five-year-old monarch settled on a compromise; she would open the climate conference via video message. Dressed in carefully chosen moss green, offset with a triple string of pearls and a butterfly brooch received as a wedding gift,* the planet's most recognisable woman reminded her virtual audience of

---

* The Queen was wearing her ruby and diamond Onslow Butterfly brooch. A wedding present from the Countess of Onslow, with other gifts, it had been on display in St James's Palace in November 1947.

their duty to protect that same planet. She kicked off her four-minute speech with a personal reference.

> The impact of the environment on human progress was a subject close to the heart of my dear late husband, Prince Philip, the Duke of Edinburgh. I remember well that in 1969, he told an academic gathering 'If the world pollution situation is not critical at the moment, it is as certain as anything can be, that the situation will become increasingly intolerable within a very short time'.[1]

She neatly ducked the issue of the Duke's scepticism concerning the scientific link (now 100% proven) between carbon emissions and global warming and cited her pride regarding his work to 'protect our fragile planet' and the environmental flame he had lit in Charles (once dismissed as 'a plant-talking oddball') and his eldest son, William.[2] The speech was testimony to the Queen's whole-hearted embrace of the need for climate action and so too the devotion she felt towards her family, particularly her late husband. This wasn't just proof that Philip's quest to keep 'busy' had paid off; it was resounding evidence that the Queen had married a man who was a pioneer and a leader. She had long known he was both.

It is worth remembering just how young and inexperienced Elizabeth was when she became Queen. She had to learn on the job and it was a very public one. During the 1953–4 Commonwealth tour, Her Majesty made 157 speeches, a tall order for a socially reticent girl in a decade when most women were stuck at home.[3] Thankfully, in Philip, she had chosen a husband very different from herself, and with good reason. She loved him and, as monarch, she needed him.

A classicist and honorary fellow at Cambridge University, Joyce Reynolds was one-hundred-and-three years old when she died three days after the Queen in September 2022. The product of aspiring middle-class parents, at the beginning of the twentieth century trail-blazing Joyce had focused her ambitions on the pursuit of academic excellence. An original thinker and a liberal, she was not a natural royalist, although, in great old age, Joyce did concede that constitutional monarchy has its benefits. Compared with Prime Minister Boris Johnson, she thought Her Majesty's appearances were flawless throughout the pandemic, and, as early as 1952, Joyce appreciated the strength of the new monarch's image overseas. 'I was studying in Rome and one day, when I was buying oranges, the fruit trader asked me: "How, my dear, is your lovely Queen?" I had no idea, so I had to make it up. She would have been disappointed if I'd said I didn't know.'[4]

It was four years later, in 1956, with a new academic post at Newnham College, Cambridge University, that Joyce met the Queen first hand. On a visit to the city under the guise of opening a Veterinary College and paying respects to her late father's college, Trinity, Elizabeth made a brief visit to Newnham (one of only three girls' colleges in Cambridge).[5] Joyce 'was charged with organising the gathering in the Senior Common Room. The guest list and sandwiches and so forth. I think it was one of those typical days when Her Majesty's schedule was very tight.' When telling this story, Joyce paused; a diplomatic woman she wanted to be fair. 'What was she like? Well, the senior members of the college liked her very much; she was good at talking to them. I think the rest of us found her . . . how can I put it? Queenly. We found her rather queenly.'

Evidently Elizabeth was not relaxed when surrounded by highly academic women her own age. She struck Joyce as someone more comfortable with older generations. This unease was picked up by writer James Pope-Hennessy when he travelled to Balmoral to interview the Queen about her grandmother, Queen Mary, in 1957. There he found a self-possessed young woman but not someone entirely comfortable in her own skin.

> She is not shy but she is clearly living at great tension, and does not give the impression of happiness. Her hands are thin and worried looking. She is extremely animated, gesticulates when telling anecdotes, makes comic or pathetic faces, and simply cannot remain still.[6]

Pope-Hennessy, keen to make a good impression and having travelled a long way, was not entirely relaxed himself – his anxiety may have exacerbated hers. And he was an unknown man in his thirties. 'One feels that the spring is wound up very tight. She is brisk, jerky and a little ungraceful.'[7] It feels almost unfair to recall these words about a young version of our late Queen, who we came to dearly love and respect. But the late 50s were a challenging time. This was before the arrival of a new decade and two more sons, when Elizabeth could embrace a role looking like the nation's mum (albeit one who wore pearls and a twin-set). The allegations about Philip had stung and Elizabeth was under considerable pressure. People wanted more from their young Queen and had started to say so.

Most famous was Lord Altrincham's personal attack in August 1957, the same month Pope-Hennessy found an awkward Elizabeth at Balmoral. The peer, only thirty-three himself, criticised the Queen for her out-of-touch manner and her courtiers, in the respected journal, *The National and English Review*. His complaints were legion: Elizabeth's entourage were 'people of the "tweedy" sort', she and her sister still bore the 'debutante stamp' (what did he expect?), her voice was a 'pain-in-the-neck' and her speeches lacked 'spontaneity', parts of which 'sound very hollow'.[8] Much has been made of this assault, which came from an esteemed journalist and a lord (he later renounced his title). Netflix drama *The Crown* dedicated an episode to the fallout and, in Sarah Bradford's cautious biography, she tries to suggest his attacks were aimed not at the monarch but her advisers.[9] I disagree. He clearly thought the Queen was a bit of a frump and said so.

It is ironic that Elizabeth carried on being a 'frump' – headscarves firmly tied beneath her chin, high pitched voice unchanged, speeches always recited word-for-word, (that never altered, not even for COP26). But by the latter years of her reign, we loved the Queen for her constancy: reassuring and nostalgic. Our monarch had become a national treasure and we didn't want her any other way. However, back in the 1950s, the criticism was raw and the future unknown. Yet despite all the wailing and gnashing of teeth (a staunch monarchist physically attacked Altrincham in front of TV cameras)[10] or perhaps because of it, a crucial part of the infamous article was overlooked – it's flattering profile of Prince Philip. Altrincham singled out the Duke as a man of 'merit'; on the cusp of a new modern era, even Philip's lack of British-ness was framed as a virtue. 'He gives the impression of being a citizen of the Commonwealth, at home wherever he goes.' Altrincham went further. While the Queen needed to improve her public speaking, not so Philip: 'who is a first-rate speaker' and 'has recently moved, not without success, into the domain of television'.[11]

History tells us that while debutante presentations were disbanded and language moderated, the Queen changed little else. Nor, as the 'bloom of youth' faded (Altrincham's words), did Elizabeth bother with his other suggestion; he wanted his Queen to 'say things people remember' and lamented 'there is little sign that such a personality is emerging'.[12] Instead the Queen stuck to a policy of less is more, with Elizabeth's often expressionless face remaining the ideal blank canvass for her subjects own thoughts and emotions. And for the most part it was a masterful decision – who needed a flamboyant monarch when walking just two steps behind was Philip? No one complained that the Queen was dull when the Duke made another of his legendary 'gaffes', and no one lamented Her Majesty lacked an opinion when Philip let rip on another pet subject (his ninetieth birthday interview with Fiona Bruce was full of them – including a recommendation for 'voluntary family limitation' to tackle unsustainable population growth).[13]

But there was one grave exception. In Altrincham's judgement were the seeds of a much later, more severe attack levelled at the Queen. It came in the immediate aftermath of Diana, the Princess of Wales's sudden death in August 1997, when Elizabeth remained tucked up in Balmoral with her grandsons (and Philip) and failed to spontaneously address the public. Then it was Prime Minister Tony Blair who led the way, intoning about Diana, 'the People's Princess'. The Queen's belated and stiff response – Diana 'was an exceptional and gifted human being' – came almost a week after the accident.

November of the same year, 1997, was Elizabeth and Philip's Golden Wedding anniversary. Together they attended a celebratory lunch at the Banqueting House and, in front of the same Prime Minister, Tony Blair, the Queen was contrite. She explained that it was sometimes difficult for the Royal Family to read the national mood, which could seem hard to reach: 'obscured as it can be by deference, rhetoric, or the conflicting current of public opinion. But read it we must.' She quietly, humbly confessed: 'I have done my best.'

And, as always, this version of Elizabeth's 'best' was framed through the prism of Philip, whose 'constant love and help' had guided her across 'the years of our marriage and of my reign as your Queen'.

Elizabeth ended that speech with the famous line about the Duke 'quite simply' being her 'strength and stay all these years'.[14] The words were a poignant reminder that while Britain's royals could no longer claim the mantle of family monarchy (three of the Windsor children were divorced), it was the dynasty's one enduring marriage, that of Philip and Elizabeth, which had sustained the Queen through the most challenging decade of her life.

◆

I was very disappointed. You can see it in my six-year-old-face – disconsolate and looking resolutely into the middle distance. Behind me my excited mother exchanges pleasantries with Charles, the then Prince of Wales; they are talking about her coronation flag. He is surprised it hasn't succumbed to moths, and she is explaining that, in Scotland, the cold keeps moths away. We have bagged a prime position on the stone dyke thanks to Mum's military-style planning. She forgot that Scotland doesn't share England's royal fervour and we arrived far too early for a forestry event in Dumfries and Galloway, where the Prince had a scheduled visit. Our photograph with him made the local paper, but that did not compensate for the absence of Lady Diana Spencer. It was early summer 1981, the year of the hotly anticipated royal wedding. A man with a tannoy said he hoped that Prince Charles would return with his beautiful new wife, but I had hoped he would bring his beautiful fiancée with him. What, I reasoned, was the point of a Prince without his (almost) Princess?

My enthusiasm for Diana was later rewarded with a Ladybird book all about the Royal Family's latest addition;

her beguiling headshot stared out from the front cover, eyes touched up with extra blue. Sitting on our neighbours' swirly carpet consuming squash and Wotsits, I'd watched Diana walk up the aisle of St Pauls Cathedral to seal her fate with Charles. Me and three-quarters of a billion other people. The country had entered a trance-like state. The papers were heavy with romantic prose and supplementary coverage. 'What a lot of balls', said Dad, and walked out of the room. But he was in the minority. For most of the country (and much of the Commonwealth and beyond), the wedding was an exciting new chapter in the story of our familial crown, a curiously old-fashioned update that looked like it had dropped straight out of a fairytale (the enormous meringue dress was partly to blame). In fact, the day took its inspiration from more recent history. This was a replay of Elizabeth and Philip's wedding on a far grander, more visual scale, as my grandmother kept reminding me. No wonder the Duke of Edinburgh was reputedly delighted. His eldest son was finally following in his footsteps; Charles, in an honorary naval uniform, walked an innocent virginal bride down the aisle into a bright royal future.

This book has deliberately focused on the early years of Elizabeth and Philip's relationship and marriage. But, in order to understand the degree to which that relationship succeeded, it is important to recall the extraordinary royal spectacle that took place on 29 July 1981. One was heavily informed by the success of the other. In a trend started by her father and grandfather, with their unusually uxorious marriages, under Elizabeth and her partnership with Philip, the popular model of family monarchy reached new heights. The couple became the symbol for all the hopes and dreams of domestic bliss that followed World War II. Diligently producing four children, they chimed with the post-war 'Breed for Britain' mantra – here were our most illustrious His and Her trend-setters. Baby boomer mothers had found their cheerleader in the Queen and, even when second-wave feminism crashed across this fraught ideal, young women couldn't charge the monarch with failing to uphold new feminist standards. Had not the Queen been working all along? It was Philip who was king of family decisions, including that fateful one to send tender Charles to rough-and-tumble Gordonstoun.

In his 1994 semi-authorised biography about the Prince, Jonathan Dimbleby explores Charles's early years; implicit is the idea that somehow the boy's remote upbringing explains the failure of his future marriage.[15] But if any blame can be apportioned to his parents, it was that they had pulled off their own marriage too successfully. The seeds of Charles and Diana's divorce partly lay in the reflective glory that Elizabeth and Philip's union cast across a rapidly changing social scene and the expectations it produced.

The vast majority of the post-war generation grew up in conventional family units (irrespective of whether they were happy or faithful). The nonagenarian voices in this book – Daphne, Barbara, Pamela, Philip J., Pat – stuck with their spouses through thick and thin. Before the 1969 reform act, divorce was considered scandalous and only available to the very rich – including Diana's father and mother, Johnnie and Frances Spencer. Although more prevalent in the early 1980s, divorce was still heavily frowned upon by the chattering classes. On 29 July 1981, as the royal carriages trundled across the television screen like large prams – Elizabeth, seated with her old equerry Johnnie Spencer and Philip with Frances – I distinctly remember the adult conversation going on over my head. 'Poor Queen, she will be upset that Diana's parents had such a nasty divorce. She's a great believer in marriage.' 'Yes, yes. Her and Philip make such a lovely couple.'

In fact, by 1981, the Queen had more experience and understanding of divorce than the vast majority; most recently her own sister Margaret had divorced in 1978. But just as Elizabeth understood that not all marriages endured, she was also aware of the complexities involved in martial failure, especially royal marital failure. Failure that involved the monarch – well, that was inconceivable. Given the high stakes, the Princess's 1947 gamble on Philip had more than paid off; it was a fantastic victory for monarchy.

The couple had begun their marriage under the gaze of a thousand lenses, behind their backs were clusters of tutting courtiers and disappointed relations. There was an unspoken murmuring campaign, in Balmoral, in Buckingham Palace and occasionally in the press: Philip would never be faithful. Philip was foreign. Philip was a little too big for his boots. Philip may well have been all those things, but, crucially, he was Elizabeth's first choice, and she was his. They didn't just have the expectations of family, church, country and Commonwealth riding on their union; they had their own expectations, for themselves and their crown, born in an era when marriage and monarchy were considered sacred institutions.

It helped that the couple were blessed with a deep affection for one another until the very end. In the final furlong of his life, the Covid-19 pandemic ensured that the Queen had the Duke all to herself inside their aptly named 'HMS Bubble'. Away from Sandringham's Wood Farm, his Land Rovers and his sometime blonde companion Penny Romsey, Philip came back to where it had all begun, Windsor Castle. He was always an independent spirit, but ultimately Philip belonged to the Queen; the Duke was crown property and had been since 1947.

Tabloids whispered that Charles was irked at his father's latter-day friendship with Penny Romsey; perhaps he was also miffed that there had been a spread featuring thirteen women in *Tatler*, entitled 'The Duke of Edinburgh's Fan Club', and yet somehow, in both cases, Philip came away with his reputation enhanced.[16] A raffish old man at worst, who could resist the outspoken Duke in his dotage, stumbling around Sandringham with gadgets and a penchant for driving when dangerously old. Like his father, Charles had also inherited Mountbatten as a pre-marriage mentor but with very different results. Times had irrevocably changed. The posh propensity to turn a blind eye no longer washed in a society where divorce was prevalent, and modern celebrity promised riches outside the royal club.

Of course it is unfair to compare father and son. Their situations were very different and there is much about Philip's private life we don't know. Unsubstantiated speculation is unhelpful, which is why I've tried to avoid it in this book. But we do know that, unlike Philip, Charles was born with the questionable luxury of extraordinary security – one day he would become King. Charles didn't put Diana first, perhaps because he never felt he really had to. While for Philip, the homeless Prince, Elizabeth was always number one. Marrying her had quite literally changed his life and he knew it.

Biographers and friends refer to the Duke's sense of loss when George VI died young and Elizabeth was catapulted to the throne prematurely, uprooting Philip and his naval ambitions. But with the benefit of hindsight, their early start was a boon. It allowed the couple to establish monarchy as a romantic idyll while they still possessed the magical sheen of youth. Beside his cherry-blossom Queen, Philip could and did wow the world with his good looks and natural charisma. Being a duke married to Her Majesty gave him lifelong platforms and access beyond his wildest dreams. Far beyond anything he might have enjoyed in the navy.

He knew he was a lucky boy, and Elizabeth felt equally fortunate with her 'strength and stay', whom she'd been devoted to from the age of thirteen. Balance is key to an enduring marriage. But if we want to really understand the glue that held this couple together, we need to return to the Queen's Silver Wedding anniversary. It was 1972 and, with the monarch in comfortable middle age, Elizabeth's reign had acquired a familiar air. The couple's image was gentrified, reassuring and family-focused – so very British. They had come a long way from those idealised, tense early years. The Queen addressed the nation, thanking people for their good wishes and taking the opportunity to impart her own counsel.

> One of the great Christian ideals is a happy and lasting
> marriage between man and wife, but no marriage can
> hope to succeed without a deliberate effort to be tolerant
> and understanding.[17]

That all-important little word 'tolerant' would be echoed exactly twenty-five years later, on the eve of their Golden Wedding anniversary. This time by a grateful Duke.

> I think the main lesson we have learnt is that tolerance is
> the one essential ingredient of any happy marriage . . .
> you can take it from me that the Queen has the quality of
> tolerance in abundance.

The speech, like the Queen's subsequent address at Banqueting House, came at a difficult time, after Diana's death. The press interpreted Philip's words as evidence that the Royal Family had 'softened' and opened up in the wake of public criticism.[18] But history tells us he was simply reaffirming what his wife had shared with the nation twenty-five years earlier. A successful marriage was built on tolerance. In 1997, Philip suggested that, in their relationship, tolerance mainly came from the Queen. Exactly what that says about the dynamics within our late monarch's marriage is open to interpretation, as the Duke no doubt intended. After all, Elizabeth and Philip came from an old-fashioned school of thought – it was important to be seen, but, where possible, royalty should not let in too much 'daylight upon the magic'.

As Walter Bagehot explained, 'its mystery is its life'.[19]

EPILOGUE

So much of the immediate aftermath of death is wrapped in convention, ceremony and occasion, and never more so than in September 2022, with the extraordinary, ornate, state funeral of our longest reigning monarch, Elizabeth II. The Queen died just weeks before this book went to print. Sometimes amid the solemn broadcasts and extensive protocol it has been hard to remember that we are saying goodbye not just to the most famous woman in the world but a real person – a Queen, yes, but also a mother, a grandmother and, perhaps most importantly, Prince Philip's wife. His Elizabeth lived a unique, full and devoted life: so many aspects of Her Majesty's ninety-six years are cause for celebration, the abundant flowers and touching messages tell us that. But responses to death are rarely rational and always unpredictable. My tears caught me by surprise when I stumbled across William, Prince of Wales's testimony to his grandmother on Instagram. He wrote: 'I thank her on behalf of my generation for providing an example of service and dignity in public life that was from a different age, but always relevant to us all.'

His comment was spot on. The Queen, with her prince, led an exemplary public life; they really were model royals for an exceptional generation who held fast on to ideals that no longer always apply in a modern era that is more transitory, vocal and flexible than its predecessor. And there is no better example of Elizabeth's unwavering faith and commitment than her seventy-three year marriage to Philip. Significantly, the Archbishop of Canterbury, Justin Welby, posted a testimony to the late Queen just one day after her death in which he commended Elizabeth's inquiring mind, intelligence, humour and kindness. But it was his observation about Elizabeth and Philip's union that stood out. The Archbishop, a man who had met them both many times, wrote: 'theirs was an inspirational example of Christian marriage – rooted in friendship, nourished by shared faith, and turned outwards in service to others'.

No doubt when there is distance between us and the Queen's death, and as people start to unbutton and share their stories, the narrative on Elizabeth and Philip's relationship will shift. But, right now, mid-September 2022, in the wake of their respective departures, it's important to focus on that idea of their marriage as a union 'turned outwards in the service of others'. Behind closed doors perhaps there is a different tale to be told, but Elizabeth and Philip were not born in an era when the private lives of monarchs were up for grabs. Their marriage, literally, worked: for us, for Britain and for the Commonwealth and the wider world. Out there, glad-handing the masses and attending their subjects, each supported the other, as they had always done from the very beginning of their married life.

Just two days after Elizabeth's death, I talked to Barbara Weatherill, the Queen's contemporary, who we met in the middle of this book. I found her contemplative and perhaps even a little bit apprehensive: 'I always wondered who would go first, the Queen or me.' Barbara's own mortality has been drawn into sharp relief by the passing of a woman who mirrored many of her own milestones, but she recognises her monarch's marriage ended very differently. 'My Stan died in 1988. I have lived thirty-five years alone. I think perhaps, because the Queen had always been in a couple, the change of direction without Philip was difficult. She had never known a life without him. I knew she wouldn't be far behind. At least now they have been reunited.'

Blessed with good health and extreme longevity, the peaches-and-cream Princess and her dashing naval husband really did live on into the sunset of life. No marriage is perfect, but their enduring bond gave the impression that occasionally fairytales really do come true. In the wake of Her Majesty's death, people have talked frequently of the Queen being a 'constant', of her presence providing us all with a sense of 'permanence' and, likewise, that, in a fast-changing world, the durability of Elizabeth marriage anchored us back in time. Certainly it was a union forged in a very different era, when the institutions of monarchy and marriage were immutable and vital. In their relationship Elizabeth and Philip prioritised both.

Barbara sighs, she is not quite ready to let her Queen go but is very glad that 'Charles seems to have been given a warm welcome as King. I was worried, but it looks like monarchy will last'. For today's remaining nonagenarians, the Royal Family is still a key marker of memory and time. Barbara is glued to her television screen: 'They keep saying the Queen is the only monarch we have known. But Charles is my fifth sovereign.' Across a century starting with George V, Elizabeth and Philip were one (extended) episode of family monarchy among many, in which the two protagonists improvised their parts in a script inherited from a world recovering from war. As grandson William observed, Elizabeth II (and her husband) and the ideas they embodied were of their generation, just as Charles III is of his.

NOTES

Introduction

1 Dr Janina Ramirez on Twitter, cited in author's article for *Mailplus*, 21 April 2022.
2 *The Queen at War: A Military Monarch*, BBC Radio 4, first aired 9 September 2022, https://www.bbc.co.uk/programmes/pocz8dg5, retrieved 16 September 2022.
3 Philip Jarman, who is fully introduced in chapter seven.

ONE: WARTIME ROMANCE

1. A Windsor Lockdown

1 Mike Brown, *The Day Peace Broke Out: The VE Day Experience* (Cheltenham: The History Press, 2005), p. 58.
2 HM Queen Elizabeth, talking in *The Way We Were*, BBC documentary, first aired in 1985.
3 Brown, *The Day Peace Broke Out*, p. 121.
4 Ben Pimlott, *The Queen: Elizabeth II and the Monarchy* (London: HarperPress, 2012, ebook), p. 112.
5 Cited in ibid.
6 Conversation and email exchange with Joanne Kavakeb, 7 June 2022.
7 *The Times*, 24 July 1939.
8 Marion Crawford, *The Little Princesses: The Extraordinary Story of the Queen's Childhood by Her Nanny*, foreword by Jennie Bond (Oxford: ISIS, 2002, ebook), pp. 111–12.
9 Alexandra, Queen Consort of Peter II, King of Yugoslavia, *Prince Philip: A Family Portrait* (London: Hodder & Stoughton, 1960), p. 53.
10 Crawford, *The Little Princesses*, p. 111.

11 Crawfie twice refers to Philip's 'Viking' look, ibid, pp. 101, 111.

12 Sarah Bradford, *George VI: The Dutiful King* (London: Penguin, 2011), p. 236.

13 *Henry 'Chips' Channon, The Diaries: 1918–38, Volume One,* Simon Heffer (ed.) (London: Penguin, 2021, ebook), p. 120.

14 Gyles Brandreth, *Philip: The Final Portrait* (London: Coronet, 2021), p. 3; Victoria to her Hesse granddaughters, in Jane Ridley, *The Heir Apparent: A Life of Edward VII, The Playboy Prince* (London: Chatto & Windus, 2012), p. 21.

15 Crawford, *The Little Princesses*, pp. 14, 17–18; Lady Martha Bruce is featured in Tessa Dunlop, *Army Girls: The Secrets and Stories of Military Service from the Final Few Women Who Fought in WWII* (London: Headline, 2021).

16 Andrew Roberts, *Churchill: Walking with Destiny* (London: Penguin, 2018), p. 475.

17 Crawford, *The Little Princesses*, pp. 117, 124.

18 Ibid, p. 112.

19 *The Times*, 30 January 1940.

20 Alathea Fitzalan Howard, *The Windsor Diaries: A Childhood with the Princesses* (London: Hodder and Stoughton, 2020, ebook), p. 69.

21 Ibid, p. 43.

22 Princess Elizabeth's first radio broadcast, 13 October 1940.

23 Fitzalan Howard, *The Windsor Diaries*, p. 87, 103, 111–12, 174, 192, 208; Crawford, *The Little Princesses*, p. 155.

24 Alathea ruefully commented that the girls were 'happier alone with their parents than with anyone else on earth', Fitzalan Howard, ibid, p. 114.

25 Ibid, pp. 78, 111–12, 214, 225.

26 *The Times*, 17 May 1943.

27 Fitzalan Howard, *The Windsor Diaries*, p. 159.

28 Letter from Princess Elizabeth to Queen Mary, *Elizabeth: The Unseen Queen*, BBC documentary, May 2022.

29 Fitzalan Howard, *The Windsor Diaries*, pp. 90, 92, 96.

30 George VI expressed his pleasure that Philip was serving in 'my navy', Brandreth, *Philip*, p. 143.

2. The Aphrodisiac of War

1 Sinclair McKay, *The Lost World Of Bletchley Park: The Illustrated History of the Wartime Codebreaking Centre* (London: Aurum Press, 2013), p. 61.

2 Incident cited in Tessa Dunlop, *The Bletchley Girls: War, Secrecy, Love and Loss, the Women of Bletchley Park Tell Their Story* (London: Hodder & Stoughton, 2015), pp. 173–4.

3 Pamela Rose's wartime story, including her time at Bletchley Park, can be read in Dunlop, *The Bletchley Girls*. The author remained a close friend of Pamela's until her death aged 103 in October 2021. Prince Philip features fleetingly in *The Bletchley Girls* (p. 136), and it was a subject Pamela returned to with the author after the Duke's death in February 2021.

4 Brandreth, *Philip*, pp. 151–2; Philip Eade, *Young Prince Philip: His Turbulent Early Life* (London: HarperPress, 2011), pp. 143–7.

5 Brandreth, ibid.

6 Sarah Baring, *The Road to Station X: From Debutante Ball to Fighter-Plane Factory to Bletchley Park, a Memoir of One Woman's Journey Through World War Two* (London: Sapere Books, 2020, ebook).

7 Ibid., p. 44.

8 *The Times*, 14 July 1939.

9 *Tatler*, 1 February 1939.

10 Eade, *Young Prince Philip*, p. 144.

11 Baring, *The Road to Station X*, pp. 52, 55.

12 Eileen Parker, *Step Aside for Royalty: Treasured Memories of the Royal Household* (Maidstone: Bachman & Turner, 1982), pp. 28, 59.

13 Jane Ridley, *George V: Never a Dull Moment* (London: Vintage, 2021), p. 17.

14 Brandreth also points out that Philip never complained about his childhood; Brandreth, *Prince Philip*, p. 7.

15 Midshipman journal, cited in Eade, *Young Prince Philip*, pp. 136–7.

16 Alexandra of Yugoslavia, *Prince Philip*, p. 64.

17 For a thorough account of this battle and Philip's role in it, see Eade, *Young Prince Philip*, pp. 135–41.

18 Interview with Pamela Rose, May 2022; testimony and Pamela and Rozanne also cited in Dunlop, *The Bletchley Girls*, pp. 222–3

19 Baring, *The Road to Station X*, pp. 44–6.

20 *Daily Telegraph*, 15 February 2013; ibid. p. 45.

21 Baring, ibid.

22 Comment cited in Brandreth, *Philip*, p. 152.

23 Baring, *The Road to Station X*, p. 45.

24 Ridley, *George V*, p. 38.

25 Bradford, *George VI*, p. 126.

26 Citation from Robin Dalton, girlfriend of David Milford Haven, Philip's first cousin, in Robin Dalton, *One Leg Over: Having Fun – Mostly – In Peace And War* (Melbourne: The Text Publishing Company, 2017, ebook), p. 12.

27 Alexandra of Yugoslavia, *Prince Philip*, pp. 55–6.

28 *Daily Mirror*, 14 November 1947.

29 Comment by Osla's daughter, cited in Eade, *Young Prince Philip*, p. 147.

Notes

3. 'Destined for Princess Elizabeth'

1 For more on Uncle David's celebrity and allure in America, see Ted Powell, *King Edward VIII: An American Life* (Oxford: Oxford University Press, 2018).
2 Cited in Tessa Dunlop, *The Century Girls: The Final Word from the Women Who've Lived the Past Hundred Years of British History* (London: Simon & Schuster, 2018), p. 119.
3 Baldwin cited in J. Gardiner, *The Thirties: An Intimate History*, (London: HarperPress, 2010, ebook), p. 378.
4 Edna Cripps in conversation with the author, parts of which are also cited in Dunlop, *The Century Girls*, pp. 119–20.
5 Edward VIII's abdication speech, 11 December 1936.
6 Crawford, *The Little Princesses*, p. 74.
7 Ibid, p. 84.
8 Margaret Rhodes, *The Final Curtsey: A Royal Memoir by the Queen's Cousin* (London: Umbria Press, 2011), p. 32.
9 Crawford, *The Little Princesses*, p. 67.
10 Princess Elizabeth to Diana Bowes-Lyons, 30 November 1943, cited in Brandreth, *Philip*, pp. 157–58.
11 The man in question was Hugh Euston, Hugh Denis Charles FitzRoy, heir to the Duke of Grafton and the incident is noted in Fitzalan Howard, *The Windsor Diaries*, p. 82.
12 *The Times*, 17 April 1943.
13 Fitzalan Howard, *The Windsor Diaries*, p. 122.
14 *Literary Review*, January 1937.
15 Ibid.
16 Henry 'Chips' Channon, *The Diaries: 1938–43, Volume Two*, Simon Heffer (ed.) (London: Penguin, 2021, ebook), p. 502.
17 Alexandra of Yugoslavia, *Prince Philip*, p. 9.
18 James Lees-Milne, *A Mingled Measure: Diaries, 1953–72* (London: John Murray, 1994), p. 183.
19 Prince Philip cited in Brandreth, *Philip*, p. 154.
20 Alexandra of Yugoslavia, *Prince Philip*, p. 66.
21 The author has written about this experience in a memoir, Tessa Dunlop, *To Romania with Love* (London: Quartet Books, 2012).
22 Pimlott, *The Queen*, p. 76; *The Times*, 18, 20 December 1943.
23 Pimlott, ibid, p. 76; Fitzalan Howard, *The Windsor Diaries*, p. 173; *The Times*, 17 April 1944.
24 *The Times*, 20 December 1943; Fitzalan Howard, ibid, p. 174.
25 Fitzalan Howard, ibid.
26 Crawford, *The Little Princesses*, p. 150.

27 The King's private secretary, Sir Alan Lascelles, and Princess Margaret, cited in Alexandra of Yugoslavia, *Prince Philip*, pp. 153–4.

28 Fitzalan Howard, *The Windsor Diaries*, p. 223.

29 Crawford, *The Little Princesses*, p. 172.

30 Alexandra of Yugoslavia, *Prince Philip*, p. 51.

31 Ibid, p. 160; Fitzalan Howard, *The Windsor Diaries*, p. 196.

32 Crawford, *The Little Princesses*, p. 160.

33 Eade, *Young Prince Philip*, pp.150–51.

34 Sir Alan Lascelles, cited in Pimlott, *The Queen*, p. 140; ibid, p. 155.

4. Demob Happy

1 For more about the role of the ATS and Barbara Weatherill's part in it, see Tessa Dunlop, *Army Girls*. For more on Elizabeth's role in that war, see the preface, pp. vii–xii, and ch. 17, pp.170–82.

2 The author has maintained contact with Barbara, and additional information about her service in relation to Princess Elizabeth's has come from interviews both in person and on the telephone throughout the course of 2022.

3 Markham Committee report, cited in Dunlop, *Army Girls*, p. 239.

4 *The Times*, 17 April 1943.

5 The correspondence is held in The National Army Museum archive and cited in Dunlop, *Army Girls*, pp. 170–82.

6 Fitzalan Howard, *The Windsor Diaries*, p. 225.

7 Dunlop, *Army Girls*, p. vii.

8 Ibid, p. xii.

9 Margaret Rhodes, *Final Curtsey*, pp. 68–9.

10 As Philip was described by a local paper in Newcastle in 1944, Eade, *Young Prince Philip*, p. 157.

11 Harry Hargreaves, cited in Brandreth, *Philip*, p.141.

12 Brandreth's own words and citation by Harry Hargreaves, ibid.

13 Parker, cited in ibid, p. 149.

14 Philip, cited by Lady Kennard in ibid, p. 54.

15 Brandreth writes about this funeral, Brandreth, *Philip*, p. 54.

16 For an excellent overview of Alice's life, see Hugo Vickers, *Alice: Princess Andrew of Greece* (London: Hamish Hamilton, 2000).

17 Alexandra of Yugoslavia, *Prince Philip*, p. 44.

18 His later valet, Dean, mentions the photograph in a battered frame that Philip kept with him during the war, John Dean, *HRH Prince Philip: Duke of Edinburgh, a Portrait by His Valet* (London: Robert Hale Limited, 1954), pp. 35–6.

19 Cited in Eade, *Young Prince Philip*, p. 154.
20 Cited in Bradford, *George VI*, p. 556.
21 Ibid, p. 178.
22 Crawford, *The Little Princesses*, p. 175.
23 Ibid.
24 *Elizabeth: The Unseen Queen*, BBC documentary, May 2022.
25 *Daily Mail*, 27 March, 29 May, 1 June 1946.
26 *Elizabeth: The Unseen Queen*, BBC documentary, May 2022.
27 Ibid.
28 Eade, *Young Prince Philip*, pp. 179–80.
29 Max Riddington and Gavan Naden, *Frances: The Remarkable Story of Princess Diana's Mother* (London: Michael O'Mara Books Ltd, 2003), p. 48.
30 Robert Hardman, *Queen Of Our Times: The Life of Elizabeth II* (London: Macmillan, 2022), p. 93.
31 Lady Kennard, cited in Brandreth, *Philip*, pp. 181–2.
32 William Shawcross, *Queen Elizabeth the Queen Mother: The Official Biography* (London: Macmillan, 2009), p. 625.
33 *Daily Express*, 12 August 1946.
34 Brandreth, *Philip*, p. 154.
35 Philip Ziegler, *Mountbatten: The Official Biography* (Glasgow, Fontana, 1986), pp. 102, 175.
36 Ibid, pp. 224, 308.
37 10 August 1944, cited in ibid, p. 308.

TWO: AUSTERITY WEDDING

5. 'Should Our Future Queen Wed Philip?'

1 Daphne Attridge, born June 1923, served in the same military service as Princess Elizabeth and her wartime story is featured in Dunlop, *Army Girls*. She is a good friend of the author and loves talking about the Royal Family. Conversations cited here took place in 2021–2.
2 *The Star*, 7 September 1946.
3 Ibid, 3 September 1945.
4 Ibid.
5 Cited in Edward Owens, *The Family Firm: Monarchy, Mass Media and the British Public, 1932–53* (London: University of London Press, Institute of Historical Research, 2019), pp. 292–93.

6 *Sunday Pictorial*, 1 December 1946.

7 Tom Driberg, cited in a letter by *Daily Express* editor Arthur Christiansen, in Owens, *The Family Firm*, p. 293.

8 *The Times*, 7 December 1946.

9 One former courtier noted this of Mountbatten in the 1940s, Pimlott, *The Queen*, p. 129; 'Nobbling' noted by *Daily Express* editor, cited in Owens, *The Family Firm*, p. 293.

10 Pimlott, ibid, pp. 134–5.

11 *Manchester Guardian*, cited in the *Sunday Pictorial*, 5 January 1947.

12 Cited in *Sunday Pictorial*, 1 December 1946.

13 *Sunday Pictorial*, 5, 12 January 1947.

14 Both newspapers cited in Owens, *The Family Firm*, p. 280.

15 Andrew Marr, *The Diamond Queen: Elizabeth II and her People* (London: Macmillan, 2011), p. 143.

16 *Sunday Pictorial* , 12 January 1947.

17 Ibid.

18 Virginia Woolf, cited in Rosalind Blunt, 'The Family Firm restored: newsreel coverage of the British monarchy 1936–45', in Christine Gledhill and Gillian Swanson (eds), *Nationalising Feminity: Culture, Sexuality and British Cinema in the Second World War* (Manchester: Manchester University Press, 1996), p. 145.

19 *Sunday Pictorial*, 19 January 1947.

20 Ibid.

21 Ibid, 12, 19 January 1947.

22 Cited in Owens, *The Family Firm*, p. 280.

23 Crawford, *The Little Princesses*, pp. 177, 181.

24 Edward VII abdication speech, 11 December 1936.

25 To understand this idea in full, see Blunt, 'The Family Firm restored' pp. 140–51.

26 James Stourton, *Kenneth Clark: Life Art and Civilisation* (London: William Collins, 2017, ebook), p. 101.

27 *News Chronicle*, 3 January 1947, also cited in *Sunday Pictorial*, 5 January 1947.

28 *Time Magazine*, May 1947, p. 18.

29 Peter Townsend, cited in Hugo Vickers, *Elizabeth, The Queen Mother* (London: Hutchinson, 2005), p. 264.

30 Brandreth, *Philip*, pp. 179–80.

31 Originally broadcast 2 June 1947, https://www.bbc.co.uk/archive/royal-tour-of-south-africa-1947/zbyrpg8.

32 Dean, *Prince Philip*, p. 38; Crawford, *The Little Princesses*, pp. 175–85.

33 Crawford, ibid, p. 186.

34 Brandreth, *Philip*, p. 175.
35 *Daily Mail*, 19 March 1947.
36 Pimlott, *The Queen*, p. 99.

6. 'People Will Say We're in Love!'

1 Crawfie also referred to it as the Princess's favourite song at that time. Crawford, *The Little Princesses*, p. 175.
2 Brandreth, *Philip*, p. 184.
3 *Sunday Pictorial*, 19 January 1947
4 Owens, *The Family Firm*, pp. 286–7.
5 As referred to in Pimlott, *The Queen*, p. 157.
6 Monteith, C. Morrah, 'Dermot Michael Macgregor (1896–1974), journalist and herald.' *Oxford Dictionary of National Biography*. Retrieved 30 June 2022, from https://www-oxforddnb-com.lonlib.idm.oclc.org/view/10.1093/ref:odnb/9780198614128.001.0001/odnb-9780198614128-e-31466.
7 Pimlott, *The Queen*, pp. 151–4.
8 Owens, *The Family Firm*, pp. 288–9.
9 Thomas, *Princess Elizabeth: Wife and Mother: A Souvenir of the Birth of Prince Charles of Edinburgh* (London: S. Evelyn Thomas, 1949), p. 47.
10 In Owens' exceptional book I particularly recommend, ch. 5, 'A happy queen is a good queen': the 1947 royal love story; in Owens, *The Family Firm*, pp. 273–330.
11 https://www.vogue.com/slideshow/iconic-photos-of-queen-elizabeth.
12 *Time* magazine, May 1947, p. 18.
13 A. Holdsworth, *Out of the Doll's House: The Story of Women in the Twentieth Century* (London: BBC Books, 1988), pp. 144–6.
14 Crawford, *The Little Princesses*, p.189; cited in Eade, *Young Prince Philip*, p. 252; Brandreth, *Philip*, p. 186.
15 Dean, *Prince Philip*, p. 41.
16 https://www.vogue.co.uk/fashion/gallery/jewellery-philip-gave-the-queen.
17 Dean, *Prince Philip*, p. 50.
18 Dalton, *One Leg Over*, p. 101.
19 Hugo Vickers, *Alice: Princess Andrew of Greece* (London: Hamish Hamilton, 2000), p. 326.
20 Crawford, *The Little Princesses*, pp. 189–90.
21 Vickers, *Alice*, p. 236.
22 Crawford, *The Little Princesses*, p. 192.
23 Vickers, *Alice*, p. 326.
24 Robin Dalton cited in Brandreth, *Philip*, p. 184; Sir Michael Duff in a letter to Ettie Desborough, cited in Eade, *Young Prince Philip*, p. 254.

25 Crawford, *The Little Princesses*, p. 203.
26 Buckingham Palace statement reported in the *Daily Mail*, 10 July 1947.
27 *Daily Mail*, 10 July 1947.
28 History books say 10,000, but all the press at the time reported the party as having 6,000 to 7,000 attendees.
29 Anecdote and letter to Mountbatten cited in Vickers, *Alice*, p. 324.
30 The couple visited Queen Mary at Marlborough House before the Palace Garden Party. Letter from Queen Mary to Prince Alice, cited in ibid; *Manchester Guardian*, 11 July 1947.
31 *Daily Mail*, 10 July 1947.
32 *Daily Express*, 10 July 1947; *Daily Mail*, ibid.
33 *Daily Mirror*, 10 July 1947.
34 'The Royal Romance', *Pathé News*, cited in Owens, *The Family Firm*, p. 304.
35 *Daily Express*, 11, 15 July 1947.
36 *Manchester Guardian*, 19 November 1947.
37 *Daily Mail*, 10 July 1947.
38 Ibid, 11 July 1947; he was 'shy' or at least reluctant about having his photograph taken, *Sunday Pictorial*, 13 July 1947.
39 Alexandra of Yugoslavia, *Prince Philip*, p. 89.
40 *Daily Mail*, 10 July 1947.
41 Gwen Watkins, cited in Dunlop, *Army Girls*, preface.
42 The pictures taken of the *Daily Mirror*'s photographers with the *Daily Mail*'s camera were featured in the *Daily Mirror*, 21 November 1947; Parker, *Step Aside for Royalty*, pp. 137–8.
43 *Elizabeth: The Unseen Queen*, BBC documentary, May 2022.
44 Dean, *Prince Philip*, p. 48.
45 Pimlot, *The Queen*, p. 162; Eade, *The Young Prince Philip*, p. 269.
46 Pimlott, ibid; the murder-in-the-dark anecdote was from courtier Edward Ford, Eade, ibid, p. 266.
47 Mountbatten to Driberg, cited in Eade, *Young Prince Philip*, pp. 259–61.
48 Pimlott, *The Queen*, pp. 167–9.
49 John Julius Norwich (ed.), *The Duff Cooper Diaries 1915–1951* (London: Weidenfeld & Nicolson, 2014, ebook), p. 665.

7. To Love, Cherish and to Obey

1 The author met Philip Jarman when writing about his wife, Cora, and her wartime role at Bletchley Park. That story is in Dunlop, *The Bletchley Girls*. Cora died in 2021 and the author has since maintained contact with Philip, including conversations about the Royal Family. In Philip's words: 'Cora was a great royalist.'

2 *Daily Mail,* 11 May 1946; *Sunday Pictorial,* 7 May 1947.
3 *Sunday Pictorial,* ibid.
4 Ibid, 11, 23 May 1946; *Sunday Pictorial,* 7 September 1947.
5 Crawford, *The Little Princesses,* p. 196.
6 Norman Hartnell, *Silver and Gold: The Autobiography of Norman Hartnell,* pp. 111–14; See also Michael Pick, *Norman Hartnell: The Biography,* (London: Zuleika, 2019)
7 Pick, ibid, p. 201.
8 *Daily Mail,* 27 October 1947.
9 Hartnell, *Silver and Gold,* pp. 111–14
10 Ibid.
11 *Daily Mail,* 27 October 1947, *Daily Mirror,* 15 November 1947.
12 Hartnell, *Silver and Gold,* p. 113.
13 *Sunday Pictorial,* 16 November 1947.
14 *Daily Mirror,* 20 November 1947.
15 Ibid, 13, 14 November 1947.
16 Eade, *Young Prince Philip,* p. 203.
17 Alexandra of Yugoslavia, *Prince Philip,* pp. 31–2.
18 *Sunday Pictorial,* 16 November 1947.
19 *Daily Mail,* 1 November 1947.
20 Alexandra of Yugoslavia, *Portrait, Prince Philip,* p. 95.
21 Smuts cited in John Colville, *The Fringes of Power: Downing Street Diaries, 1939-1955* (London: Hodder & Stoughton, 1985), p. 584; second citation from Sir Michael Duff in Vickers, *Elizabeth, The Queen Mother,* p. 270.
22 *Manchester Guardian,* 23 November 1947.
23 Ibid, 21 November 1947.
24 *The Observer,* 23 November 1947.
25 Marion Crawford, aka Crawfie, writes of how touched Elizabeth was by all the letters and gifts she received from the public before the wedding, Crawford, *The Little Princesses,* p. 206.
26 *The Observer,* 23 November 1947.
27 Alexandra of Yugoslavia, *Prince Philip,* pp. 97–8.
28 Ibid, p. 97; Sir Michael Duff, cited in Vickers, *Elizabeth, The Queen Mother,* p. 270.
29 Vickers, ibid.
30 *Manchester Guardian,* 21 November 1947.
31 Bridesmaid Pamela Hicks née Mountbatten, cited in Pimlott, *The Queen,* p. 177.
32 *The Observer,* 23 November 1947.
33 Ibid.
34 Daphne Attridge in conversation with the author, June 2022.

35 *Daily Mail*, 21 November 1947.

36 Lucy Worsley, *Queen Victoria: Daughter, Wife, Mother, Widow* (London: Hodder & Stoughton, 2018), p. 148.

37 Footage shown in *Elizabeth: The Unseen Queen*, BBC documentary, May 2022.

38 *Daily Mail*, 20 November 1947.

39 Thomas, *Princess Elizabeth, Wife and Mother*, pp. 14–20; Mrs Fisher, wife of the Archbishop of Canterbury, cited in Pimlot, *The Queen*, p. 178.

40 *Sunday Pictorial*, 12 January 1947.

41 George VI to Princess Elizabeth, cited in Bradford, *George VI*, p. 559.

42 Cited in Worsley, *Queen Victoria*, p. 148.

43 Alexandra of Yugoslavia, *Prince Philip*, pp. 97, 99.

44 *Daily Mirror*, 21 November 1947.

45 Ibid.

46 *Daily Mirror*, 24 November 1947.

47 Rhodes, *The Final Curtsey*, p. 36.

48 Alexandra of Yugoslavia, *Prince Philip*, p. 99.

49 *Daily Mirror*, 21 November 1947.

50 Ibid.

51 He refers to it as a 'a kind of misreporting' that came to define the coverage of the royal honeymoon, Owens, *The Family Firm*, p. 325.

52 Mass Observation commentators (who tended to have a left-of-centre bias), cited in Owens, *The Family Firm*, p. 324.

53 *Daily Mirror*, 21 November 1947.

8. Married Life

1 The word that John Dean, Philip's valet, used to describe the media invasion at Broadlands, Dean, *Prince Philip*, p. 61.

2 Elizabeth to the Queen, 22 November 1947, cited in William Shawcross, *Queen Elizabeth, the Queen Mother: The Official Biography* (London: Macmillan, 2009), p. 630.

3 Rhodes, *Final Curtsey*, p. 35.

4 Elizabeth to the Queen, 30 November 1947, cited in Shawcross, *Queen Elizabeth, the Queen Mother*, p. 631.

5 Queen Elizabeth to Philip, 1 December 1947, cited in William Shawcross (ed.), *Counting One's Blessings: The Collected Letters of Queen Elizabeth the Queen Mother* (London: Macmillan, 2012, ebook), loc. 7250.

6 Cited in Alexandra of Yugoslavia's book, she also comments on the irony, Alexandra of Yugoslavia, *Prince Philip*, p. 100.

7   Cited in Shawcross, *Queen Elizabeth, the Queen Mother*, p. 786.
8   Dean, *Prince Philip*, p. 139.
9   Elizabeth cited in Shawcross, *Queen Elizabeth, the Queen Mother*, p. 785.
10 *Daily Mail*, 10 July 1947.
11 Several references to the house and its refurbishment are made, *Daily Mail*, 10, 12 July 1947.
12 Alexandra of Yugoslavia, *Prince Philip*, p. 93.
13 *Sunday Pictorial*, 30 August 1947.
14 Crawford, *The Little Princesses*, p. 230.
15 Dean, *Prince Philip*, p. 139.
16 Colville, 15 December 1947, cited in Pimlott, *The Queen*, p. 144.
17 Dean, *Prince Philip*, p. 52.
18 Ibid, pp. 52–3.
19 Vickers, *Alice: Princess Andrew of Greece*, p. 345.
20 Patricia Mountbatten's husband, Lord Brabourne, cited in Brandreth, *Philip*, p. 207.
21 James Pope-Hennessy, Hugo Vickers (ed.), *The Quest for Queen Mary* (London: Hodder & Stoughton, 2018), p.87.
22 *Sunday Pictorial*, 2 November 1947.
23 Dean, *Prince Philip*, p. 93.
24 Ibid, p. 43.
25 Crawford, *Little Princesses*, p. 208–9.
26 Dean, *Prince Philip*, pp. 46–7, 93.
27 *Sunday Pictorial*, 2 November 1947; ibid, pp. 93–5.
28 https://www.townandcountrymag.com/society/tradition/a27241862/prince-philip-driving-private-road-photo-2019/.
29 *Sunday Pictorial*, 2 November 1947.
30 Parker, *Step Aside for Royalty*, p. 35.
31 Colville, *The Fringes of Power*, p. 582.
32 Norwich (ed.), *The Duff Cooper Diaries*, pp. 665, 681.
33 *Daily Mirror*, 6 May 1948.
34 Ibid, 18 May 1948; Bradford, *Elizabeth*, p. 140.
35 Colville, *The Fringes of Power*, p. 588; Valet John Dean also commented on Philip's endurance in the face of illness, news of which never broke in the press, Dean, *Prince Philip*, p. 78; Bradford, *Elizabeth*, p. 140.
36 Dean, *Prince Philip*, p. 77.
37 *Daily Mirror*, 18 May 1948.
38 Colville, *The Fringes of Power*, p. 588; *Daily Mirror*, 15 May 1948.
39 Hartnell, *Silver and Gold*, p. 116.

Notes

9. Domestic Bliss?

1 *The New Standard*, 30 July 1981.
2 Cartland cited in Dunlop, *The Century Girls*, p. 190.
3 Beveridge Report cited in ibid, p. 181.
4 Thomas, *Princess Elizabeth, Wife and Mother*, p. 3.
5 Crawford, *The Little Princesses*, p. 233.
6 Ibid, p. 237.
7 In his introduction to the 1993 reprint of the book, A. N Wilson referred to it as mawkish but 'written with obvious love'. Cited in Pimlott, *The Queen*, pp. 204–5; in Jennie Bond's foreword in the latest edition of *The Little Princesses*, she refers to it as a 'charming, hopelessly romantic chronicle', Jennie Bond, Foreword, ibid, p. 5; for the most reliable detailed account of the book's publication, see Vickers, *Elizabeth, the Queen Mother*, pp. 279–91.
8 Crawford, ibid, p. 39.
9 Vickers, *Elizabeth, the Queen Mother*, p. 92.
10 Information from a private conversation with a royal biographer.
11 *Daily Mail*, 15 November 1948.
12 Ibid.
13 Harold Nicolson to Vita Sackville-West, 8 June 1948, cited in Bradford, *Elizabeth*, p. 133.
14 Thomas, *Princess Elizabeth, Wife and Mother*, pp. 22–9.
15 *Sunday Graphic*, 19 April 1953.
16 *Daily Mail*, 15 November 1947; Thomas, *Princess Elizabeth, Wife and Mother*, pp. 8–9.
17 Parker, *Step Aside for Royalty*, p. 51; Thomas, ibid, pp. 3–13.
18 Dean, *Prince Philip*, p. 50.
19 https://youtu.be/44J4_ESXGWI, retrieved 25 July 2022.
20 Mellor, R. 'Kirkwood, Patricia [Pat] (1921–2007), actress and singer.' *Oxford Dictionary of National Biography*, https://www-oxforddnb-com. lonlib.idm.oclc.org/view/10.1093/ref:odnb/9780198614128.001.0001/ odnb-9780198614128-e-99293 retrieved 25 July 2022.
21 Robin Dalton provides a useful summary of Browning's Thursday Club, Dalton, *One Leg Over*, pp. 887–8.
22 There are numerous accounts of this meeting in most biographies, and it also resurfaced in the press in 1957. For a reliable overview, see Eade, *Young Prince Philip*, pp. 218–19.
23 *Independent on Sunday*, 4 April 1993.
24 *Daily Express*, 27 December 2007.
25 *Daily Mirror*, 15 January 1996.

26 Brandreth, *Philip*, pp. 59–62.

27 As described in ibid, p. 59.

28 See particularly Dean, *Prince Philip*, p. 75; Anne Glenconner, *Lady In Waiting: My Extraordinary Life in the Shadow of Royalty* (London: Hodder & Stoughton, 2019, ebook), p. 187.

29 Colville unpublished diary, 30 Oct 1947, cited in Pimlott, *The Queen*, p. 176.

30 Ibid, p. 318.

31 1988 photograph and David Bailey citation featured at the 'Life Through a Lens' exhibition, Kensington Palace, 2022.

32 There is a comprehensive book that covered the exhibition but, interestingly, the Holyoak photograph of Elizabeth and Philip is omitted, Claudia Acott Williams, *The Crown in Focus: Two Centuries of Royal Photography* (London, New York: Merrell, 2020).

33 Eade, *Young Philip*, pp. 199–200.

34 *Daily Mail*, 15 July 1982.

35 Marie Stopes, cited in Claire Langhamer, *The English in Love: The Intimate Story of an Emotional Revolution* (Oxford: Oxford University Press, 2013), p. 185.

36 Dean, *Prince Philip*, p. 112.

37 Langhamer, *The English in Love*, p. 185.

38 For example Eade, *Young Philip*, p. 228.

39 Vickers, *Elizabeth, the Queen Mother*, p. 309; Parker, *Step Aside for Royalty*, p. 74.

40 Pope-Hennessy, *The Quest of Queen Mary*, p. 94.

41 Crawford, *The Little Princesses*, p. 181.

42 Crawfie said as much to Alathea during their time at Windsor during World War II, Fitzalan Howard, *The Windsor Diaries*, p. 225.

43 James Stourton, *Kenneth Clark*, pp. 288–9.

44 Crawford, *The Little Princesses*, pp. 181, 207.

45 Dean, *Prince Philip*, pp. 98–99.

46 Pope-Hennessy, *The Quest of Queen Mary*, p. 94.

47 Marie, Queen of Roumania, *The Story of My Life*, vol. 1 (London: Cassell and Company, 1934), p. 105.

48 Ibid, pp. 103, 105.

49 Brandreth, *Prince Philip*, p. 233.

50 Basil Boothroyd, *Prince Philip: An Informal Biography* (Harlow: Longman, 1971), p. 144; Eade, *Young Prince Philip*, p. 237.

51 This much repeated 'happiest time' description was valet John Dean's. Certainly, 'it was a good time', as described by Philip and one clearly enjoyed by the staff (including Parker, for whom it

was a 'fabulous time'). Dean, *Prince Philip*, p. 117; Brandeth, *Philip*, p. 233; Eade, *Young Philip*, ch.18 'Their Happiest Time', pp. 227–40.

52 Ziegler, *Mountbatten*, pp. 491–2.
53 Brandreth, *Prince Philip*, p. 232; *Elizabeth: The Unseen Queen*, BBC documentary, May 2022.
54 Janet Morgan, *Edwina Mountbatten: A Life of Her Own* (London: HarperCollins, 1991), p. 444; Dean, *Prince Philip*, p. 121.
55 Ziegler, *Mountbatten*, p. 492.
56 Morgan, *Edwina Mountbatten*, p. 440.
57 Ibid, p. 444.

THREE: MONARCHY

10. 'Good Health is a Precious Gift'

1 Conversation with the author, 8 May 2022. Pat and Jean Owtram also feature in Dunlop, *The Bletchley Girls* and *Army Girls* respectively. See also Pat and Jean Owtram, *Codebreaking Sisters, Our Secret War* (London: Mirror Books, 2020).
2 Bradford, *George VI*, pp. 600–1
3 Ibid, p. 594.
4 The King did not seek medical help until October 1948, ibid. A royal aide cited in Pimlott, *The Queen*, p. 198.
5 Crawford, *The Little Princesses*, pp. 16, 194, 239.
6 Winston Churchill, broadcast 7 February 1952.
7 Professor Harold Ellis, cited in the *Guardian*, 28 April 2015.
8 Dean, *Prince Philip*, pp. 46, 56.
9 This report appeared in April 1953, but according to Philip's valet, the Duke gave up smoking for his wedding, *Sunday Graphic*, 19 April 1953.
10 Dean, *Prince Philip*, p. 56.
11 Ibid, p. 101.
12 Ibid.
13 An Alan Lascelles comment recalled by James Pope-Hennessy, cited in Pope-Hennessy, *The Quest for Queen Mary*, Vicker (ed.), p. 18.
14 *Sunday Graphic*, 24 May 1953.
15 *The Sun*, 22 August 2021; *Daily Mail*, 19 August 2021.
16 Conversation with Hugo Vickers, 30 May 2022.
17 Brandreth, *Prince Philip*, pp. 23–4.

18 Pierre Berton, 'The Family in the Palace: the first taste of queenship', *Maclean's*, 1 May 1953.

19 Ibid.

20 *Life*, 12 November 1951.

21 Berton, *Maclean's*, 1 May 1953.

22 Ibid.

23 Dean, *Prince Philip*, p. 132.

24 Berton, *Maclean's*, 1 May 1953; *The Des Moines Register*, Iowa, 1 November 1951.

25 *The Des Moines Register*, ibid.

26 *Life*, 1 October 1951.

27 For a scholarly examination of 1950s marriage, see Janet Finch and Penny Summerfield, 'Social reconstruction and the emergence of companionate marriage, 1945–59', David Clark (ed.), *Marriage, Domestic Life and Social Change:, Writings for Jacqueline Burgoyne, 1944–88* (London: Routledge, May 1991), pp. 7–31.

28 Berton, *Maclean's*, 1 May 1953.

29 Princess Elizabeth to George VI, cited in *Elizabeth: The Unseen Queen*, BBC documentary, May 2022.

30 Ibid.

31 Pimlott, *The Queen*, p. 526.

32 Cited in ibid, p. 553.

33 *Life*, 1 October 1951; Berton, *Maclean's*, 1 May 1953.

34 *Life*, 12 November 1951; Martin Charteris, cited in Pimlott, *The Queen*, p. 213.

35 Roberts, *Churchill*, pp. 928–9.

36 Cited in ibid.

37 Newsreel footage in *Elizabeth: The Unseen Queen*, BBC documentary, May 2022.

38 His Majesty's Christmas Broadcast, December 1951.

39 Newsreel footage in *Elizabeth: The Unseen Queen*, BBC documentary, May 2022.

40 Archive footage, *Royal Beat*, True Royalty TV, 3 February 2022.

41 *Daily Express*, 7 February 1952.

42 Roberts, *Churchill*, p. 929.

43 First quote from the Queen's Private Secretary Martin Charteris, and second from Sarah Bradford in the same book, Bradford, *Elizabeth*, p. 166.

44 Parker, *Step Aside for Royalty*, p. 104.

11. An Elizabethan 'Golden Age'

1   Wesley Kerr, 'Long to reign over us?', *Tatler*, July 2022, p. 104.
2   *Royal Beat*, True Royalty TV, 3 February 2022.
3   Ibid.
4   James Pope-Hennessy, cited in Bradford, *Elizabeth*, p. 172.
5   Parker, *Step Aside for Royalty*, p. 106.
6   *Daily Express*, 8 February 1952.
7   Winston Churchill, cited in Bradford, *Elizabeth*, p. 174.
8   *Sunday Graphic*, 17 February 1952.
9   Ibid.
10 Bradford, *Elizabeth*, p. 168; Pimlott, *The Queen*, p. 222.
11 Bradford, ibid.
12 David Cannadine, 'Churchill and the British Monarchy', *Transactions of the Royal Historical Society*, 2001, vol. 11, p. 267.
13 A female clerk, cited in Bradford, *Elizabeth*, p. 179.
14 Ibid, p. 174.
15 David Cannadine makes this point, Cannadine, 'Churchill and the British Monarchy', p. 267.
16 Worsley, *Queen Victoria*, p. 111.
17 Cited in ibid.
18 Cannadine, 'Churchill and the British Monarchy', p. 267.
19 Brandreth, *Prince Philip*, p. 66.
20 Bradford, *Elizabeth*, pp. 177–8.
21 Ibid, pp. 176–7; Cannadine, 'Churchill and the Monarchy', p. 269.
22 Basil Boothroyd, *Philip*, p. 39.
23 Cited in Pimlott, *The Queen*, p. 228.
24 In spite of the difficulties that Churchill threw up for the Duke, Dean believed that the latter was 'very fond' of the Prime Minister. Dean, *Prince Philip*, p. 162.
25 Jonathan Dimbleby, *The Prince of Wales: A Biography* (London: Warner Books, 1994), p. 53.
26 Boothroyd, *Philip*, p. 49.
27 Parker, *Step Aside for Royalty*, pp. 74–75, 84.
28 Dean, *Prince Philip*, pp. 154–55.
29 Cited in Bradford, *Elizabeth*, p. 179.
30 Dean, *Prince Philip*, p. 157.
31 Parker, *Step Aside For Royalty*, p. 113.
32 Ibid, p. 122.
33 J. Bowlby, *Maternal Care and Mental Health* (New York: Schocken Books, 1966; 1st edn, 1950). His work was soon converted into the new mother's bible, *Childcare and the Growth of Love*.

34 Dunlop, *The Century Girls*, p. 187.

35 Dean, *Prince Philip*, p. 172.

36 In the early chapters of his biography, Jonathan Dimbleby makes pointed references to Elizabeth and Philip's absences; Dimbleby, *The Prince of Wales*, pp. 19, 26–7.

37 Prince Harry, broadcast, 13 May 2021.

38 Parker, *Step Aside for Royalty*, p. 89.

39 Duke of Edinburgh, cited in James Wilkinson, *The Queen's Coronation: The Inside Story* (London: Scala, 2011), foreword.

40 Winston Churchill, cited in Roberts, *Churchill*, p. 935.

41 Winston Churchill, cited in Bradford, *Elizabeth*, p. 180.

42 Cited in Wilkinson, *The Queen's Coronation*, foreword.

43 *Good Housekeeping*, 13 April 2020.

44 Wilkinson, *The Queen's Coronation*, p. 12.

45 Owens, *The Family Firm*, p. 336.

46 Ibid, pp. 337–8; Cannadine, 'Churchill and the Monarchy', p. 267.

47 Owens, *The Family Firm*, pp. 338–9.

48 Ibid, pp. 339–40

49 Photograph and broadcast in *The Platinum Queen: Over 75 Speeches Given by Britain's Longest-Reigning Monarch*, with a foreword by Jennie Bond (London: Allen and Unwin, 2022), pp. 16–17.

50 Philip's library contained several hundred volumes on religious and spiritual matters, Brandreth, *Philip*, p. 34.

51 James Pope-Hennessy, *The Quest for Queen Mary*, p. 115.

52 For Philip's input into the service, see Wilkinson, *The Queen's Coronation*.

53 Dean, *Prince Philip*, pp. 163–4.

54 Parker, *Step Aside for Monarchy*, pp. 119–21.

55 Cited in *Elizabeth: The Unseen Queen*, BBC documentary, May 2022.

56 Dean, *Prince Philip*, p. 164.

12. 'I Have My Husband to Support Me'

1 Glenconner, *Lady in Waiting*, pp. 61–2.

2 *The Times*, cited in https://www.bbc.co.uk/news/magazine-22688498 retrieved 23 August 2022; Charles, cited in Dimbleby, *Prince Charles*, p. 23.

3 Author's interview with her mother, Anthea Dunlop, 18 August 2022.

4 Statistics from https://www.bbc.co.uk/news/magazine-22688498 retrieved 23 August 2022.

5 *Daily Mirror*, 1 June 1953.

6 Owens, *The Family Firm*, p. 361.

7 Ibid, pp. 356–69.

8 Cited in Brandreth, *Prince Philip*, p. 261.

9 Dimbleby, *Prince Charles*, p. 23.

10 Cecil Beaton, *The Strenuous Years: 1948–55, Cecil Beaton's Diaries, Book 4*, (London: Sapere Books, London, 2018, ebook), p. 180; Glenconner, *Lady in Waiting*, pp. 62, 68.

11 *Daily Mirror*, 1 June 1953.

12 Glenconner, *Lady in Waiting*, p. 60.

13 Ibid, p. 68.

14 *Daily Mirror*, 3 June 1953.

15 Beaton, *The Strenuous Years*, pp. 185–7.

16 Beaton, ibid, pp. 184–5; Glenconner, *Lady in Waiting*, p. 76.

17 Beaton, ibid, p. 184.

18 Brandreth, *Prince Philip*, pp. 267–9.

19 Beaton, *The Strenuous Years*, p. 187.

20 HM the Queen, broadcast, 2 June 1953.

21 *Daily Express*, cited in Ruth P. Feingold, 'Marketing the Modern Empire: Elizabeth II and the 1953–54 World Tour', *Antipodes*, December 2009, vol. 23. no. 2, p. 149.

22 HM the Queen, Christmas broadcast, 1953.

23 *Daily Mirror*, 3 June 1953.

24 *The People*, 14 June 1953.

25 Ibid.

26 *Sunday Graphic*, 20 April 1952.

27 Roberts, *Churchill*, pp. 937–8.

28 *Sunday Graphic*, 19 July 1953.

29 Crawford, *The Little Princesses*, p. 98.

30 Parker, *Step Aside for Royalty*, pp. 146–8.

31 *Sunday Graphic*, 26 July 1953.

32 Glenconner, *Lady in Waiting*, p. 75.

33 Cited in Bradford, *Elizabeth*, p. 205.

34 Cited in ibid, p. 203.

35 Cited in ibid, p. 211.

13. Keeping Up Appearances

1 Cited in Feingold, 'Marketing the Modern Empire', p. 150.

2 This point is made and quotations cited in ibid.

3　Conversation with Sheila and Jon Albrecht, 20 August 2022. Conversation supplemented with references to Shelia's unpublished memoir: *Those Were the Best Days – and the Rest*, 2018.

4　For more on the significance of coronation souvenirs see Feingold, 'Marketing the Modern Empire', pp. 147–54.

5　*Sydney Morning Herald*, 27 January, 2 February 1954.

6　*Sunday Graphic*, 10 February 1952.

7　H. V. Nelles, cited in Feingold, 'Marketing the Modern Empire', p. 149; Feingold cites a similar argument but focuses on the reciprocity of Imperial/Commonwealth identities.

8　*Sydney Morning Herald*, 22, 28 January, 1 February 1954.

9　Ibid, 16 January 1954; Robert Hardman, *Queen of the World* (London, Century, London, 2018), p. 188.

10　Hardman, ibid, pp. 188–9.

11　*Woman's Day* ran the extracts advertised in *Sydney Morning Herald*, 19 January 1954; Feingold, 'Marketing the Modern Empire', p. 152.

12　Cited in Feingold, 'Marketing the Modern Empire', p. 151.

13　Footage of the decommissioning ceremony can be seen here: https://www.youtube.com/watch?v=4uL_eiiHNVU, accessed 22 August 2022.

14　Alan Bennett described the Queen as obliged to go on a 'mournabout', Alan Bennett, *Untold Stories* (London: Faber and Faber, 2005), pp. 215–16.

15　Hardman, *Queen of the World*, pp. 350–1.

16　Dimbleby, *The Prince of Wales*, p. 26.

17　Hardman, *Queen of the World*, p. 352; Bradford, *Elizabeth*, pp. 219–20.

18　Hardman, ibid, p. 366; Jellyfish detail from Viacom research team filming 'The Royal Yacht Britannia'.

19　Deborah Clarke and Sally Goodsir, *Prince Philip, 1921–2021: A Celebration* (London: Royal Collection Trust, 2021), pp. 60–63; Hardman, *Queen of the World*, pp. 366–7.

20　Hardman, ibid, p. 366; the *Daily Express* talked about the single bed being replaced with a king-sized one for Charles and Diana's honeymoon, *Daily Express*, 30 July 1981.

21　Elieen Parker describes her husband as a court jester, Parker, *Step Aside for Royalty*, p. 64.

22　Ibid.

23　Ibid, p. 63.

24　Valet John Dean explains that Daphne du Maurier wrote all her novels in their Cornwall home while Browning was up in London, Dean, *Prince Philip*, p. 113; ibid, p. 63; *Daily Mail*, 15 October 2020.

25　http://www.uffafox.com/uffabiog.htm, accessed 23 August 2022.

26　Parker, *Step Aside For Royalty*, pp. 63–7.

27 Ibid.
28 Cited in Langhamer, *The English in Love*, p. 178.
29 Parker, *Step Aside for Royalty*, p. 67; Hardman, *Queen of the World*, p. 367.
30 Langhamer, *The English in Love*, pp. 185–6.
31 Pimlott, *The Queen*, pp. 142–3.
32 *Radio Times*, 18 November 2019.
33 *Guardian*, 29 July 2022.
34 Ibid, 18 November 2021.
35 Clarke and Goodsir, *Prince Philip*, p. 72.
36 Parker, *Step Aside for Royalty*, pp. 175–8.
37 Langhamer, *The English in Love*, pp. 177–8.
38 The *Tatler* family photograph is featured in Parker's book. Parker, *Step Aside for Royalty*.
39 Ibid, p. 178.
40 *Sunday Pictorial*, 2 February 1957.
41 *Daily Mirror*, 7 February 1957.
42 Brandreth, *Prince Philip*, pp. 290–91.
43 Parker, *Step Aside for Royalty*, p. 181.
44 *Baltimore Sun*, cited in *Daily Mirror*, 12 February 1957.
45 Said to members of the Mothers' Union in 1949, cited in Brandreth, *Prince Philip*, p. 233; *Daily Mirror*, 12 February 1957.
46 *Sunday Graphic*, cited in *Daily Mirror*, 11, 12 February 1957.
47 Brandreth, *Prince Philip*, p. 292.
48 Ibid, p. 293.

14. A 'Tolerant and Understanding' Marriage

1 Her Majesty the Queen, broadcast, 1 November 2021.
2 Ibid; *Daily Telegraph*, 3 November 2021; *Daily Mirror*, 3 November 2021; *Washington Post*, 1 November 2011.
3 Hardman, *Queen of the World*, p. 188.
4 Author's conversation with Joyce Reynolds, 14 May 2022, and further citations from Dunlop, *The Century Girls*, p. 216.
5 *The New Yorker*, 14 January 1956.
6 Pope-Hennessy, *The Quest for Queen Mary*, p. 222.
7 Ibid.
8 Lord Altrincham, 'The Monarchy Today', *The National and English Review*, vol. 149, August 1957, pp. 61–6.
9 Bradford, *Elizabeth*, p. 240.
10 Ibid, p. 241.
11 Altrincham, 'The Monarchy Today', pp. 62, 65.

12 Ibid, p. 63.
13 BBC online, 9 June 2011; https://www.bbc.co.uk/news/uk-13682432, accessed 26 August 2022.
14 Ibid.
15 Dimblely, *Prince Charles*, pp. 3–114.
16 *The Sun*, 22 August 2021; *Tatler*, cited in Brandreth, *Prince Philip*, p. 19.
17 Her Majesty, cited in *The Platinum Queen*, p. 78.
18 Duke of Edinburgh, 19 November 1997, https://www.youtube.com/watch?v=xRx6dSrkk6o, accessed 27 August 2022.
19 Walter Bagehot, cited in: Walter Bagehot - Oxford Reference, accessed 27 August 2022.

BIBLIOGRAPHY

◆◇◆

A staggering number of books have been written on the subject Her Majesty the Queen, and that's just in the duration of her (admittedly long) lifetime – many more will follow in the decades to come. I suspect she was not only one of the most photographed women in the world but also one of the most written about. Needless to say, certain biographies and histories stand out in terms of research and quality and it is to them that I owe the greatest debt in the writing of this book. A particular mention must go to Sarah Bradford's and Ben Pimlott's respective biographies. I also found Robert Hardman's *Queen of the World* a very useful resource.

Although the late Duke will never catch up with his wife, a glut of books about his life have appeared in recent years – I found both Philip Eade's interpretation of Philip's early years and Gyles Brandreth's comprehensive and intimate portrait invaluable, and strongly recommend them to any reader on a quest to find out more.

Beyond Elizabeth and Philip, this is also a story both about a family and an era – and again certain books proved immensely helpful. Hugo Vickers' affectionate biography *Elizabeth, the Queen Mother* has been a constant companion; ditto his edited edition of James Pope-Hennessy's *Quest for Queen Mary* – full of glorious descriptions and anecdotes. Academic interpretations always produce more light than heat and I was grateful for Edward Owens thought-provoking *The Family Firm*. Alongside interviews with those who have lived our most recent history, I also lent heavily on memoirs from individuals who served and worked alongside Elizabeth and Philip – including, most recently, Alathea Fitzalan Howard's wonderful *The Windsor Diaries*. As well as Marion Crawford's better known text *The Little Princesses*, I found equerry Mike Parker's ex-wife Eileen's memoir, *Step Aside for Royalty*, particularly helpful.

To ensure this book captured the feel and tone of the 1940s–50s, contemporary newspaper and newsreel coverage are firmly embedded within the text. All the publications accessed are cited below as well as helpful websites.

BOOKS

Acott Williams, Claudia, *The Crown in Focus: Two Centuries of Royal Photography* (London, New York: Merrell, 2020)

Alexandra, Queen Consort of Peter II, King of Yugoslavia, *Prince Philip: A Family Portrait* (London: Hodder & Stoughton, 1959)

Arbiter, Dickie and Lynne, *On Duty with the Queen* (London: Blink Publishing, 2014)

Baring, Sarah, *The Road to Station X: From Debutante Ball to Fighter-Plane Factory to Bletchley Park, a Memoir of One Woman's Journey Through World War Two* (London: Sapere Books, 2020)

Bradford, Sarah, *Elizabeth: A Biography of Britain's Queen* (London: William Heinemann, 1996)

Bradford, Sarah, *Elizabeth II, Her Life in Our Times* (London: Penguin, 2011)

Bradford, Sarah, *George VI* (London: Penguin, 2011)

Beaton, Cecil, *The Strenuous Years: 1948–55, Cecil Beaton's Diaries, Book 4* (London: Sapere Books, 2018)

Beaton, Cecil, *The Happy Years, 1944–48, Cecil Beaton's Diaries, Book 3* (London: Sapere Books, 2018)

Bennett, Alan, *Untold Stories* (London: Faber & Faber, 2005)

Birt, Catherine, *The Royal Sisters,* vol. 1, (London: A. H & W. L. Pitkin Ltd, 1949)

Brandreth, Gyles, *Philip: The Final Portrait* (London: Coronet, 2021)

Brendon, Piers, *Edward VIII: The Uncrowned King* (London: Allen Lane, 2016)

Boothroyd, Basil, *Prince Philip: An Informal Biography* (Harlow: Longman, 1971)

Brown, Mike, *The Day Peace Broke Out: The VE Day Experience* (Stroud: Sutton Publishing, 2005)

Bowlby, J., *Maternal Care and Mental Health* (New York: Schocken Books, 1966)

Channon, Henry 'Chips', *The Diaries: 1918–38, Volume 1,* Simon Heffer (ed.) (London: Penguin, 2021)

Channon, Henry 'Chips', *The Diaries: 1938–43, Volume 2,* Simon Heffer (ed.) (London: Penguin, 2022)

Clarke, Deborah and Goodsir, Sally, *Prince Philip, 1921–2021: A Celebration* (London: Royal Collection Trust, 2021)

Colville, John, *The Fringes of Power: Downing Street Diaries 1939–1955* (London: Hodder & Stoughton, 1985)

Crawford, Marion, *The Little Princesses: The Story of the Queen's Childhood by her Governess,* foreword by Jennie Bond (Oxford: ISIS, 2002)

Dalton, Robin, *One Leg Over: Having Fun – Mostly – In Peace And War* (Melbourne: The Text Publishing Company, 2017)

Dimbleby, Jonathan, *The Prince of Wales: A Biography* (London: Warner Books, 1994)

Dean, John, *HRH Prince Philip: Duke of Edinburgh, a Portrait by His Valet* (London: Robert Hale Limited, 1954)

Dunlop, Tessa, *Army Girls: The Secrets and Stories of Military Service from the Final Few Women Who Fought in WWII* (London: Headline, 2021)

Dunlop, Tessa, *The Bletchley Girls: War, Secrecy, Love and Loss, the Women of Bletchley Park Tell Their Story* (London: Hodder & Stoughton, 2015)

Dunlop, Tessa, *The Century Girls: The Final Word from the Women Who've Lived the Past Hundred Years of British History* (London: Simon & Schuster, 2018)

Eade, Philip, *Young Prince Philip: His Turbulent Early Life* (London: HarperPress, 2011)

Finch, David (ed.), *Marriage, Domestic Life and Social Change: Writings for Jacqueline Burgoyne, 1944–88* (London: Routledge, May 1991)

Gardiner, J., *The Thirties: An Intimate History* (London: HarperPress, 2010)

Gledhill, Christine and Swanson, Gillian, (eds) *Nationalising Feminity: Culture, Sexuality and British Cinema in the Second World War* (Manchester: Manchester University Press, 1996)

Glenconner, Anne, *Lady In Waiting: My Extraordinary Life in the Shadow of Royalty* (London: Hodder & Stoughton, 2019)

Hardman, Robert, *Queen of the World* (London: Century, 2018)

Hardman, Robert, *Queen of Our Times: The Life of Elizabeth II* (London: Macmillan, 2022)

Hartnell, Norman, *Silver and Gold: The Autobiography of Norman Hartnell* (London: V&A Publishing, 2019)

HRH The Duke of Kent and Vickers, Hugo, *A Royal Life* (London: Hodder & Stoughton, 2022)

Holdsworth, Angela, *Out of the Doll's House: The Story of Women in the Twentieth Century* (London: BBC Books, 1988)

Howard, Alathea Fitzalan, *The Windsor Diaries: A Childhood with the Princesses* (London: Hodder & Stoughton, 2020)

Lacey, Robert, *Majesty: Elizabeth II and the House of Windsor* (London: Hutchinson, 1977)

Langhamer, Claire, *The English in Love: The Intimate Story of an Emotional Revolution* (Oxford: Oxford University Press, 2013)

Lees-Milne, James, *A Mingled Pleasure: Diaries, 1953–72* (London: John Murray, 1994)

Marie, Queen of Roumania, *The Story of my Life*, vol. 1 (London: Cassell and Company, 1934)

Marr, Andrew, *The Diamond Queen: Elizabeth II and her People* (London: Macmillan, 2011)

McKay, Sinclair, *The Lost World Of Bletchley Park: An Illustrated History of the Wartime Codebreaking Centre*(London: Aurum Press, 2013)

Morgan, Janet, *Edwina Mountbatten: A Life of Her Own* (London: HarperCollins, 1991)

Murphy, Deirdre and Davies-Strodder, Cassie, *Modern Royal Fashion: Seven Royal Women and Their Style* (London: Historic Royal Palaces, 2015)

Nicholson, Virginia, *Perfect Wives in Ideal Homes: The Story of Women in the 1950s* (London: Penguin, 2015)

Norwich, John Julius (ed.), *The Duff Cooper Diaries 1915–1951* (London: Weidenfeld & Nicolson, 2014)

Owens, Edward, *The Family Firm: Monarchy, Mass Media and the British Public, 1932–53* (London: University of London Press, Institute of Historical Research, 2019)

Parker, Eileen, *Step Aside for Royalty: Treasured Memories of the Royal Household* (Maidstone: Bachman & Turner, 1982)

Pick, Michael, *Norman Hartnell: The Biography* (London: Zuleika, 2019)

Pimlott, Ben, *The Queen: Elizabeth II and the Monarchy* (London: HarperPress, 2012)

Pope-Hennessy, James, *The Quest for Queen Mary*, Hugo Vickers (ed.) (London: Hodder & Stoughton, 2018)

Porter, Ivor, *Michael of Romania: The King and the Country* (Stroud: Sutton Publishing, 2005)

Riddington, Max, and Naden, Gavan, *Frances: The Remarkable Story of Princess Diana's Mother* (London: Michael O'Mara Books Ltd, 2003)

Powell, Ted, *King Edward VIII: An American Life* (Oxford: Oxford University Press, 2018)

Rhodes, Margaret, *The Final Curtsey: A Royal Memoir by the Queen's Cousin* (London: Umbria Press, 2011)

Ridley, Jane, *The Heir Apparent: A Life of Edward VII, The Playboy Prince* (London: Chatto & Windus, 2012)

Ridley, Jane, *George V: Never a Dull Moment* (London: Vintage, 2021)

Roberts, Andrew, *Churchill: Walking with Destiny* (London: Penguin, 2018)

Shawcross, William (ed.), *Counting One's Blessings: The Collected Letters of Queen Elizabeth the Queen Mother* (London: Macmillan, 2012)

Shawcross, William, *Queen Elizabeth, the Queen Mother: The Official Biography* (London: MacMillan, 2009)

Starkey, David, *Monarchy from the Middle Ages to Modernity* (London: HarperCollins, 2006)

Stourton, James, *Kenneth Clark: Life Art and Civilisation* (London: William Collins, 2017)

Thomas, Evelyn, *Princess Elizabeth, Wife and Mother; A Souvenir of the Birth of Prince Charles of Edinburgh* (London: S. Evelyn Thomas, 1949)

Townsend, Peter, *Time and Chance: An Autobiography* (London: Silvertail Books, 2022)

Vickers, Hugo, *Alice: Princess Andrew of Greece* (London: Hamish Hamilton, 2000)

Vickers, Hugo, *Cecil Beaton* (London: Phoenix Press, 1985)

Vickers, Hugo, *Elizabeth, The Queen Mother* (London: Hutchinson, 2005)

Williams, Kate, *Young Elizabeth: The Making of our Queen*, (London: Weidenfeld & Nicolson, 2012)

Wilkinson, James, *The Queen's Coronation: The Inside Story* (London: Scala, 2011)

Worsley, Lucy, *Queen Victoria: Daughter, Wife, Mother, Widow* (London: Hodder & Stoughton, 2018)

Wyatt, Derek, *The Platinum Queen: Over 75 Speeches Given by Britain's Longest-Reigning Monarch*, with a foreword by Jennie Bond (London: Allen and Unwin, 2022)

Ziegler, Philip, *Mountbatten: The Official Biography* (Glasgow: Fontana, 1986)

ACADEMIC ARTICLES

Cannadine, David, 'Churchill and the British Monarchy', *Transactions of the Royal Historical Society*, 2001, vol. 11.

Feingold, Ruth P., 'Marketing the Modern Empire: Elizabeth II and the 1953–54 World Tour, *Antipodes*, December 2009, vol. 23. no. 2.

NEWSPAPERS, MAGAZINES, JOURNALS

Daily Express
Daily Mail
Daily Mirror
Daily Telegraph
Des Moines Register
National and English Review
Evening Standard
Independent on Sunday
Good Housekeeping
Guardian/Manchester Guardian

Life Magazine
Literary Review
Maclean's
News Chronicle
Observer
People
Radio Times
Star
Sun
Sunday Graphic
Sunday Pictorial
Sydney Morning Herald
Tatler
The New Standard
The New York Times
The Times
Time Magazine
Vogue
Washington Post
Woman's Own
Yorkshire Post

WEBSITES

www.bbc.co.uk
www.britishpathe.com
www.oxforddnb.com
www.townandcountrymag.com
www.youtube.com

ACKNOWLEDGEMENTS

I could not have written this book without extraordinary friendships among the oldest and most majestic in society. I benefitted hugely from a breadth of knowledge and understanding about an era which was not my own, thanks to their generous and vivid story-telling. In need of name checks are Barbara Weatherill, who insists I once again make clear she did not train at Camberley MTTC alongside HRH Princess Elizabeth in World War II – the Princess came later. However, Barbara was one of the late Queen's fellow time-travellers and, at ninety-seven, her recall is phenomenal. Stan was a lucky man. Likewise Daphne Attridge – thank you for your candour and good humour. Philip was your sort of prince!

Philip Jarman, as well as being the only one-hundred-year-old man I know, has furnished me with an invaluable male perspective of the post-war years and came up trumps as a research assistant. He sent me his late wife Cora's newspaper collection – I am now the proud owner of a lot of wedding bumf from 1981. The British Library and London Library were, as always, on hand to help with the earlier 1940s–50s' editions. Pat Owtram – thank you for your 'post-war presentation' saga (I wish we had a picture of your mauve cocktail dress), and Shelia Albrecht – thank goodness for Zoom. Talking to you in Australia was the earliest and best way to start the day. I can't believe you are one hundred! Thank you, Jon, for connecting us.

I met Joanne Kavakeb in a television studio talking about her late stepfather, Ronald Thomas, and realised there was no better way to begin the book. Thank you for letting me do just that, Joanne. Joyce Reynolds, I am so sad to hear of your death just days after Her Majesty's and weeks before this book went to print. I feel extremely lucky to have called you a friend and to have featured your voice in two books. You were the Baby Spice of *The Century Girls,* but, at one-hundred-and-three, you're the oldest cameo in *Elizabeth and Philip.* RIP Joyce, and thank you always.

First-hand memories from the era, wonderful as they are, can only tell so much. I also needed royal expertise and historical perspective, which I received in abundance from Hugo Vickers. Thank you, Hugo, your contributions and brilliant books were, of course, invaluable. Wesley Kerr OBE, it was a great pleasure to meet you on set at True Royalty TV – thank you for your insights, so ebulliently told. Kerene Barefield – thank you for giving me access to individuals from your little black book, and Basia Briggs – supper in Chelsea was the highlight of my summer. There are others, some of whom prefer to remain nameless.

I was commissioned to write this book by my wonderful (visionary!) publisher Iain McGregor in the Jubilee year – the timeline was tight, especially if I wanted to hit what would have been Elizabeth and Philip's seventy-fifth wedding anniversary in November 2022. I could not have contemplated it without the help of the extraordinary (overqualified) Dr Jack Clift, whose tireless newspaper research has given this book much of its original content. I also received assistance from doctoral student Yashashwani Srinivas, for which many thanks, and David Charter, your American insights were much appreciated. I look forward to the 2024 publication of your own book about Her Majesty the Queen. Emeritus Professor

Bruce Collins, thank you for being the most amazing friend and mentor and for judiciously going through the text, including pointing out every time I had failed to upscale Louis Mountbatten's title with his latest promotion! The book has relied heavily on your unparalleled historical knowledge.

I know that as I type there is a Headline team smashing this text into shape, led by the inimitable Holly Purdham, with Emily Patience waiting to work her PR wonders. Thank you. And Emily and I both learned so much from you, Simon Robinson – thank you always, and for giving me the courage to take on this book. Ditto Alessandra Covino. I like writing to a deadline, but writing to a deadline with a toddler is a different ball game. In no particular order, thank you Dan Luca, Mara Luca, Miruna Fantanescu, Violeta Ciobanu, Cathy Hazar, Sanae Chentouf. At times I was so remote I almost felt like the Queen! Other names who were instrumental in royal lift off include Dr Katherine Schofield, Professor Will Gould, Rebecca Rideal and Oliver Webb-Carter.

I am very excited to be writing this book with my amazing new agent, Caroline Michel, and her team at PFD. Thank you, Saul David, for the introduction. May there be many more (books that is, not introductions!). From new support to old, and a special mention for my own mother, who, at eighty, is finally featured in one of my books. Thank you, Mum, for your deliciously Anglican royalist views and flag waving accounts – how have you survived in Scotland all these years?!

And finally I would like to dedicate this book to my erstwhile and dearest friend Pamela Rose, who died last November aged one-hundred-and-three. She was a liberal, an actress and a contrarian. Together we sat and watched Harry and Meghan's wedding in the summer of 2018, when she turned to me and said 'monarchy's big events are a great fusion of old and new. What a glorious spectacle.' That afternoon was a spent tripping through a staggering Who's Who of history in which the Queen and Philip both featured. We were lucky to have them walk alongside us for almost a century; an extraordinary couple with a unique story and deep unwavering commitment to public service, constitutional monarchy and each other.

IMAGE CREDITS

Page 1: George VI, Queen Elizabeth and Princess Elizabeth and
         Margaret – Sydney Morning Herald/Superstock/Alamy
         Prince Philip, Hopeman Harbour – Paul Popper/Popper-
         foto via Getty Images
         Princess Elizabeth, *Tatler* © Illustrated London News Ltd/
         Mary Evans

Page 2: Princess Elizabeth, HMS *Vanguard* – Paul Popper/Popper-
         foto via Getty Images
         Princess Elizabeth, Cape Town – Topical Press/Superstock/
         Alamy
         Lieutenant Philip Mountbatten – Photograph by B/S, Camera
         Press London

Page 3: Lieutenant Philip Mountbatten and Princess Elizabeth, wed-
         ding of Louis Mountbatten's daughter – AP/Shutterstock
         Princess Elizabeth and Lieutenant Philip Mountbatten,
         engagement – PA Images/Alamy
         Lieutenant Philip Mountbatten and Louis Mountbatten,
         stag – Keystone/Hulton Archive/Getty Images

Page 4: Prince Philip, Greek costume – Trinity Mirror/Mirrorpix/
         Alamy
         Prince Philip and King Michael – PA Images/Alamy

Image Credits

Page 5: Duke of Edinburgh and Princess Elizabeth, wedding – ITV/
Shutterstock
Lieutenant Philip Mountbatten, Corsham, Wiltshire – Sydney
Morning Herald/Superstock/Alamy
Queen Elizabeth, Copenhagen – Paul Popper/Popperfoto via
Getty Images

Page 6: Lieutenant Commander the Duke of Edinburgh, Malta –
photograph by Baron, Camera Press London
Duke of Edinburgh and Princess Elizabeth, Paris –
Paul Popper/Popperfoto via Getty Images
Duke of Edinburgh and Princess Elizabeth, America – PA
Images/Alamy

Page 7: Princess Elizabeth and Prince Charles © Cecil Beaton/
Victoria and Albert Museum, London
Duke of Edinburgh and Prince Charles – PA Images/
Alamy
Queen Elizabeth, coronation © Illustrated London News
Ltd/Mary Evans

Page 8: Duke of Edinburgh and Queen Elizabeth, Queensland –
Historic Collection/Alamy
Duke of Edinburgh and Mike Parker – Trinity Mirror/
Mirrorpix/Alamy
Duke of Edinburgh and Queen Elizabeth, portrait – photo-
graph by Matt Holyoak, Camera Press London

INDEX

285

Index

Index

Index

Index